Matlab by Example: Programming Basics

Matlab by Example: Programming Basics

Munther Gdeisat
Department of Information Technology,
College of Applied Sciences,
Sohar, Sultanate of Oman

Francis Lilley
Liverpool John Moores University,
General Engineering Research Institute (GERI),
Liverpool, UK

AMSTERDAM • BOSTON • HEIDELBERG • LONDON • NEW YORK • OXFORD
PARIS • SAN DIEGO • SAN FRANCISCO • SINGAPORE • SYDNEY • TOKYO

ELSEVIER

Elsevier
32 Jamestown Road, London NW1 7BY
225 Wyman Street, Waltham, MA 02451, USA

First edition 2013

British Library Cataloguing-in-Publication Data
A catalogue record for this book is available from the British Library

Library of Congress Cataloging-in-Publication Data
A catalog record for this book is available from the Library of Congress

ISBN: 978-0-12-405212-3

For information on all Elsevier publications
visit our website at store.elsevier.com

This book has been manufactured using Print On Demand technology. Each copy is produced to order and is limited to black ink. The online version of this book will show color figures where appropriate.

Working together to grow
libraries in developing countries

www.elsevier.com | www.bookaid.org | www.sabre.org

ELSEVIER   BOOK AID   Sabre Foundation
                International

Contents

Preface

When something can be read without effort, great effort has gone into its writing.
Enrique Jardiel Poncela

Matlab is a powerful software package that has seen massive uptake and popularity among the science and engineering communities. In addition to its ease of use, Matlab can perform complex matrix, mathematical, and graphics operations, while requiring minimal programming effort from the user. It can also be used to build complete stand-alone applications using its graphical user-interface capabilities. For these reasons, most universities around the world teach Matlab to their engineering and science students. This is probably the reason why you are reading this book, in order to learn Matlab!

This book is designed to guide you, in a step-by-step manner, how to write Matlab programs. We suppose here that you do not have any previous programming experience. After reading this book, you will note that your programming capabilities in Matlab are considerably and noticeably improved within a short time-frame. Although this book is written to help novice users, even advanced Matlab professionals will find much of its contents useful and easier to access than the online Matlab help facility, or indeed most other published books and tutorials about Matlab.

The best way to learn any sort of programming is by way of examples. Reading the principles of a programming language without making use of examples makes that programming language both difficult to understand and easy to forget. In this book, we use the power of examples to introduce the concepts of Matlab programming. This simplifies many of the more complex aspects in Matlab and facilitates its application for your own use.

Programming is like driving a car; you learn it by practicing rather than by reading about it or watching others doing it. So if you keep on practicing Matlab concepts while you are reading this book, then this will significantly improve your programming capabilities and will also help you in memorizing the numerous concepts to be found in Matlab. Remember that there is no substitute for experimenting, and as Confucius says, *"I hear and I forget. I see and I remember. I do and I understand."*

The book comprises 10 chapters. Each chapter is divided into lessons. Every lesson starts with a set of learning objectives and topics. The objectives inform you of what you are actually going to learn by studying this lesson. The topics inform you which Matlab-related subjects are discussed in that particular lesson.

This book includes many examples and exercises that are specifically designed to build up your programming skills in Matlab and to help you overcome the pitfalls in programming that most new Matlab users face. In this book, Matlab version 7.12 (R2011a) is used to produce the figures; however, this book can be used for most versions of Matlab.

We hope that you will enjoy reading this book and that you will find it useful. If you have any comments, we would like to hear from you. You can contact us at our e-mail address gdeisat@hotmail.com.

Acknowledgments

The idea of writing this book first began when teaching Matlab at Liverpool John Moores University to students who had no previous programming background at all. We searched through many different potential teaching resources, such as published books and tutorials, to use in the teaching of Matlab to our students, but we could not find very much that was helpful. So we decided to write a book ourselves to help both our own students and also any other Matlab users who would like to learn how to use Matlab but who do not have any significant previous programming background. Our students have already used some of the material from this book to learn Matlab, and they have stated that they found learning Matlab much easier when using this type of example driven approach.

So, here we would like to thank the students at Liverpool John Moores University, especially the weaker students amongst the cohorts that we have taught, for their helpful suggestions in the development of this book that has made following the tutorials much easier for others.

We would like to thank Gary Johnson, an experienced programmer for his help in reviewing this book and for his invaluable suggestions.

We would also like to thank Dr. Laila Mahasneh for reviewing the book and for taking the time to solve the various programming exercises. She is a dentist and has had nothing at all to do with Matlab programming in her professional career; hence, her perspective as a complete novice in the field and her suggestions were very valuable to us in terms of improving the readability of this book for beginners.

Why This Book Is Different

There are hundreds of books and tutorials that have been written to teach programming in Matlab. Many of these books cover the basics of Matlab, while other books explain more advanced topics. This raises two questions: What are the features in this book that make it different from other Matlab books that are available? And how can this book help novice Matlab learners more than other similar books or tutorials?

We have long-term experience of using and teaching Matlab and have taught the subject for more than a decade. During this period, we have used many different books and Internet tutorials in order to teach our students and have noted many deficiencies in the various published materials. Most of the books and tutorials assume that the reader has some sort of previous experience in programming languages other than Matlab. In other words, they do not explain basic programming principles, such as vectors, arrays, while/for loops, and if statements, and so on, in detail, thereby assuming that the reader already knows these programming principles. This makes reading such books and tutorials difficult for a beginner who does not have any prior experience in computer programming. To overcome this deficiency, we decided to write this book in order to teach such beginners programming in Matlab.

Most of the published books and tutorials that explain Matlab topics do not provide their readers with exercises, or questions, to enhance their Matlab programming skills. During our teaching experience, we have noted that most students study and remember the basic Matlab principles quite well but are often not as competent in using this knowledge to solve problems during examinations, course work, or projects. In order to fill this gap, we have included many examples and exercises to support the readers' new knowledge of Matlab. Some of these exercises require only knowledge of the material that is explained in this book, whereas others require the reader to use Matlab's online help facility to answer them. This ensures that the reader thinks "outside the box" and also ensures that they will be able to use Matlab's online help facility efficiently to solve their programming problems. We have also ranked the exercises into three difficulty levels: basic, intermediate, and advanced, denoted by "1", "2," and "3," respectively, with "1" being the simplest and "3" the most challenging. These will appear as superscripts to the exercise number, for example, Exercise 2^3 would denote that Exercise 2 is an advanced-level task. The solutions for selected exercises are given at the end of each individual chapter.

In this book, we have included a number of challenging projects. The solution of these projects includes two separate steps. The first step is to think how to solve the problem in hand. The second step is to program the solution. Programming these projects requires the understanding of many different aspects of Matlab, which will considerably improve your Matlab skills. We advise you to test your skills in Matlab by using the projects that are presented in this book.

Although many novice students already have excellent logical programming skills, their Matlab code is sometimes not well organized. This makes the code difficult to understand. Therefore, we have written this book in such a way to teach students to use a good programming style. This makes their code "readable" both for themselves and for others, for example, by commenting Matlab code, using proper spacing, and using meaningful variable names.

Another motivation that encouraged us to write this book was the requirement to teach students about the Matlab integrated development environment (IDE). Matlab has a very advanced IDE that is designed to help you to solve programming problems, optimize your code, and make it readable. Most existing Matlab books completely ignore the task of explaining the important features of the IDE. Through our experience of teaching Matlab, we have noticed that students often require a significant amount of time to both discover and effectively use certain key IDE features.

We hope that by providing you with this book, we have done our best to simplify the task of learning Matlab programming from scratch. We hope you will enjoy reading it!

How This Book Is Organized

This book is organized into 10 chapters. Each chapter teaches you an important aspect to improve your skills in both programming and using Matlab.

Chapter 1 discusses the Matlab integrated development environment (IDE). The Matlab IDE has many advanced features that are designed to simplify writing programs, improve the readability of your code, highlight syntax errors in your code, give you suggestions to improve the speed of your programs, help you to organize your Matlab files, allow you to inspect values of variables, and much more. Learning these important features right from the beginning helps you to understand programming in Matlab more efficiently and quickly.

Chapter 2 is written specifically for readers who do not have any previous programming experience. Some of the topics discussed in this part are common to other programming languages, such as C, Java, and FORTRAN, for example, naming variables, converting mathematical expressions to Matlab expressions, approximating real numbers, and so on. Readers with some previous programming experience can skim some of these initial topics. The rest of the topics in this chapter are uniquely related to Matlab, such as arithmetical operations on complex numbers, and should not be skimmed even if you have previous programming knowledge of other languages.

Chapter 3 discusses the topic of vectors in Matlab. The name of Matlab is derived from an abbreviation of **Mat**rix **Lab**oratory. Processing matrices is the heart of the Matlab programming language. Matrices can be divided into 1D, 2D, 3D, and so on. One-dimensional (1D) matrices are called vectors. In this part, you will learn about creating and plotting vectors. Additionally, accessing elements in vectors, relational, logical, and arithmetical operations for vectors are all explained here using examples.

Chapter 4 is similar in its organization to the third part of the book, but here the discussion is carried out for arrays rather than vectors. The fourth part explains in detail issues such as accessing elements in arrays, relational, logical, and arithmetical operations for arrays and plotting arrays.

Chapter 5 explains the techniques of structured programming, which here means the process of dividing your code into a script file and a number of functions. The use of functions improves code readability, reusability, and maintainability. This part also explains the purpose of functions in programming, how to write a Matlab function, and the scope of variables in a function.

Chapter 6 explains conditional statements in Matlab. This part explains two conditional statements in Matlab: `if` and `switch`. A number of examples that explain the syntax and the use of both conditional statements are given here. This section also explains the principle of recursive functions.

Chapter 7 discusses the `for` and `while` loop statements. This part also introduces the syntax of both loop statements. Additionally, a number of examples are given in order to explain the concept behind and the use of loops for beginners in programming. This part concludes with two programming projects. Here you will write a Matlab program to implement Conway's Game of Life. This requires the extensive use of loops and conditional statements.

Chapter 8 teaches you two important tools of the Matlab IDE, which are debugging and profiling. The debugging tools help programmers to fix runtime bugs in their code. Examples of debugging tools are **Breakpoint, Conditional Breakpoint, Step In, Step Out**, and **Continue**. The Profiling tool helps programmers to time their code, determine sections in the code that require long execution times, and optimize these sections.

Chapter 9 discusses the use of structures in programming. Structures simplify the programming task and improve the readability of your programs. A number of examples are given to explain the concept and the advantages of using structures in Matlab. This part concludes by programming a fox and rabbit game using structures.

Chapter 10 discusses the use of the Matlab Symbolic Math toolbox to solve calculus problems. For example, solving algebraic equations, differentiation, integration, differential equations, and Laplace and Fourier transforms. The Symbolic Math toolbox produces an exact solution (an equation) for a calculus problem. This is different from a numerical solution of a calculus problem, which normally produces numerical data.

1 Matlab Integrated Development Environment

Chapter Outline

Lesson 1.1   Basics of the Matlab Integrated Development Environment

Objectives
- To familiarize beginners in Matlab with its programming environment.
- To learn how to use Matlab to execute simple commands, create variables, and display their values.

Topics
1.1.1 Matlab Integrated Development Environment
1.1.2 Creating Scalar Variables
1.1.3 Creating Vector Variables
1.1.4 Creating Array Variables

1.1.1   Matlab Integrated Development Environment

Matlab version 7.12 (R2011a) is used here to explain the integrated development environment (IDE). Even though this specific version of Matlab has been used here, other Matlab versions can still be used to follow the discussions presented in this book if you do not have this exact version.

First launch Matlab. When MATLAB opens you should see four windows: the **Command Window**, the **Command History**, the **Workspace**, and the **Current**

Matlab by Example. DOI: http://dx.doi.org/10.1016/B978-0-12-405212-3.00001-3

Folder. If you do not see these windows, you can direct Matlab to display them by going to the **Menu→Desktop** and then click the window you would like to display, so that it has a tick ✓ next to it. For example, if you would like to display the **Command Window**, go to **Menu→Desktop** and then click the **Command Window**.

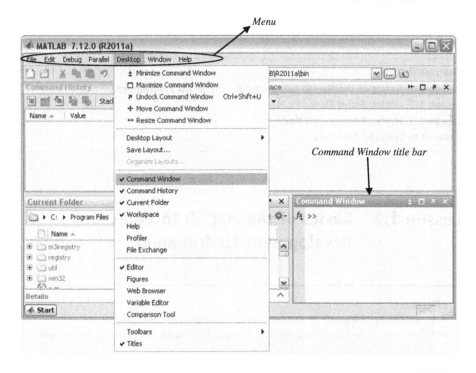

In addition to your ability to display the required windows, you can arrange them in any way you prefer. This can be achieved by clicking the **title bar** of any window, dragging it, and placing it in the required location within the Matlab main window.

---

‡**Exercise 1**[1]

Display the four windows and arrange them as shown. Remember, the four windows are the **Command Window**, the **Command History**, the **Workspace**, and the **Current Folder**.

---

‡ The superscript after the exercise number denotes the exercise difficulty level: 1 being basic, 2 intermediate, and 3 being an advanced task.

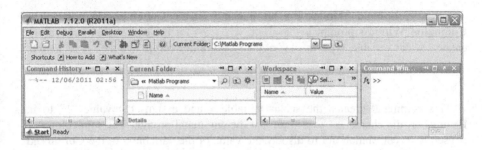

The **Command Prompt** "$>>$" is displayed in the **Command Window**. When the **Command Window** is active, a blinking cursor appears to the right of the prompt. The cursor and the prompt signify that Matlab is ready to perform a computational operation.

The **Workspace** lists all the variables that you have created so far and their values. Other information is also displayed here, such as the maximum and minimum values of any variables that are created.

The **Command History** records all of the commands that you have previously typed at the **Command Prompt**. You can select one of these commands using the mouse and execute it in the **Command Window** by double-clicking it from within the **Command History** window.

Current Folder: You can direct Matlab to set up a folder of your choice to be a current folder. This will then be your working folder, where you can save your programs.

The main window that contains these four windows is called the **Matlab Desktop.**

As mentioned earlier, the **Matlab Desktop** contains four windows: the **Command Window**, the **Command History**, the **Current Folder**, and the **Workspace**. When one of these windows is active, the remaining windows become inactive, but the contents of the remaining windows may still be updated if a script is running. The title bar of the active window appears in a dark gray color, whereas the title bar of the inactive window appears in light gray color. In the preceding figure, the **Command Window** is active and the title bars of the other three windows are grayed out (inactive).

The **Menu** in the **Matlab Desktop** dynamically changes according to the window selected (the active window).

Click on the **Workspace** window and note the change in the **Menu**.

Click another time on the **Command History** window and note the change in the **Menu**.

1.1.2   Creating Scalar Variables

Matlab is a short name for **Matrix lab**oratory. As the name indicates, Matlab is a matrix-based software package, which, infact, considers the scalar variable to be a 1×1 matrix. A scalar here means a number such as "2" or " -100."

Select **Command Window** by left-clicking on the **Command Window**. The **Command Window** prompt is "$>>$" or "$EDU>>$" for the educational version. To create a scalar variable, type "$x = 1;$" at the **Command Prompt** and then press **Enter**.

    >> x = 1;

This command creates the scalar variable x and assigns the value "1" to it. Remember, the characters "$>>$" are just the command prompt. The semicolon ";" is used to direct Matlab not to display the value of the variable x in the **Command Window**. If you leave the semicolon off the end of a command, then it will be echoed straightaway to the display, which can sometimes be cumbersome for very large arrays. Alternatively, it sometimes can be useful to see the results displayed.

Note the changes that happened in the **Command Window**, the **Command History**, and the **Workspace** windows. The **Workspace** displays the x variable, its value, and the maximum and minimum values of the variable. The **Command History** records the $x = 1;$ command.

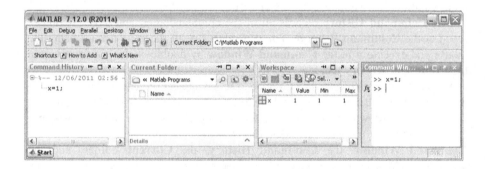

Double-click the variable x in the **Workspace**. The **Variable Editor** pops up and shows the value of the variable. To change the value of the variable x, double-click on the cell indicated by the black arrow in the following figure and change it to another value, for example, by typing the numeral "2". Press **Enter**. Close the **Variable Editor** window by clicking the X at the top right of the **Variable Editor** window.

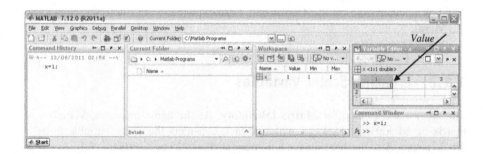

You should get the following figure.

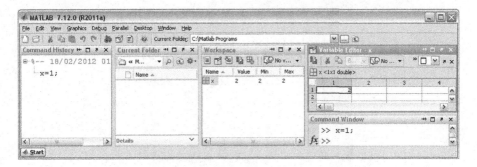

1.1.3   Creating Vector Variables

To create a vector variable, type the Matlab command

$$>>y=[2,3,6,9,11,8,5,3,2,-1];$$

at the **Command Prompt** and then press **Enter**.
This command creates a vector variable with the values

$$y=[2,3,6,9,11,8,5,3,2,-1].$$

The Matlab desktop responds to this command as shown in the following figure.

In order to draw the vector variable y, click on the y variable in the **Workspace** so that it is highlighted as in the following figure, then go to **Menu** →**Graphics**→ **plot(y)**. A pop-up window appears and plots the vector y.

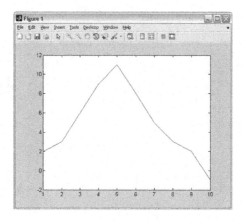

Exercise 2[1]

In the **Workspace** window double-click the variable y. The **Variable Editor** pops up and shows you the contents of this variable. Change the contents of the vector y to be as follows:

    2,3,6,9,1,8,5,3,2,-1

Draw the vector. You should get the following figure.

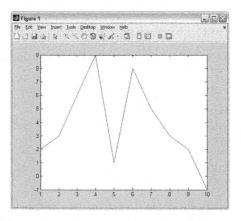

1.1.4   Creating Array Variables

To create an array variable, type the following Matlab command

    >> Z = [1,2;3,4];

at the **Command Prompt** and then press **Enter**.

Note and make sure that you include the two semicolons and the commas in the command.

This command creates an array variable with the following values:

```
Z = [1  2
     3  4]
```

The Matlab desktop responds as shown in the following figure. In this book, we will use uppercase letters to name arrays.

To draw the array variable Z, click on the Z variable in the **Workspace** so as to highlight it (as shown in the following figure), then go to **Menu→Graphics→ mesh(Z)**. A pop-up window appears and displays the array variable Z as a 3D mesh. An alternative to using the pop-up menu is to right-click on the Z array in the **Workspace** and select **mesh(Z)** from that menu.

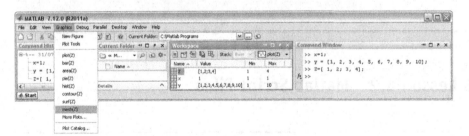

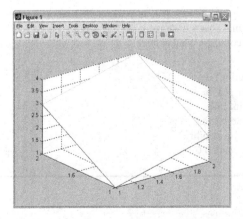

Exercise 3[1]

In the **Workspace,** double-click the array variable Z. The **Variable Editor** pops up and shows you the contents of this variable. Change the contents of this variable to the following:

```
Z = [1   6
     3   4]
```

Draw the array variable Z. You should now get the following figure.

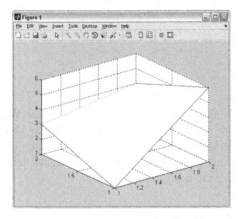

Lesson 1.2   Matlab Script Files

Objectives
- To learn how to create, name, save, and execute Matlab script files.
- To learn how to make your code readable for others.
- To learn how to comment Matlab code.

Topics
1.2.1 Creating a Script File
1.2.2 Naming a Script File
1.2.3 Saving a Script File
1.2.4 Executing a Script File
1.2.5 Matlab Code Readability
1.2.6 Commenting Matlab Code

1.2.1   Creating a Script File

An M-file is a text file that contains a collection of commands that Matlab executes in a sequential order. A script file has the following properties:

- It has no arguments (input data) and it does not return any values (outputs).
- The commands executed in the script file have the same effect as if these commands were executed in the **Command Window.**
- The variables created by the script file are displayed in the **Workspace** window.

Suppose that we would like to create a script file that contains the following Matlab commands.

```
x = 1;
y = 2;
```

To carry out this task, do the following.
Launch Matlab. Then go to **Menu→ File→New→Script**.

The Matlab window **Editor** pops up. In this window, type the Matlab commands shown in the **Editor**.

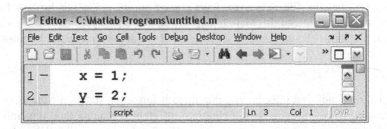

1.2.2   Naming a Script File

Choose a name for this file. The extension for the file must be *.m*. The following restrictions must be taken into consideration when a script file is named.

- The file name must **not** contain spaces or hyphens (-).
- The file name **must** start with an alphabetical character (a−z or A−Z).
- The file name **must** contain only alphabetical characters (a−z or A−Z), numbers (1−9) or underscores (_).
- Punctuation characters such as commas (,) or apostrophes (') are not allowed, because many of them have special meanings in Matlab.
- The file name must be neither a **Matlab variable** nor an existing **Matlab function**.
- The use of a **Matlab reserved word** as a file name is not allowed. A list of **Matlab reserved words** are given below.

```
'name'                  'across_variable'
'node'                  'build'
'output'                'description'
'parameter'             'descriptor'
'setup'                 'element'
'signal'                'input'
'source'                'interface_input'
'terminal'              'interface_node'
'through_variable'      'interface_output'
'variable'              'item_type'
                        'local_variable'
```

- The use of a **Matlab keyword** as a file name is not allowed. A list of **Matlab keywords** are given below.

```
'break'        'global'
'case'         'if'
'catch'        'otherwise'
'classdef'     'parfor'
'continue'     'persistent'
'else'         'return'
'elseif'       'spmd'
'end'          'switch'
'for'          'try'
'function'     'while'
```

To check that the file name you have chosen is not a **Matlab keyword** or a **Matlab function**, you can use Matlab help and search under your chosen file name. For example, let us choose *cat.m* as a file name. Type at the **Command Prompt**

```
>>help cat
```

Matlab responds and informs you that there is already a function called cat that concatenates arrays. So you should choose a different file name (and remember to check that this new name is not restricted in the same way too!). Matlab will warn against using names that are existing Matlab keywords, but it will not produce a warning when generating a script with certain function names, for example, the *cat* function above. Therefore, for this reason you should always test new user-defined names that you are unsure about by using the help facility, as shown previously, to avoid potential problems with name clashes when debugging.

Let's try a different name, such as *cat1.m*. Type at the **Command Prompt**

```
>>help cat1
```

Matlab responds and informs you that there is no function called *cat1* as shown in the following window. So we can save the file with the name *cat1.m*.

Remember: It can be very helpful to use meaningful and descriptive file names.

Exercise 1[1]

Which of the following is a suitable file name that can be used to save a script file? Explain your answer.

1. *det.m*   2. *cars.m*   3. *two jars.m*   4. *2D.m*
5. *r$.m*   6. *_long.m*   7. *−long.m*   8. *for.m*

Exercise 2[3]

Why would naming the following script file as *a.m* be incorrect?

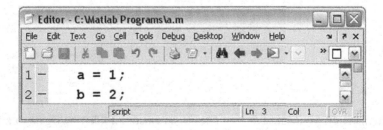

1.2.3   Saving a Script File

The next step is to save the script file to a specific folder. Here we will create a folder called *Lesson 2*, and we will make it Matlab's current folder. To perform this task, click on the icon [...] (indicated by the arrow in the following screenshot) and choose the location where you would like to save the folder *Lesson 2*.

Click on **Make New Folder**. Change the name of the folder to *Lesson 2*. Click **OK**.

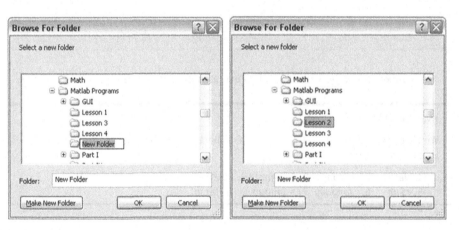

This creates a new folder called *Lesson 2* and makes it the current folder for use by Matlab as indicated by the arrow shown in the following screenshot.

Alternatively, you can save your files to an existing folder. Navigate to a folder of your choice and set it to be the current folder for Matlab.

The last step is to save the file. In the Matlab **Editor**, go to **Menu→File→Save As**. Type the file name; in this case type *cat1.m* and click **Save**.

The file that has just been saved appears in the **Current Folder** window. In the following screenshot figure, an arrow points to this file as it appears on the **Matlab Desktop**.

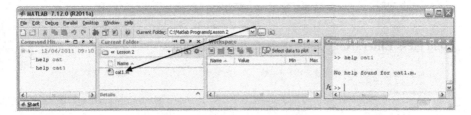

1.2.4   Executing a Script File

There are two methods available for executing the script file *cat1.m*.

Method 1

In the first method, go to the **Matlab Editor** and click on the **Run** icon ▶, as indicated by the arrow in the following figure.

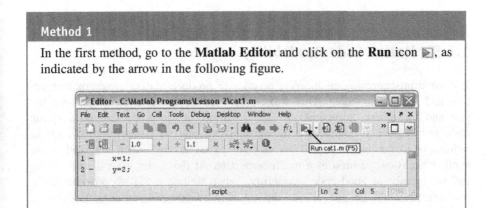

Note the changes in the **Workspace**.

Method 2

The second method is to type the name of the M-file at the **Command Prompt** without the file extension. For example, to run the M-file *cat1.m*, type at the **Command Prompt**

```
>> cat1
```

and press **Enter**. Note the changes in the **Workspace**.

1.2.5   Matlab Code Readability

It is good programming/engineering practice to produce Matlab programs that are tidy and well commented. This makes the code easier to understand, both for you and for others. Sometimes we get involved in the process of writing our code and neglect to comment it, to make it tidy and well structured. If code is written in this manner, it will be difficult to understand when we read it on another occasion, perhaps at a much later date. At that point we will realize the full importance of good code readability. When writing a Matlab program, code readability should be one of our top priorities. Good programming practice is best learned by an example.

Example 1

It is good programming practice to use meaningful names for variables. For example, Chris bought three rulers, two rubbers, and four books. The price for each ruler is £6, for each rubbers £8, and for each book £25. Write a Matlab program that calculates the total price paid by Chris.

Answer
Go to **Menu→File→New→Script**. Type the code below into the **Editor**.

```
price_of_ruler = 6;
price_of_rubber = 8;
price_of_book = 25;
No_of_rulers = 3;
No_of_rubbers = 2;
No_of_books = 4;
Total_price_paid_by_Chris = ...
    price_of_ruler * No_of_rulers +...
    price_of_rubber * No_of_rubbers +...
    price_of_book * No_of_books
```

Note that the code is self-explained. The continuation characters "..." at the end of the line makes the code continue onto the next line.

Compare the preceding code with the following code in terms of readability. Both programs produce the same results.

```
x = 6;
y = 8;
z = 25;
a = 3;
b = 2;
c = 4;
r = x * a + y * b + z * c
```

Which version of the code do you think is easier to understand?

1.2.6 Commenting Matlab Code

Method 1

You can add a comment to Matlab code by inserting a percentage sign "%" at the beginning of the line. For example,

```
% Chris bought three rulers, two rubbers, and four books.
% The price of a ruler is £6. The price of a rubber is £8.
% The price for a book is £25.
% This Matlab program calculates the total price paid by
% Chris.
```

```
price_of_ruler = 6;
price_of_rubber = 8;
price_of_book = 25;
No_of_rulers = 3;
No_of_rubbers = 2;
No_of_books = 4;
Total_price_paid_by_Chris = ...
   price_of_ruler * No_of_rulers + ...
   price_of_rubber * No_of_rubbers + ...
   price_of_book * No_of_books
```

When Matlab encounters a percentage sign "%" within a line of code, Matlab ignores any text after this point until the end of the line. This commenting method can be tedious and can make it cumbersome to modify large sections of comments. However, there is another alternative method of commenting code.

Method 2

A more elaborate method for commenting code is performed by using block commenting. In this method, add the textual characters "%{" before the first line of the comments and add the characters "%}" after the last line of the comments. This is illustrated by the following example.

```
%{
Chris bought three rulers, two rubbers, and four books.
The price of a ruler is £6. The price of a rubber is £8.
The price for a book is £25. This Matlab program calculates the total
price paid by Chris.
%}
price_of_ruler = 6;
price_of_rubber = 8;
price_of_book = 25;
No_of_rulers = 3;
No_of_rubbers = 2;
No_of_books = 4;
Total_price_paid_by_Chris = ...
   price_of_ruler * No_of_rulers + ...
   price_of_rubber * No_of_rubbers + ...
   price_of_book * No_of_books
```

This technique is best used for larger comment blocks.

Lesson 1.3   Matlab Editor—Cell Mode

Objective
* To learn how to use the **Cell Mode** in the Matlab **Editor**.

Topics
1.3.1 Enabling Cell Mode
1.3.2 Separating a Program into Cells
1.3.3 Evaluating Code in a Cell

1.3.1   Enabling Cell Mode

Create a new folder and name it **Lesson 3**. Make **Lesson 3** the current folder of Matlab.

Suppose that you have the following program that can be divided into three individual parts. Also, suppose that you would like to run the code one part at a time. In order to do this, you can use the **Cell Mode** in Matlab. Type the code below in the **Editor** window. Save the file as *find_y.m*.

```
clear; clc;
%part 1
x1 = 10
y1 = x1.^2
%part 2
x2 = 20
y2 = 3*x2.^3
%part 3
x3 = 30
y3 = 5*x3.^2
```

Initially, ensure that the **Cell Mode** in the **Editor** is enabled. To do this, go to **Menu→Cell**. The figure below on the left shows that the **Cell Mode** is disabled, and you need to enable it. The figure below on the right shows that the **Cell Mode** is already enabled, and you need to do nothing to enable it.

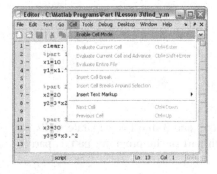
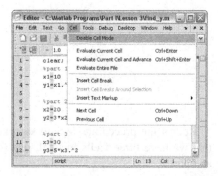

Ensure that the **Cell Mode** is enabled.

The Matlab command `clear` removes all the variables from Matlab memory.

The Matlab command `clc` clears the **Command Window**.

We advise you to start your Matlab program with both commands.

1.3.2   Separating a Program into Cells

Using the mouse, click on line 5. This is the separation between part 1 and part 2 of the program. Go to **Menu→Cell→Insert Cell Break**.

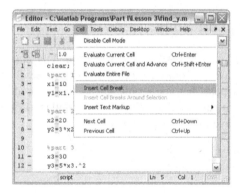

This separates the program into two separate **Cells**. The first **Cell** comprises part 1, and the second **Cell** comprises both parts 2 and 3.

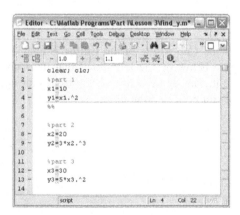

Repeat the preceding steps to separate parts 2 and 3 into two separate **Cells**, so that we have three **Cells** in total, one for each part of the program: part 1, part 2, and part 3.

1.3.3   Evaluating Code in a Cell

To evaluate the code in the first **Cell**, click anywhere inside the first **Cell by using the mouse**. This changes the color of the **Cell** to yellow. Then go to **Menu→Cell→Evaluate Current Cell.**

Matlab runs the code in the first **Cell** and produces the result shown in the following figure.

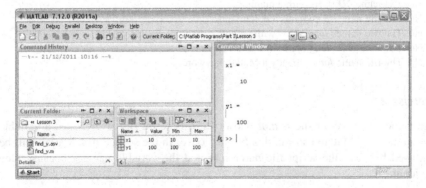

You can evaluate the code in any **Cell** and in any order that you choose. For example, you could start by evaluating the code in the third **Cell**, then the first **Cell**, and then the second **Cell**.

Exercise 1[1]

Evaluate the code in the third **Cell**. Then evaluate the code in the second **Cell**.

It is important to note code dependency among code sections. For example, in the following program, you cannot run the code in part 1 and then the code in part 3 as you did before. This is because the value of x2 in part 3 depends on the code in part 2.

```
clear; clc;
%part 1
x1 = 10
y1 = x1.^2
%part 2
x2 = 20
y2 = 3*x2.^3
%part 3
x3 = 30
y3 = 5*x3.^2 + 4*x2
```

Answers to Selected Exercises

Lesson 1.2

Exercise 1

Can these file names be used, yes or no ?

1. No. *det*. There is already a function in Matlab with this name.
2. Yes. *cars* can be used. But ask yourself whether it could be more descriptive.
3. No. The name *two jars* contains a space.
4. No. The name *2D* starts with a number.
5. No. The file name *r$* contains a dollar sign.
6. No. The file name *_long* starts with an underscore.
7. No. The file name *-long* starts with a dash.
8. No. The file name *for* is already a Matlab keyword.

Exercise 2

The name of the script file is *a.m*. However, this script file also creates a variable and names it a. Matlab can run this file just once. In the second run, Matlab will be confused between the script file name *a.m* and the variable name a because they are identical.

2 Scalars in Matlab

Chapter Outline

Lesson 2.1 Creating and Naming Matlab Scalar Variables

Objectives
- To learn how to create scalar variables using Matlab.
- To differentiate between Matlab special variables and user-defined variables.

Topics

2.1.1 Matlab Special Variables
    2.1.1.1 Using Matlab Special Variables
    2.1.1.2 Changing the Values of Matlab Special Variables

2.1.2 User-Defined Variables
    2.1.2.1 Naming a User-Defined Variable
    2.1.2.2 Matlab is Case Sensitive
    2.1.2.3 Clearing a User-Defined Variable

2.1.1 Matlab Special Variables

2.1.1.1 Using Matlab Special Variables

In Matlab, every variable created should have a value. Variables are created either by Matlab or by the user. Variables created by Matlab are considered to be special

Matlab by Example. DOI: http://dx.doi.org/10.1016/B978-0-12-405212-3.00002-5

variables, whose values are assigned by Matlab. For example, the special variable pi (π), whose value is approximated here to 3.1416. To find the value of the special variable pi, type at the **Command Prompt**

```
>>pi
```

Then press **Enter**. Matlab responds with

```
ans =
      3.1416
```

This command generates another special variable ans and assigns the value 3.1416 to it. The special variable ans saves the result of any Matlab operation if the value of the result is not specifically assigned to a variable. For example, type at the **Command Prompt**

```
>>1 + 2
```

Then press **Enter**. Matlab responds with

```
ans =
      3
```

Other examples of special variables are i and j. The value for both variables is defined as $\sqrt{-1}$. Normally, mathematicians use the term i to represent $\sqrt{-1}$, whereas engineers use the term j to represent the same thing.

To find the value of the special variable i, type at the **Command Prompt**

```
>>i
```

Then press **Enter**. Matlab responds with

```
>>ans
      0 + 1.0000i
```

To get some help about the variable i, type at the **Command Prompt**

```
>>help i
```

Then press **Enter**. Matlab responds and gives you some information about the special variable i as follows.

To find the value of the special variable j, type at the **Command Prompt**

```
>>j
```

Then press **Enter**. Matlab responds with

```
>>ans
        0 + 1.0000i
```

2.1.1.2 Changing the Values of Matlab Special Variables

The user can change the value of the special variables. For example, type at the **Command Prompt**

```
>>pi = 1
```

Then press **Enter**. Matlab responds with

```
pi =
     1
```

Now the value for the special variable pi has been changed to 1.
To restore the value of the special variable pi, type at the **Command Prompt**

```
>>clear pi
```

Then press **Enter**.
To display the value of the variable pi, type at the **Command Prompt**

```
>>pi
```

Then press **Enter**. Matlab responds with

```
ans =
       3.1416
```

2.1.2 User-Defined Variables

2.1.2.1 Naming a User-Defined Variable

The user can also create Matlab variables and assign values to the created variables. The variable name should satisfy the following requirements:

- A variable name must not contain spaces or hyphens (-).
- A variable name can contain up to 63 characters.
- A variable name must start with a letter (a−z or A−Z), followed by any number of letters, digits (0−9), or underscores (_).

- Punctuation characters such commas (,) or apostrophes (') are not allowed, because many of them have special meanings in Matlab.
- A variable name must not be a **Script M-file** name or an existing **Matlab function** name.
- The use of a **Matlab reserved word** as a variable name is not allowed. A list of **Matlab reserved words** is given below.

```
'name'                  'across_variable'
'node'                  'build'
'output'                'description'
'parameter'             'descriptor'
'setup'                 'element'
'signal'                'input'
'source'                'interface_input'
'terminal'              'interface_node'
'through_variable'      'interface_output'
'variable'              'item_type'
                        'local_variable'
```

- The use of a **Matlab keyword** as a variable name is not allowed. A list of **Matlab keywords** is given below.

```
'break'      'global'
'case'       'if'
'catch'      'otherwise'
'classdef'   'parfor'
'continue'   'persistent'
'else'       'return'
'elseif'     'spmd'
'end'        'switch'
'for'        'try'
'function'   'while'
```

The following variable names are acceptable

```
x,y,z,hello,let_us_name_this_variable_x,letter1,letter2.
```

The following names are not suitable to be used as variable names:

3x: This variable name starts with a number, not an alphabetical character.
_y: This variable name starts with an underscore.
r$: This variable name contains the dollar sign.
sum: This variable name is a Matlab function. To check this, type at the **Command Prompt**

```
>>help sum
```

Matlab responds by displaying some information about the sum function.

2.1.2.2 Matlab is Case Sensitive

Matlab is a case-sensitive programming language as it distinguishes lowercase from uppercase. The variable name x is considered to be different from the variable name X, which can lead to confusion, so be careful! For example, type at the **Command Prompt**

>> x = 1;

Then Press **Enter**. Matlab responds by creating the variable x and assigning the value "1" to it.

To display the content of the x variable, type at the **Command Prompt**

>> x

Then Press **Enter**. Matlab responds by displaying the value of the variable x as

x = 1
   1

To find the value of X, type at the **Command Prompt**

>> X

Then Press **Enter**. Matlab gives the results

???Undefined function or variable 'X'.

In Matlab, the variable x is different from the variable X. Matlab is case sensitive. For example, cost, Cost and COST are viewed as being three different variables in Matlab.

2.1.2.3   Clearing a User-Defined Variable

Create a variable y

>> y = 10;

To display the content of y, type at the **Command Prompt**

>> y

Then Press **Enter**. Matlab responds by displaying the value of y as

y =
   10

To clear the variable y, type at the **Command Prompt**

```
>>clear y
```

Then Press **Enter**. To be sure that the variable y is cleared, type at the **Command Prompt**

```
>>y
```

Then Press **Enter**. Matlab responds with

```
???Undefined function or variable 'y'.
```

Exercise 1[1]

Explain why the following Matlab code is incorrect.

```
number_of_red_and_new_cars_that_have_been_used_in_the_year_2007_by_Chris_are = 10
number_of_red_and_new_cars_that_have_been_used_in_the_year_2007_by_John_are = 11
```

Lesson 2.2   Approximation of Numbers and Discrete Mathematical Operations

Objectives
- To learn how to approximate numbers in Matlab.
- To learn a few of Matlab's discrete mathematical operations.

Topics
2.2.1 Approximating Numbers
    2.2.1.1 round Function
    2.2.1.2 fix Function
    2.2.1.3 ceil Function
    2.2.1.4 floor Function
2.2.2 Discrete Mathematical Operations
    2.2.2.1 Factorizing a Number
    2.2.2.2 Greatest Common Divisor
    2.2.2.3 Least Common Multiple

2.2.1 Approximating Numbers

A real number consists of integer and decimal parts, and it can be approximated by an integer number. For example, the real number 2.5 can be approximated by the integer number 2. This approximation process requires the elimination of the decimal part of the number, and it may also affect the integer part. Matlab supports four functions to approximate real numbers: round, fix, ceil, and floor.

2.2.1.1 round *Function*

This function rounds a real number upward, or downward, toward the nearest integer. The operation of this function is best explained by way of examples. Type at the **Command Prompt**

```
>>x = round(2.51)
```

Then press **Enter**. Matlab responds with

```
x =
    3
```

A second example, type at the **Command Prompt**

```
>>y = round(2.49)
```

Then press **Enter**. Matlab responds with

```
y =
    2
```

2.2.1.2 fix *Function*

This function truncates (eliminates) the decimal part of a real number, leaving the integer part unchanged. The operation of this function is best explained by way of examples. Type at the **Command Prompt**

```
>>x = fix(2.51)
```

Then press **Enter**. Matlab responds with

```
x =
    2
```

A second example, type at the **Command Prompt**

```
>>y = fix(-2.51)
```

Then press **Enter**. Matlab responds with

```
y =
    -2
```

2.2.1.3   ceil *Function*

This function rounds up a real number toward the nearest higher integer. For example, type at the **Command Prompt**

>> x = ceil(2.51)

Then press **Enter**. Matlab responds with

x =
   3

A second example, type at the **Command Prompt**

>> y = ceil(2.49)

Then press **Enter**. Matlab also responds with

y =
   3

2.2.1.4   floor *Function*

This function rounds down a real number toward the nearest lower integer. For example, type at the **Command Prompt**

>> x = floor(2.51)

Then press **Enter**. Matlab responds with

x =
   2

A second example, type at the **Command Prompt**

>> y = floor(2.49)

Then press **Enter**. Matlab also responds with

y =
   2

Exercise 1[1]

For each of the following cases, either on paper or in your head, find the value of x using the rules explained in this lesson. Then use Matlab to check your answer.

1. x = round(pi)
2. x = fix(pi)
3. x = ceil(pi)

4. x = floor(pi)
5. x = round(-pi)
6. x = fix(-pi)
7. x = ceil(-pi)
8. x = floor(-pi)

2.2.2 Discrete Mathematical Operations

2.2.2.1 Factorizing a Number

The factor function factorizes a positive integer number into its prime factors. For example, to factorize the number 6, type at the **Command Prompt**

>>x = factor(6)

Then press **Enter**. Matlab returns a vector that contains the prime factors of x as follows:

x =
    2 3

2.2.2.2 Greatest Common Divisor

The greatest common divisor for two positive integer numbers is calculated by using the gcd function. For example, to find the greatest common divisor to the numbers 6 and 9, type at the **Command Prompt**

>>x = gcd(6,9)

Then press **Enter**. Matlab responds with

x =
    3

Note that the order of the numbers is not important here.

2.2.2.3 Least Common Multiple

The least common multiple for two positive integer numbers is calculated by using the lcm function. For example, to find the least common multiple of the numbers 6 and 9, type at the **Command Prompt**

>>x = lcm(6,9)

Then press **Enter**. Matlab responds with

x =
    18

Note that the order of the numbers is not important here.

Lesson 2.3   Mathematical Expressions for Scalar Variables

Objectives
- To learn how to assign a value to a variable.
- To learn the precedence principle for mathematical operations in Matlab.

Topics

2.3.1 Creating Variables
2.3.2 Precedence of Mathematical Operations
2.3.3 From Mathematical Expressions to Matlab expressions
2.3.4 From Matlab Expressions to Mathematical Expressions
2.3.5 Exercises

2.3.1 Creating Variables

In Matlab, every created variable should have a value. For example, type the following Matlab code at the **Command Prompt**.

```
>> x   = 1;
>> y   = 2*x;
```

This creates two variables x and y. To display the content of the x and y variables, type at the **Command Prompt**

```
>> x,y
```

Then press **Enter**. Matlab responds with

```
x =
    1
y =
    2
```

Now change the value of x to 4 as follows:

```
>> x = 4
```

Then press **Enter**. Matlab responds with

```
x =
    4
```

Note here that the value of y has not changed, although the value of x has changed from 1 to 4 and remembering that y is a function of x, in that $y = 2*x$. However, this expression was calculated when the value of x was 1, and it has not been reevaluated yet. To display the contents of the variable y, type at the **Command Prompt**

>> y

Then press **Enter**. Matlab responds with

y =
  2

In order to change the value of y to $2*x$, using the new value of $x = 4$, you should execute the command $y = 2*x$ a second time. To do this, type at the **Command Prompt**

>> y = 2*x

Then press **Enter**. Matlab now responds with

y =
  8

2.3.2 Precedence of Mathematical Operations

Matlab evaluates mathematical expressions from left to right. Mathematical expressions may contain addition, subtraction, multiplication, division, and exponential mathematical operations as well as parentheses. These mathematical operations are evaluated in the following order in Matlab:

I. Parentheses, by starting with the innermost set and proceeding outward
II. The exponentiation operation
III. Multiplication and division
IV. Addition and subtraction.

2.3.3 From Mathematical Expressions to Matlab Expressions

Example 1

Write a Matlab program to evaluate r using the minimum number of parentheses,

$$r = \frac{x+y}{z}, \quad where \quad x = 1, \ y = 2, \ z = 3$$

Answer
In this mathematical expression, the addition operation needs to be evaluated first followed by the division.

$$r = \left\{ \frac{\{x+y\}_1}{z} \right\}_2$$

The mathematical operations in $\{\}_1$ must be performed before the mathematical operations in $\{\}_2$. However, as you have just learned, the division operation has a higher priority in Matlab than the addition operation. To alter this priority order, parentheses are used to give the addition operation a higher priority than that of the division operation.

```
x = 1;
y = 2;
z = 3;
r = (x + y)/z;
```

Example 2

Write a Matlab program to evaluate r using the minimum number of parentheses,

$$r = x + \frac{y}{z}, \quad \text{where} \quad x = 1,\ y = 2,\ z = 3$$

Answer
In this mathematical expression, the division has a higher priority than the addition operation.

$$r = \left\{ x + \left\{ \frac{y}{z} \right\}_1 \right\}_2$$

The order of evaluating this mathematical expression exactly follows the priority of mathematical operations in Matlab: division has a higher priority than addition, both mathematically and also in Matlab. So you should not use parentheses here.

```
x = 1;
y = 2;
z = 3;
r = x + y/z;
```

Example 3

Write a Matlab program to evaluate r using the minimum number of parentheses,

$$r = \frac{x+y^2}{z^3+y^4}, \quad \text{where} \quad x = 1,\ y = 2,\ z = 3$$

Answer

In this mathematical expression, the exponent has the highest precedence, followed by the additions and then by the division.

$$r = \left\{ \frac{\{x + \{y^2\}_1\}_2}{\{\{z^3\}_1 + \{y^4\}_1\}_2} \right\}_3$$

The order of evaluating mathematical operations in Matlab is exponentiation, division, and then addition. So we need parentheses here to give the addition operation higher priority than the division operation.

```
x = 1;
y = 2;
z = 3;
r = (x + y^2)/(z^3 + y^4);
```

Example 4

Write a Matlab program to evaluate r using the minimum number of parentheses,

$$r = \frac{x + y^2}{z^3 + y^4} + \frac{x^3 + y^3}{x^2}, \quad \text{where} \quad x = 1, \ y = 2, \ z = 3$$

Answer

The order of evaluating the mathematical expression above is as shown below.

$$r = \left\{ \left\{ \frac{\{x + \{y^2\}_1\}_2}{\{\{z^3\}_1 + \{y^4\}_1\}_2} \right\}_3 + \left\{ \frac{\{\{x^3\}_1 + \{y^3\}_1\}_2}{\{x^2\}_1} \right\}_3 \right\}_4$$

In Matlab, division has a higher priority than addition. But in this mathematical expression, three of the additions should be performed before the two divisions. So parentheses should be used to give the three specific additions higher priority than the two divisions.

```
x = 1;
y = 2;
z = 3;
r = (x + y^2)/(z^3 + y^4) + (x^3 + y^3)/x^2;
```

Example 5

Write a Matlab program to evaluate r using the minimum number of parentheses,

$$r = \cfrac{\cfrac{x+y^2}{z^3+y^4} + \cfrac{x^3+y^3}{x^2}}{\cfrac{x^2+1}{y^3}}, \quad \text{where} \quad x=1,\ y=2,\ z=3$$

Answer

The order of evaluating the mathematical expression above is shown below.

$$r = \left\{ \cfrac{\left\{\cfrac{\{x+\{y^2\}_1\}_2}{\{\{z^3\}_1+\{y^4\}_1\}_2}\right\}_3 + \left\{\cfrac{\{\{x^3\}_1+\{y^3\}_1\}_2}{\{x^2\}_1}\right\}_3}{\left\{\cfrac{\{\{x^2\}_1+1\}_2}{\{y^3\}_1}\right\}_3} \right\}_4$$

In Matlab, division has a higher priority than addition. But in this mathematical expression, most of the addition operations should be performed before the divisions. So in these specific cases, parentheses should again be used to give the additions higher priority than the divisions.

```
x = 1;
y = 2;
z = 3;
r = ((x + y^2)/(z^3 + y^4) + (x^3 + y^3)/x^2)/((x^2 + 1)/y^3);
```

Example 6

Write a Matlab program to evaluate r using the minimum number of parentheses, where

$$r = \cfrac{\cfrac{x}{z^3+y^4} + \cfrac{x^3+y^3}{x^2}}{\cfrac{x^2+1}{y^3} - 3}, \quad \text{where} \quad x=1,\ y=2,\ z=3$$

Answer

The order of evaluating the mathematical expression above is shown below.

$$r = \left\{ \cfrac{\left\{\left\{\cfrac{x}{\{\{z^3\}_1+\{y^4\}_1\}_2}\right\}_3 + \left\{\cfrac{\{\{x^3\}_1+\{y^3\}_1\}_2}{\{x^2\}_1}\right\}_3\right\}_4}{\left\{\left\{\cfrac{\{\{x^2\}_1+1\}_2}{\{y^3\}_1}\right\}_3 - 3\right\}_4} \right\}_5$$

```
x = 1;
y = 2;
z = 3;
r = (x/(z^3 + y^4) + (x^3 + y^3)/x^2)/((x^2 + 1)/y^3 - 3);
```

Example 7

Write a Matlab program to evaluate r using the minimum number of parentheses,

$$r = \frac{\sin(2x^2 + 1)}{\cos(x^2 - 2) + 1}, \quad \text{where} \quad x = 1$$

Answer

$$r = \left\{ \frac{\{\sin(\{\{2\{x^2\}_1\}_2 + 1\}_3)\}_4}{\{\{\cos(\{\{x^2\}_1 - 2\}_2)\}_3 + 1\}_4} \right\}_5$$

```
x = 1;
r = sin(2*x^2 + 1)/(cos(x^2 - 2) + 1);
```

Example 8

Write a Matlab program to evaluate r using the minimum number of parentheses,

$$r = \frac{\frac{x^2 + \sqrt{y}}{z^2 + 1} + \frac{z^2 + x^4}{y^3}}{\frac{\cos(2x^2 + 1)\sin(x^2)}{3x^2 + 2} + \sin^2(x^3)}, \quad \text{where} \quad x = 1, \; y = 2$$

Answer

$$r = \left\{ \frac{\left\{ \left\{ \frac{\{\{x^2\}_1 + \{\sqrt{y}\}_1\}_2}{\{\{z^2\}_1 + 1\}_2} \right\}_3 + \left\{ \frac{\{\{z^2\}_1 + \{x^4\}_1\}_2}{\{y^3\}_1} \right\}_3 \right\}_4}{\left\{ \left\{ \frac{\{\{\cos(\{\{2\{x^2\}_1\}_2 + 1\}_3)\}_4\{\sin(\{x^2\}_1)\}_2\}_3}{\{\{3\{x^2\}_1\}_2 + 2\}_3} \right\}_5 + \{((\sin(\{x^3\}_1)\}_2)^2\}_3 \right\}_6} \right\}_7$$

```
x = 1;
y = 2;
r1 = (x^2 + sqrt(y))/(z^2 + 1) + (z^2 + x^4)/y^3;
r2 = cos(2*x^2 + 1)*sin(x^2)/(3*x^2 + 2) + sin(x^3)^2;
r = r1/r2
```

Example 9

Write a Matlab program to evaluate r using the minimum number of parentheses,

$$r = \frac{\log(x^2 + 1)}{2e^x + \tan^{-1}(x^2)}, \quad \textit{where} \quad x = 1$$

log(x) is the logarithm to the base 10 for the number *x*.

Answer

$$r = \left\{ \frac{\{\log((\{x^2\}_1 + 1\}_2))\}_3}{\{\{2\{e^x\}_1\}_2 + \{\tan^{-1}(\{x^2\}_1)\}_2\}_3} \right\}_4$$

```
x = 1;
r = log10(x^2 + 1)/(2*exp(x) + atan(x^2));
```

Example 10

Write a Matlab program to evaluate r using the minimum number of parentheses,

$$r = \frac{\log(x)}{\ln(x)}, \quad \textit{where} \quad x = 1$$

ln(x) is the natural logarithm for the number *x*.

Answer

```
x = 1;
r = log10(x)/log(x);
```

Example 11

Write a Matlab program to evaluate r using the minimum number of parentheses,

$$r = \frac{\tan^{-1}(x^2 - 2)}{\cos^{-1}(x) + \sin^{-1}(\sin^3(x^2))}, \quad \textit{where} \quad x = 1$$

Answer

$$r = \left\{ \frac{\{\tan^{-1}((\{x^2\}_1 - 2\}_2))\}_3}{\{\{\cos^{-1}(x)\}_1 + \{\sin^{-1}((\{(\{\sin(\{x^2\}_1)\}_2)^3\}_3)\}_4\}_5} \right\}_6$$

```
x = 1;
r = atan(x^2 - 2)/(acos(x) + asin(sin(x^2)^3));
```

Example 12

Write a Matlab program to evaluate r using the minimum number of parentheses,

$$r = \frac{\sqrt[3]{\log(x^2 + 1)}}{(2e^x + \tan^{-1}(x^2))^{-0.5}}, \quad where \quad x = 1$$

Answer

$$r = \left\{ \frac{\left\{ \sqrt[3]{\{\log((\{x^2\}_1 + 1\}_2))\}_3} \right\}_4}{\{((\{\{2\{e^x\}_1\}_2 + \{\tan^{-1}(\{x^2\}_1)\}_2\}_3)^{-0.5}\}_4} \right\}_5$$

```
x = 1;
r = log10(x^2 + 1)^(1/3)/(2*exp(x) + atan(x^2))^(-0.5);
```

2.3.4 From Matlab Expressions to Mathematical Expressions

Now we are going to go the opposite way and convert Matlab coded mathematical expressions back to their equivalent mathematical expressions.

Example 13

Write the mathematical expression to find r that is equivalent to the following Matlab program, where a = 2, b = 3, c = 4, d = 5.

```
>>r = a + b * (c + d);
```

Answer

$$r = a + b(c + d)$$

Example 14

Write the mathematical expression to find r that is equivalent to the following Matlab program, where a = 2, b = 3, c = 4, d = 5.

```
>>r = a + b + c * d;
```

Answer

$$r = a + b + c * d$$

Example 15

Write the mathematical expression to find r that is equivalent to the following Matlab program, where a = 2, b = 3, c = 4, d = 5.

```
>>r = (a + b)/(c + d);
```

Answer

$$r = \frac{a+b}{c+d}$$

Example 16

Write the mathematical expression to find r that is equivalent to the following Matlab program, where a = 2, b = 3, c = 4, d = 5, e = 6.

```
>>r = (a + b)/(c + d) + e;
```

Answer

$$r = \frac{a+b}{c+d} + e$$

Example 17

Write the mathematical expression to find r that is equivalent to the following Matlab program, where a = 2, b = 3, c = 4.

```
>>r = a * b/c;
```

Answer

$$r = a\left(\frac{b}{c}\right) = \frac{ab}{c}$$

Example 18

Write the mathematical expression to find r that is equivalent to the following Matlab program, where a = 2, b = 3, c = 4.

```
>>r = a/b * c;
```

Answer

$$r = \left(\frac{a}{b}\right) \times c = \frac{ac}{b}$$

Example 19

Write the mathematical expression to find r that is equivalent to the following Matlab program, where a = 2, b = 3, c = 4.

$$>>r = a/b/c;$$

Answer

$$r = \frac{a/b}{c} = \frac{a}{bc}$$

Example 20

Write the mathematical expression to find r that is equivalent to the following Matlab program, where a = 2, b = 3, c = 4.

$$>>r = a/(b/c);$$

Answer

$$r = \frac{a}{b/c} = \frac{ac}{b}$$

Example 21

Write the mathematical expression to find r that is equivalent to the following Matlab program, where a = 2, b = 3, c = 4, d = 5.

$$>>r = (a/b)/(c/d);$$

Answer

$$r = \frac{a/b}{c/d} = \frac{ad}{bc}$$

Example 22

Write the mathematical expression to find r that is equivalent to the following Matlab program, where a = 2, b = 3, c = 4, d = 5.

$$>>r = ((a + b)/(c + d) + (a - b)/(c - d))/((a + b + c)/d);$$

Answer

$$r = \frac{\frac{a+b}{c+d} + \frac{a-b}{c-d}}{\frac{a+b+c}{d}}$$

Example 23

Write the mathematical expression to find r that is equivalent to the following Matlab program, where a = 2, b = 3, c = 4, d = 5.

>>r = ((a + b)/(c + d) + (a − b)/(c − d))/((a + b + c)/d) + a;

Answer

$$r = \frac{\frac{a+b}{c+d} + \frac{a-b}{c-d}}{\frac{a+b+c}{d}} + a$$

Example 24

Write the mathematical expression to find r that is equivalent to the following Matlab program, where a = 2, b = 3, c = 4, d = 5.

>>r = ((a + b)/(c + d) + (a − b)/(c − d))/((a + b + c)/(d + a));

Answer

$$r = \frac{\frac{a+b}{c+d} + \frac{a-b}{c-d}}{\frac{a+b+c}{d+a}}$$

Example 25

Write the mathematical expression to find r that is equivalent to the following Matlab program, where a = 2, b = 3, c = 4, d = 5.

>>r = ((a + b^2)^3/(c + d) + (a − b)/(c − d))/((a + b + c)^4/(d + a));

Answer

$$r = \frac{\frac{(a+b^2)^3}{c+d} + \frac{a-b}{c-d}}{\frac{(a+b+c)^4}{d+a}}$$

Example 26

Write the mathematical expression to find r that is equivalent to the following Matlab program, where a = 2, b = 3, c = 4, d = 5.

```
>>r = ((a + b)^2/(c + d) + (a − b)^3/(c − d))/((a + b + c)/d) + a^4;
```

Answer

$$r = \frac{\dfrac{(a+b)^2}{c+d} + \dfrac{(a-b)^3}{c-d}}{\dfrac{a+b+c}{d}} + a^4$$

Example 27

Write the mathematical expression to find r that is equivalent to the following Matlab program, where $a = 2$, $b = 3$, $c = 4$, $d = 5$.

```
>>r = ((a + b)^2/(c + d) + (a − b)^3/(c − d))/((a + b + c)^4/(d + a)^4);
```

Answer

$$r = \frac{\dfrac{(a+b)^2}{c+d} + \dfrac{(a-b)^3}{c-d}}{\dfrac{(a+b+c)^4}{(d+a)^4}}$$

2.3.5 Exercises

Write a Matlab program to evaluate r using the minimum number of parentheses, where $x = 2$, $y = 3$, $z = 4$

1. $r = \dfrac{x + \dfrac{y}{z}}{y^2} - 1$

2. $r = \dfrac{x + \dfrac{y}{z}}{y^2 + 3z} - 1$

3. $r = \dfrac{e^{\cos(2x)+1} + 2x}{\ln(x^2 + 1) + 2}$

4. $r = \tan^{-1}(x\tan(x^{\frac{1}{3}}))$

5. $r = \dfrac{-x + \sqrt{x^2 - 4yz}}{2y}$

6. $r = \dfrac{\dfrac{\cos(2x + 1) + 2}{3x^2 - 4}}{\dfrac{2\sqrt{y}}{\sin^{-1}(0.1z)}}$

Write the mathematical expression to find r that is equivalent to the following
Matlab program, where a = 2, b = 3, c = 4, d = 5.

7. r = (a + 1)/b^2 − 3
8. r = a + 1/b^2 − 3
9. r = a + 1/(b^2 − 3)
10. r = a + (1/b^2 − 3)
11. r = a + 1/(b^2) − 3
12. r = (a + b)/(c + d)^2
13. r = cos(2*a^2)^3/b − 4
14. r = log(acos(0.2*b) + sin(a))
15. r = log(acos(0.2*b)) + sin(a)

Lesson 2.4   Relational and Logical Operations for Scalar Variables

Objectives
- To learn the logical class in Matlab.
- To learn the main six relational operators in Matlab.
- To learn the main three logical operators in Matlab.

Topics
2.4.1 The logical Class
2.4.2 The Relational Operators
2.4.3 The Logical Operators
    2.4.3.1 AND "&" Logical Operator
    2.4.3.2 OR "|" Logical Operator
    2.4.3.3 NOT "~" Logical Operator
2.4.4 Combining Logical and Relational Operators

2.4.1 The logical Class

Any variable with a logical class has a value of either true or false. Matlab
represents true as 1, and false as 0. For example, type at the **Command Prompt**

>> r = true

Matlab responds with

r =
    1

To check the class of r, type at the **Command Prompt**

```
>>whos r
```

Matlab responds with

```
Name  Size  Bytes  Class      Attributes
r     1×1   1      logical
```

Another example, type at the **Command Prompt**

```
>>s = false
```

Matlab responds with

```
s =
    0
```

To check the class of s, type at the **Command Prompt**

```
>>whos s
```

Matlab responds with

```
Name  Size  Bytes  Class      Attributes
s     1×1   1      logical
```

2.4.2   The Relational Operators

The relational operators require two operands, and they compare two values. For example, is the value of b greater than 10? The answer for such a question could be either 1 or 0. The relational operators produce variables with a logical class. As mentioned earlier, the logical class variable represents true as 1 and false as 0.

Matlab has six relational operators which are

1. Greater than " > "
2. Less than " < "
3. Greater than or equal " >= "
4. Less than or equal " <= "
5. Equal " == "
6. Not equal " ~= "

We will explain some of these relational operators using some examples. First, create a scalar variable x and set it to a value of 1.

```
>>x = 1;
```

Create a second scalar variable y and set it to a value of 2.

```
>>y = 2;
```

The following Matlab command determines whether the value of the x is greater than the value of y. The result of this comparison is saved in a variable called a.

```
>> a = x > y
```

Matlab responds and displays the value of a as

```
a =
   0
```

Since the value of x is less than the value of y, the execution of the Matlab command x > y produces 0, which is equivalent to false. The result of this comparison is assigned to the logical variable a. The Matlab command x > y is equivalent of asking the question: Is x greater than y? Matlab answers by giving the value 0 and assigns this value to a. The value of 0 is equivalent to the answer false.

The variable a has a logical class. The value of a variable with the logical class is either 1 or 0. Since a is a logical scalar variable, Matlab uses one byte of your computer memory to save a. To check the class of a, type at the **Command Prompt**

```
>>whos a
```

Matlab responds with

```
Name  Size  Bytes  Class     Attributes
a     1×1   1      logical
```

Exercise 1[1]

Explain the operation of the Matlab commands

1. x = 1;
   y = −2;
   b = x < y;
2. x = 1;
   y = 2;
   c = x <= y;
3. x = 1;
   y = 2;
   d = x >= y;

4. x = -1;
   y = 2;
   e = x == y;
5. x = 1;
   y = 2;
   f = x ~= y;
6. x = 1;
   f = x ~= 1;

2.4.3   The Logical Operators

Matlab has three logical operators which are

1. AND "&"
2. OR "|"
3. NOT "~"

The logical operators produce variables with the `logical` class.

2.4.3.1   AND "&" Logical Operator

The Matlab AND logical operator & has two operands. It produces 1 if both of its operands have nonzero values. Otherwise, it produces 0. This is shown in the following table.

Operand 1	Operand 2	&
0	0	0
0	nonzero	0
nonzero	0	0
nonzero	nonzero	1

An operand of a logical operator with nonzero value is considered to be `true`. An operand with a negative value is also considered `true`. While an operand of a logical operator with a 0 value is considered to be `false`. For example,

   x = 1;
   y = 2;
   g = x&y

Matlab responds with

   g =
       1

Another example,

```
x   = 1;
y   = 0;
h   = x&y
```

Matlab responds with

```
h =
    0
```

Another example,

```
x   = 1;
y   = -1;
k   = x&y
```

Matlab responds with

```
k =
    1
```

Another example,

```
x   = 0;
y   = 0;
m   = x&y
```

Matlab responds with

```
m =
    0
```

Exercise 2[1]

Complete the table below with the appropriate answers, first without using Matlab. Then, check your answers using Matlab.

x	y	x & y
1	0	0
-1	-1	
0	3	
0	0	

2.4.3.2 OR "|" Logical Operator

The Matlab OR logical operator "|" has two operands and it produces an output of 1 if one of its operands has nonzero value. This is shown in the following table:

x	y	x | y
0	0	0
0	nonzero	1
nonzero	0	1
nonzero	nonzero	1

For example,

```
x = 1;
y = 2;
n = x|y
```

Matlab responds with

```
n =
   1
```

Another example,

```
x = 1;
y = 0;
p = x|y
```

Matlab responds with

```
p =
   1
```

Another example,

```
x = 0;
y = 0;
q = x|y
```

Matlab responds with

```
q =
   0
```

Another example,

```
x = 0 ;
y = -1 ;
r = x|y
```

Matlab responds with

```
r =
    1
```

2.4.3.3   NOT "~" Logical Operator

The NOT "~" logical operator has one operand and it produces 1 if its operand has a zero value. For example,

```
x = 0 ;
z = ~x
```

Matlab responds with

```
z =
    1
```

The NOT "~"operator produces 0 if its operand has a nonzero value. For example,

```
x = 1 ;
w = ~x
```

Matlab responds with

```
w =
    0
```

Another example,

```
x = -1 ;
y = ~x
```

Matlab responds with

```
y =
    0
```

2.4.4   Combining Logical and Rational Operators

Logical and rational operators can be combined. For example,

```
x = 1;
y = 2;
n = (x < 3)&(y < 0)
```

Matlab responds with

```
n  =
   0
```

The relational expression $x < 3$ produces 1, since x is less than 3.
The relational expression $y < 0$ produces 0, since y is greater than 0.
The & logical operation for 1 and 0 produces 0.

Exercise 3[1]

Explain the operation of the Matlab commands

```
x = - 1;
y = 2;
r = x&~y;
```

Exercise 4[1]

Explain the operation of the Matlab commands

```
x = 1;
y = 2;
m = (x > y)|(y < - x);
```

Exercise 5[1]

Explain the operation of the Matlab commands

```
x = 1;
y = - 2;
n = (x > y)&(y < x)
```

Exercise 6[1]

Determine the value of x first without using Matlab. Then, check your answers using Matlab.

1. $x = (1 < 2) \,\&\, (3 > 4)$
2. $x = 1 < 2 \,\&\, 3 > 4$
3. $x = -1 \,\&\, -1$
4. $x = \sim\!-1$
5. $x = \sim\!1$
6. $x = (1 < 2) \,|\, (3 > 4)$

Lesson 2.5 Complex Scalar Variables

Objectives
- To learn how to create complex scalar variables in Matlab.
- To learn how to do arithmetical operations for complex scalar variables using Matlab.

Topics

2.5.1 Introduction
2.5.2 Creating Complex Scalar Variables
2.5.3 Addition of Complex Numbers
2.5.4 Subtraction of Complex Numbers
2.5.5 Multiplication of Complex Numbers
2.5.6 Division of Complex Numbers
2.5.7 Conjugate of a Complex Number
2.5.8 Modulus and Angle of a Complex Number
2.5.9 Plotting of a Complex Number in Cartesian Coordinates
2.5.10 Plotting of a Complex Number in Polar Coordinates

2.5.1 Introduction

Matlab has a built-in capability to deal with complex numbers. Creating complex numbers, complex vectors, and complex arrays is simple using Matlab. Additionally, performing addition, subtraction, multiplication, and division for complex numbers is also easy using Matlab. Other operations such as calculating the modulus and angle of complex numbers can also be performed easily using Matlab.

2.5.2   Creating Complex Scalar Variables

To create the complex number $1 + i2$ in Matlab and assign it to the variable z, type at the **Command Prompt**

```
>> z = 1 + 2i
```

Matlab responds as follows:

```
z =
   1.0000 + 2.0000i
```

You can use j instead of i to represent $\sqrt{-1}$. For example,

```
>> z = 1 + 2j;
```

A third method to create a complex number is

```
>> z = 1 + 2*i;
```

A fourth method to create a complex number is

```
>> z = 1 + 2*j;
```

All the four commands above are equivalent. The value 1 is the real part of the complex number. The imaginary part of the complex number is 2. We refer to both parts as complex.

You can use either i or j to create complex numbers. Note that i and j are special variables in Matlab and their value is equal to $\sqrt{-1}$. Normally, mathematicians use i to represent $\sqrt{-1}$, whereas engineers use j to represent $\sqrt{-1}$.

Matlab considers the value of both i and j variables to be $\sqrt{-1}$ unless you specifically act to change their values. In the following example, the value of i is changed to 1. In this case, you cannot use i to create complex numbers. To illustrate this, type at the **Command Prompt**

```
>> i = 1;
>> z = 1 + 2*i
```

Matlab responds as follows

```
z =
   3
```

Another example, type at the **Command Prompt**

```
>> j = 2;
>> x = 1 + 2*j
```

Matlab responds as follows

```
x =
   5
```

To return the values of the i and j Matlab variables to their original states of $\sqrt{-1}$, type at the **Command Prompt**

```
>> clear i, j
```

Therefore, be very careful **not** to use the terms i and j elsewhere as variable names, loop count indices, and so on, or you may find unexpected errors in your use of complex numbers.

2.5.3   Addition of Complex Numbers

In Matlab, adding two complex numbers together is similar to the addition of two real numbers. For example, to add the two complex numbers z1 and z2, type at the **Command Prompt**

```
>> z1 = 1 + 2i;
>> z2 = 3 + 4i;
>> z = z1 + z2
```

Matlab responds with

```
z =
   4.0000 + 6.0000i
```

Mathematically, the addition of the two complex numbers

$$z_1 = x_1 + iy_1$$

and

$$z_2 = x_2 + iy_2$$

is

$$z = z_1 + z_2 = (x_1 + x_2) + i(y_1 + y_2)$$

2.5.4 Subtraction of Complex Numbers

In Matlab, subtracting two complex numbers is similar to the subtraction of two real numbers. For example, to subtract the complex number z2 from the complex number z1, type at the **Command Prompt**

```
>> z1 = 1 + 2i ;
>> z2 = 3 + 4i ;
>> z = z1 - z2
```

Matlab responds with

```
z =
    - 2.0000 - 2.0000i
```

Mathematically, the subtraction of the two complex numbers

$$z_1 = x_1 + iy_1$$

and

$$z_2 = x_2 + iy_2$$

is

$$z = z_1 - z_2 = (x_1 - x_2) + i(y_1 - y_2)$$

2.5.5 Multiplication of Complex Numbers

Matlab enables you to easily multiply complex numbers. For example, to multiply the two complex numbers z1 and z2, type at the **Command Prompt**

```
>> z1 = 1 + 2i ;
>> z2 = 3 + 4i ;
>> z = z1*z2
```

Matlab responds with

```
z =
    - 5.0000 + 10.0000i
```

Mathematically, the multiplication of the two complex numbers

$$z_1 = x_1 + iy_1$$

and

$$z_2 = x_2 + iy_2$$

is

$$
\begin{aligned}
z = z_1 z_2 &= (x_1 + iy_1)(x_2 + iy_2) \\
&= x_1 x_2 + ix_1 y_2 + iy_1 x_2 + i^2 y_1 y_2 \\
&= (x_1 x_2 - y_1 y_2) + i(x_1 y_2 + y_1 x_2)
\end{aligned}
$$

Remember that $i^2 = -1$

2.5.6 Division of Complex Numbers

Matlab enables you to easily divide complex numbers. For example, to divide the complex number z1 by the complex number z2, type at the **Command Prompt**

```
>> z1 = 1 + 2i ;
>> z2 = 3 + 4i ;
>> z = z1/z2
```

Matlab responds with

```
z =
    0.4400 + 0.0800i
```

Mathematically, the division of the complex number

$$z_1 = x_1 + iy_1$$

by the complex number

$$z_2 = x_2 + iy_2$$

is

$$z = \frac{z_1}{z_2} = \frac{x_1 + iy_1}{x_2 + iy_2}$$

Multiplying by the conjugate of the denominator

$$z = \frac{x_1 + iy_1}{x_2 + iy_2} \frac{x_2 - iy_2}{x_2 - iy_2}$$

$$= \frac{(x_1x_2 + y_1y_2) + i(x_2y_1 - x_1y_2)}{x_2^2 + y_2^2}$$

$$= \frac{(x_1x_2 + y_1y_2)}{x_2^2 + y_2^2} + i\frac{(x_2y_1 - x_1y_2)}{x_2^2 + y_2^2}$$

2.5.7 Conjugate of a Complex Number

The conjugate of the complex number z is computed by changing the sign of its imaginary part, and it is given the symbol z^*. For example, the conjugate of the complex number $z = 1 + i2$ is $z^* = 1 - i2$. In Matlab, the command conj is used to calculate the conjugate of complex numbers. For example, type at the **Command Prompt**

```
>> z = 1 + 2i;
>> z1 = conj(z)
```

Matlab responds as follows:

```
z1 =
    1.0000 - 2.0000i
```

2.5.8 Modulus and Angle of a Complex Number

Mathematically, the modulus of the complex number $z = x + iy$ is given by $\sqrt{x^2 + y^2}$.

The angle of the complex number z is given by

$$\text{angle}(x + iy) = \begin{cases} \tan^{-1}\left(\dfrac{y}{x}\right) & x > 0 \ \text{and} \ y > 0 \\[2ex] \pi - \tan^{-1}\left(\dfrac{y}{|x|}\right) & x < 0 \ \text{and} \ y > 0 \\[2ex] -\left(\pi - \tan^{-1}\left(\dfrac{|y|}{|x|}\right)\right) & x < 0 \ \text{and} \ y < 0 \\[2ex] -\tan^{-1}\left(\dfrac{|y|}{x}\right) & x > 0 \ \text{and} \ y < 0 \end{cases}$$

The first equation above corresponds to the first quadrant. The second equation corresponds to the second quadrant and so on... |y| refers to the absolute value of y. For example, $|-3| = 3$.

In Matlab, the modulus of a complex number z is determined using the command abs. For example, type at the **Command Prompt**

```
>> z = 3 + 4i;
>> a = abs(z)
```

Matlab responds as follows

```
a =
    5
```

To calculate the angle of the complex number z in Matlab, use the command angle(z). For example, type at the **Command Prompt**

```
>> b = angle(z)
```

Matlab responds with

```
b =
    0.9273
```

Note that the angle is given here in radians. To convert the angle from radians to degrees, multiply it by 180/π. For example,

```
>> angle_in_degrees = angle(z)*180/pi
angle_in_degrees =
    53.1301
```

2.5.9   Plotting a Complex Number in Cartesian Coordinates

To plot the complex number z in Cartesian coordinates, use the command plot as follows, type at the **Command Prompt**

```
>> z = 3 + 4i;
>> plot(z,'o');
>> xlabel('Real axis');
>> ylabel('Imaginary axis')
```

Matlab produces the following figure. The complex number is drawn as a circle here, denoted by the "o" argument (lower case letter o, not a zero!) that is supplied to the plot command. Note that the x axis corresponds to the real part of the complex number, whereas the y axis corresponds to the imaginary part of the complex number.

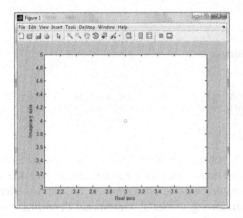

2.5.10   Plotting a Complex Number in Polar Coordinates

To plot the complex number z in polar coordinates, use the command `compass`. For example, type at the **Command Prompt**

```
>> z = 3 + 4i;
>> compass(z);
```

Matlab produces the following figure. Note that the length of the arrow corresponds to the modulus of the complex number z, and it is equal to 5. The angle of the arrow corresponds to the angle of the complex number z and it is equal to an angular value of 53.1301°.

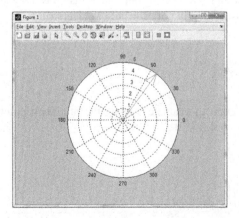

Answers to Selected Exercises

Lesson 2.1

Exercise 1

The two variable names

```
number_of_red_and_new_cars_that_have_been_used_in_the_year_2007_by_Chris_are = 10;
number_of_red_and_new_cars_that_have_been_used_in_the_year_2007_by_John_are = 11;
```

are both more than 63 characters long. Matlab will consider only the first 63 characters of any variable name and then ignores the rest of the characters. So for Matlab, the two variables will be considered to be just one identical variable. To show this, type the following at Matlab **Command Prompt.**

```
clear
number_of_red_and_new_cars_that_have_been_used_in_the_year_2007_by_Chris_are = 10;
number_of_red_and_new_cars_that_have_been_used_in_the_year_2007_by_John_are = 11;
whos
```

Matlab responds with

```
Name
number_of_red_and_new_cars_that_have_been_used_in_the_year_2007
Size  Bytes  Class    Attributes
1×1   8      double
```

Matlab reports that there is only one variable saved in Matlab memory.

Incidentally, it would have the second value that was assigned to it, that is, 11, as the previously assigned value of 10 would be overwritten.

Lesson 2.4

Write a Matlab program to evaluate r using the minimum number of parentheses, where $x = 2$, $y = 3$, $z = 4$.

1. $r = \dfrac{x + \frac{y}{z}}{y^2} - 1$

```
x = 2; y = 3; z = 4;
r = (x + y/z)/y^2 - 1
```

2. $r = \dfrac{x + \frac{y}{z}}{y^2 + 3z} - 1$

```
x = 2; y = 3; z = 4;
r = (x + y/z)/(y^2 + 3*z) - 1
```

3. $r = \dfrac{e^{\cos(2x)+1} + 2x}{\ln(x^2 + 1) + 2}$

```
x = 2; y = 3; z = 4;
r = (exp(cos(2*x) + 1) + 2*x) / (log(x^2 + 1) + 2)
```

4. $r = \tan^{-1}(x\tan(x^{1/3}))$

```
x = 2; y = 3; z = 4;
r = atan(x*tan(x^(1/3)))
```

5. $r = \dfrac{-x + \sqrt{x^2 - 4yz}}{2y}$

```
x = 2; y = 3; z = 4;
r = (-x + sqrt(x^2 - 4*y*z))/(2*y)
```

6. $r = \dfrac{\dfrac{\cos(2x + 1) + 2}{3x^2 - 4}}{\dfrac{2\sqrt{y}}{\sin^{-1}(0.1z)}}$

```
x = 2; y = 3; z = 4;
r = ((cos(2*x + 1) + 2)/(3*x^2 - 4))/(2*sqrt(y)/asin(0.1*z))
```

Write the mathematical expression to find r that is equivalent to the following Matlab program, where $a = 2$, $b = 3$, $c = 4$, $d = 5$.

7. `>> r = (a + 1)/b^2 - 3`

$r = \dfrac{a + 1}{b^2} - 3$

8. `>> r = a + 1/b^2 - 3`

$r = a + \dfrac{1}{b^2} - 3$

9. `>> r = a + 1/(b^2 - 3)`

$r = a + \dfrac{1}{b^2 - 3}$

10. `>> r = a + (1/b^2 - 3)`

$r = a + \dfrac{1}{b^2} - 3$

11. `>> r = a + 1/(b^2) - 3`

$$r = a + \frac{1}{b^2} - 3$$

12. `>> r = (a + b)/(c + d)^2`

$$r = \frac{a + b}{(c + d)^2}$$

13. `>> r = cos(2*a^2)^3/b - 4`

$$r = \frac{\cos(2a^2)^3}{b} - 4$$

14. `>> r = log(acos(0.2*b) + sin(a))`

$$r = \ln(\cos^{-1}(0.2b) + \sin(a))$$

15. `>> r = log(acos(0.2*b)) + sin(a)`

$$r = \ln(\cos^{-1}(0.2b)) + \sin(a)$$

3 Vectors in Matlab

Chapter Outline

Lesson 3.1   Creating Vectors

Objective
- To learn how to create vectors in Matlab using four different methods.

Topics

3.1.1 Introduction

3.1.2 Method 1: Creating Vectors Manually
    3.1.2.1 Creating Row Vectors Manually
    3.1.2.2 Creating Column Vectors Manually
    3.1.2.3 Transpose Operation
    3.1.2.4 Determining the Number of Elements in a Vector
    3.1.2.5 Converting a Vector to a Column Vector

3.1.3 Method 2: Creating Vectors Using the Linear Method

3.1.4 Method 3: Creating Vectors Using the Linear Spacing Method

3.1.5 Method 4: Creating Vectors Using the Logarithmic Spacing Method

3.1.6 Empty Vectors

3.1.7 Vectors Concatenation

3.1.8 Creating Complex Vectors
    3.1.8.1 Method 1: Creating Complex Vectors Manually
        3.1.8.1.1 Creating Complex Row Vectors Manually
        3.1.8.1.2 Creating Complex Column Vectors Manually
        3.1.8.1.3 Transpose Operation
    3.1.8.2 Method 2: Creating Complex Vectors Using the Linear Method
    3.1.8.3 Method 3: Creating Complex Vectors Using the Linear Spacing Method

Matlab by Example. DOI: http://dx.doi.org/10.1016/B978-0-12-405212-3.00003-7

3.1.1   Introduction

As explained in the previous lessons, Matlab can create scalar variables which are single numbers. Matlab also can create vector variables. A vector is an array that contains only one row or one column. For example, the row vector

x = [1,2,3,4]

and the column vector

y =   [5
        6
        7
        8]

There are four different methods to create vectors, and they are all covered in this lesson.

3.1.2   Method 1: Creating Vectors Manually

3.1.2.1   Creating Row Vectors Manually

To create the row vector **x** = [2, 3, 5], type at Matlab **Command Prompt**

    >>x = [2,3,5];

This creates a row vector variable with the name x. The first element in this vector is 2. The second element is 3, and the third element is 5. Note that in this book that we use bold fonts to distinguish vector variables from scalar variables.

To display the contents of x, type at Matlab **Command Prompt**

    >>x

Matlab responds with

    x =
        2   3   5

To get more information about the vector x, type at Matlab **Command Prompt**

>>whos x

Matlab responds with

```
Name  Size  Bytes  Class
x     1×3   24     double array
Grand total is 3 elements using 24 bytes
```

Matlab informs you that x is a vector with the size of 1 row and 3 columns.

Matlab is the abbreviation of **Mat**rix **lab**oratory and is a matrix-based software package. A scalar variable is considered by Matlab to actually be a 1×1 matrix, while the vector x is considered to be a 1×3 matrix.

3.1.2.2 Creating Column Vectors Manually

To create the column vector

$$\mathbf{y} = \begin{bmatrix} 4 \\ 9 \\ 7 \\ 12 \end{bmatrix}$$

type at the Matlab **Command Prompt**

>>y = [4;9;7;12];

Note the repeated use of semicolons here. This creates a column vector variable with the name y. The first element in this vector is 4. The second element is 9, the third element is 7, and so on.

To display the contents of y, type at the Matlab **Command Prompt**

>>y

Matlab responds with

```
y =
    4
    9
    7
   12
```

To get more information about the column vector y, type at the **Command Prompt**

>>whos y

Matlab responds with

```
Name  Size  Bytes  Class
y     4×1   32     double array
Grand total is 4 elements using 32 bytes
```

Matlab informs you that y is a vector with the size of four rows and one column. Remember once again that Matlab is matrix-based software. The column vector y is considered to be a 4 × 1 matrix.

3.1.2.3   Transpose Operation

Consider the three-element column vector **x** that is shown below.

$$\mathbf{x} = \begin{bmatrix} 2 \\ 3 \\ 4 \end{bmatrix}$$

Mathematically, we can refer to the three-element column vector **x** in the form of the transpose of a three-element row vector, for example, as $\mathbf{x} = [2, 3, 4]^{T}$ where ^{T} refers to the matrix transpose operation. This operation involves changing all the rows in a matrix to columns and all the columns to rows.

Applying the transpose operation to vectors changes a row vector to a column vector and vice versa. To transpose the row vector **x** = [2, 3, 5], type at the **Command Prompt**

```
>> x = [2, 3, 5];
>> x = x';
```

where (') refers to the Matlab transpose operation.

To display the contents of the column vector x, type at the **Command Prompt**

```
>> x
```

Matlab responds with

```
x =
   2
   3
   5
```

3.1.2.4   Determining the Number of Elements in a Vector

The Matlab command length() is used to determine the number of elements in a vector. For example, to determine the number of elements in the vector x, type at the **Command Prompt**

```
>>x  =  [2,3,5];
>>n  =  length(x)
```

Matlab responds and displays the result as

```
n =
   3
```

Exercise 1[1]

Create the following vectors:

1. $x = [1, 2, 3, 4, 5]$
2. $y = [1, 2, 3, 4, 5]^\mathsf{T}$

Exercise 2[1]

Using Matlab, determine the number of elements in the vectors **x** and **y**.

Exercise 3[1]

Explain the Matlab command x = [1 2 3]; Note here that the vector elements are separated using spaces only, not commas.

3.1.2.5 Converting a Vector to a Column Vector

The Matlab colon operator, ":", can be used to convert a vector to a column vector. For example, the row vector

```
>> y = [1,2,3,4,5];
```

can be converted to column vector as follows:

```
>> y = y(:)
```

Matlab responds and displays the result as

```
y =
   1
   2
   3
   4
   5
```

3.1.3 Method 2: Creating Vectors Using the Linear Method

The linear method can be used to create a row vector that has linearly spaced elements, that is, the difference between two successive elements in the vector is constant. To create a vector using this method, you need to determine the start value, the increment, and the final value for the vector. For example, for the vector **x** = [0, 2, 4, 6, 8, 10], the start value is 0, the increment is 2, and the final value is 10. Remember that the difference between two successive elements in the vector is the increment: $2 - 0 = 2, 4 - 2 = 2, 6 - 4 = 2$, and so on.

The first element of the **x** vector is the start value, which is 0. To calculate the second element, the increment is added to the first element, which gives 2. The third element is calculated by adding the increment to the second element, and this produces 4. The fourth element is calculated by adding the increment to the third element, and this produces 6. This operation is repeated until the final value is reached or not exceeded.

To create the vector **x** = [0, 2, 4, 6, 8, 10], type at the **Command Prompt**

```
>> x = 0:2:10
```

Note that the start value is 0, the increment is 2, and the final value is 10.

Since this command has not ended with a semicolon (;), Matlab displays the contents of the vector x and produces the result

```
x =
     0   2   4   6   8   10
```

Let us try to create the vector **y** = [10, 8, 6, 4, 2, 0] using the linear method. Here the start value is 10. The increment is equal to $8 - 10 = -2$, which is the difference between each two successive elements in the vector. The final value is 0. To create the vector y, type at Matlab **Command Prompt**

```
>> y = 10: - 2:0;
```

To display the contents of the vector y, type at Matlab **Command Prompt**

```
>> y
```

Matlab produces the output

```
y =
    10  8  6  4  2  0
```

Exercise 4[1]

Write a Matlab command that creates the following vectors using the linear method.

1. $x = [-5, -4, -3, -2, -1, 0, 1, 2, 3, 4, 5]$.
2. $y = [5, 4, 3, 2, 1, 0, -1, -2, -3, -4, -5]$.
3. $z = [10, 8, 6, 4, 2, 0, -2, -4]$.

Exercise 5[1]

Explain the reason that the following two Matlab commands give the same result.

1. x = 1:2:9;
2. y = 1:2:10;

Exercise 6[1]

Write a Matlab command that creates a vector of the even whole numbers between 10 and 20 using the linear method.

Exercise 7[1]

Write a Matlab command that creates a vector of the odd whole numbers between 11 and 21 using the linear method.

Exercise 8[1]

Explain the reason that the following two Matlab commands give the same result.

1. x = 1:10;
2. y = 1:1:10;

3.1.4   Method 3: Creating Vectors Using the Linear Spacing Method

The Matlab function linspace(x1,x2,N) can be used to create a row vector. This command has three arguments which are

- x1 is the start value.
- x2 is the final value.
- N is the number of elements in a vector.

For example, to create the vector x = [0, 2, 4, 6, 8, 10], type at Matlab **Command Prompt**

```
>>x=linspace(0,10,6)
```

Matlab responds and produces the output

```
x =
    0   2   4   6   8   10
```

Exercise 9[1]

Write a Matlab command that creates the following vectors using the linear spacing method.

1. $x = [-5, -4, -3, -2, -1, 0, 1, 2, 3, 4, 5]$.
2. $y = [5, 4, 3, 2, 1, 0, -1, -2, -3, -4, -5]$.
3. $z = [10, 8, 6, 4, 2, 0, -2, -4]$.
4. $r = [\frac{1}{2}, \frac{1}{4}, \frac{1}{6}, \frac{1}{8}]$.
5. $s = [0, \frac{1}{2}, \frac{2}{3}, \frac{3}{4}, \frac{4}{5}]$.

Exercise 10[1]

Write a Matlab command that creates a vector of the even whole numbers between 10 and 20 using the linear spacing method.

Exercise 11[1]

Write a Matlab command that creates a vector of the odd whole numbers between 11 and 21 using the linear spacing method.

3.1.5 Method 4: Creating Vectors Using the Logarithmic Spacing Method

The `logspace(a1,a2,N)` function creates a row vector of logarithmically equally spaced points between 10^{a1} and 10^{a2}. This function takes three arguments that determine vector creation as follows:

1. The start value for the created vector is 10^{a1}.
2. The final value for the created vector is 10^{a2}.
3. The number of elements in the created vector is N.

For example, to create the vector $\mathbf{x} = [10, 100, 1000, 10000, 100000]$, type at the Matlab **Command Prompt**

```
>> x = logspace(log10(10),log10(100000),5)
```

Matlab responds and produce the output

```
x =
    10  100  1000  10000  100000
```

To show that the vector x is logarithmically equally spaced, type at the **Command Prompt**

```
>> y = log10(x)
```

Matlab responds with

```
y =
    1  2  3  4  5
```

Remember: Mathematically, if $x = 10^y$. Then $y = \log_{10}(x)$.

Exercise 12[1]

Write a Matlab command that creates the following vector using the logarithmically spacing method.
$\mathbf{x} = [1.0000, 1.2915, 1.6681, 2.1544, 2.7826, 3.5938, 4.6416, 5.9948, 7.7426, 10.0000]$

Exercise 13[1]

Explain the results produced by the Matlab command `logspace(0,pi,10)`

3.1.6   Empty Vectors

An empty vector is a vector that does not contain any elements. To create an empty vector, type at the **Command Prompt**

```
>> x = [];
```

The empty vector is very useful in simplifying programming in Matlab.

3.1.7 Vector Concatenation

Two vectors can be concatenated and become a single vector. For example, the concatenation of the vectors **x1** = [1, 2, 3] and **x2** = [4, 5, 6] can be performed in Matlab as follows. Type at the **Command Prompt**

```
>> x1 = [1,2,3];
>> x2 = [4,5,6];
>> x  = [x1,x2]
```

Matlab responds and produces the output

```
x =
    1  2  3  4  5  6
```

Exercise 14[1]

Explain the operation of the Matlab commands

```
x1 = [1,2,3];
x2 = [4,5,6];
x  = [x2 × 1]
```

Exercise 15[1]

Explain the operation of the Matlab commands

```
x1 = [1,2,3];
x2 = [4,5,6];
x  = [x1;x2]
```

Exercise 16[1]

Explain the operation of the Matlab commands

```
y1 = [1,2,3];
y2 = [4,5,6];
y3 = cat(1,y1,y2)
y4 = cat(2,y1,y2)
```

Exercise 17[1]

Explain the operation of the Matlab commands

```
s1 = [1;2;3];
s2 = [4;5;6];
s3 = [s2,s1]
```

Exercise 18[1]

Explain the operation of the Matlab commands

```
x1 = [1 2 3];
x2 = [4,5,6];
x3 = [x2;x1]
```

3.1.8 Creating Complex Vectors

Consider a complex number c that is represented mathematically as $c = a + ib$. The same number is represented in Matlab as $c = a + bi$. For example, the complex number $1 + i2$ is represented in Matlab as $1 + 2i$.

Matlab can be used to create complex vectors. Complex vectors are classified into row vectors and column vectors. There are three methods that can be used to create complex vectors, which are discussed next.

3.1.8.1 Method 1: Creating Complex Vectors Manually

3.1.8.1.1 Creating Complex Row Vectors Manually

To create the complex row vector $\mathbf{x} = [2 + i2, \ 3 + i4, \ 5 + i6]$, type at the **Command Prompt**

```
>> x = [2 + 2i,3 + 4i,5 + 6i];
```

To display the contents of x, type at Matlab **Command Prompt**

```
>> x
```

Matlab responds with

```
x =
    2.0000 + 2.0000i   3.0000 + 4.0000i   5.0000 + 6.0000i
```

3.1.8.1.2   Creating Complex Column Vectors Manually

To create the complex column vector

$$\mathbf{y} = \quad [4 + i3$$
$$9 + i4$$
$$7 + i5$$
$$12 + i11],$$

type at the Matlab **Command Prompt**

>> y = [4 + 3i ; 9 + 4i ; 7 + 5i ; 12 + 11i];

This creates a column vector variable with the name y. The first element in this vector is $4 + i3$. The second element is $9 + i4$, the third element is $7 + i5$, and so on. To display the contents of y, type at Matlab **Command Prompt**

>> y

Matlab responds with

```
y =
    4.0000  + 3.0000i
    9.0000  + 4.0000i
    7.0000  + 5.0000i
   12.0000 + 11.0000i
```

To get more information about the column vector y, type at Matlab **Command Prompt**

>> whos y

Matlab responds with

```
Name  Size  Bytes  Class
y     4×1   64     double array(complex)
Grand total is 4 elements using 64 bytes
```

Matlab informs you that y is a complex vector with the size of four rows and one column.

Remember that Matlab is matrix-based software. The column vector y is considered to be a 4×1 matrix.

3.1.8.1.3   Transpose Operation for Complex Vectors

Applying the transpose operation to a complex vector not only changes rows to columns and vice versa, but also conjugates the vector's elements. Remember, the conjugate operation changes the sign of the imaginary parts in the complex vector.

To transpose the row vector $\mathbf{x} = [2 + i, \ 3 - i2, \ 5 + i3]$, type at Matlab **Command Prompt**

```
>> x = [2 + i, 3 - 2i, 5 + 3i]
>> z = x';
```

where (') refers to the transpose operation.

To display the contents of the column vector z, type at Matlab **Command Prompt**

```
>> z
```

Matlab responds with

```
z =
    2.0000 - 1.0000i
    3.0000 + 2.0000i
    5.0000 - 3.0000i
```

Exercise 19[1]

Explain the operation of the Matlab commands

```
y   =   [4 - 3i; 9 + 4i; 7 - 5i; 12 + 11i];
z   =   y.';
```

Applying the command y.' changes rows to columns and columns to rows only. It does not conjugate the vector y elements.

3.1.8.2   Method 2: Creating Complex Vectors Using the Linear Method

To create the vector $\mathbf{x} = [0 + i2, \ 2 + i3, \ 4 + i4, \ 6 + i5, \ 8 + i6, \ 10 + i7]$, type at Matlab **Command Prompt**

```
>> x = (0:2:10) + i*(2:1:7)
```

Note that for the real part, the start value is 0, the increment is 2, and the final value is 10. For the imaginary part, the start value is 2, the increment is 1, and the final value is 7. Since this command has not ended with a semicolon (;), Matlab displays the contents of the vector x and produces the result

```
x =
    0 + 2.0000i       2.0000 + 3.0000i    4.0000 + 4.0000i
    6.0000 + 5.0000i  8.0000 + 6.0000i    10.0000 + 7.0000i
```

Exercise 20[1]

Write a Matlab command that creates the following vectors using the linear spacing method.

1. $x = [-5 + i5, -4 + i4, -3 + i3, -2 + i2, -1 + i]$.
2. $y = [1/2, 1/4 + i1/2, 1/6 + i2/3, 1/8 + i3/4, 1/10 + i4/5]$.

3.1.8.3 Method 3: Creating Complex Vectors Using the Linear Spacing Method

The Matlab function `linspace(x1,x2,N)` can be used to create a row complex vector. This command has three arguments.

1. The first argument `x1` is the start value.
2. The second argument `x2` is the final value.
3. The third argument `N` is the number of elements in a vector.

For example, to create the vector $x = [0 + i0.1, 2 + i0.2, 4 + i0.3, 6 + i0.4]$, type at the Matlab **Command Prompt**

```
>>x = linspace(0 + 0.1i, 6 + 0.4i, 4)
```

Matlab responds with

```
x =
    0 + 0.1000i   2.0000 + 0.2000i   4.0000 + 0.3000i   6.0000 + 0.4000i
```

Exercise 21[1]

Write a Matlab command that creates the following vectors using the linear spacing method.

1. $x = [-5 + i5, -4 + i4, -3 + i3, -2 + i2, -1 + i1]$.
2. $y = [1/2, 1/4 + i1/2, 1/6 + i2/3, 1/8 + i3/4, 1/10 + i4/5]$.

Exercise 22[1]

Explain why representing the complex number $r = 1 + i2$ using the following code is correct.

```
>>r = 1 + 2*i;
```

Exercise 23[1]

Explain why representing the complex number $r = 1 + i2$ using the following code is correct.

```
>> r = 1 + 2*j;
```

Exercise 24[1]

Explain why representing the complex number $r = 1 + i2$ using the following code is correct.

```
>> r = 1 + 2j;
```

Exercise 25[1]

Explain why representing the complex number $r = 1 + i2$ using the following code is not correct.

```
>> i = 1;
>> r = 1 + 2 * i;
```

Lesson 3.2   Relational and Logical Operations on Vectors

Objectives
- To learn the main six relational operators on vectors.
- To learn the main three logical operators on vectors.
- To learn the `logical` class in Matlab.

Topics
3.2.1 The Relational Operators on Vectors
3.2.2 The Logical Operators on Vectors
      3.2.2.1 AND "&" Logical Operator
      3.2.2.2 OR "|" Logical Operator
      3.2.2.3 NOT "~" Logical Operator
3.2.3 Combining Logical and Relational Operators

3.2.1   Relational Operations on Vectors

As you learned in Lesson 2.4, Matlab has six relational operators which are

1. Greater than " > "
2. Less than " < "
3. Greater than or equal to " >= "
4. Less than or equal to " <= "
5. Equal to " == "
6. Not equal to " ~= "

Here we will explain the use of these relational operators for vectors using examples. First, create a vector x as follows:

```
>>x = [2,4,7,9, - 1,2];
```

Also, create a second vector y as follows.

```
>>y = [ - 1,4,8,1, - 4,6];
```

The following Matlab command determines whether the value of each element in the vector x is greater than the corresponding element in the vector y. The results of this comparison are saved in the vector z.

```
>>z = x>y
```

Matlab responds and displays the value of z as.

```
z =
    1   0   0   1   1   0
```

The value of the first element of x is 2. The value of the first element of y is −1. The execution of the command $z = x > y$ is the equivalent of asking Matlab the following question: "Are the elements in the vector x greater than the elements in the vector y?" The answer is true(1) for the first element in the x and y vectors, since 2 is greater than −1. So Matlab assigns the first value of z to 1, which means true.

To determine the value of the second element in z, Matlab compares the value of the second element of vector x with the second element of vector y to evaluate the logical expression x>y. The value of the second element of x is 4, and the value of the second element of y is 4. Since both values are equal, the evaluation of the logical expression x>y is false. So Matlab assigns the second value of z to 0, which means false.

The same operation is repeated for the rest of the elements in both the x and y vectors.

The class of the vector z is logical. The values of a logical class vector can only be either 1 or 0. Since z is a six-element logical vector, Matlab uses six bytes of your computer memory to save z. To check the class of z, type at Matlab **Command Prompt**

```
>>whos z
```

Matlab responds with

```
Name  Size  Bytes  Class    Attributes
z     1×6   6      logical
```

Exercise 1[1]

Given the following two different vectors

$$x = [2,4,7,9,-1,2], \quad and \quad y = [-1,4,8,1,-4,6],$$

explain the operation of the following Matlab commands:

1. z = x < y
2. z = x == y
3. z = y < x
4. z = x <= y
5. z = y >= x

3.2.2 The Logical Operations on Vectors

As you learned in Lesson 2.4, Matlab has three logical operators, which are

1. AND "&"
2. OR "|"
3. NOT "~"

3.2.2.1 AND "&" Logical Operator

AND logical operator "&" produces true if both of its operands are true. For example, create the two vectors x and y as follows. Type at Matlab **Command Prompt**

```
x = [0,4,7,0,-1,2];
y = [1,2,8,0,-4,6];
z = x&y
```

Matlab produces the output

```
z =
   0  1  1  0  1  1
```

Matlab evaluates the expression x&y and assigns the results to the vector z.
The first element in z is evaluated as follows. The first element in vector x is 0,
and it is considered to be false. The first element in y is 1, and it is considered to
be true. Evaluating the "&" logical operation false&true produces false because
the first operand for the "&" logical operator is false. A value of 0, which means
false, is therefore assigned to the first element of the vector z.

The second element of z is evaluated as follows. The second element of x is 4,
and it is therefore considered to be true. The second element of y is 2, and it is
therefore also considered to be true. Evaluating the "&" logical operation produces
true, since both operands for "&" logical operator are true. A value of 1, which is
true, is therefore assigned to the second element in the vector z. And so on.

Remember: An input to relational and logical operators is considered to be true
if it has a nonzero value, while an input with a 0 value is considered to be false.
An input with a negative value is considered to be true.

3.2.2.2   OR "|" Logical Operator

The OR logical operator "|" produces true if one of its operands is true. For
example, type at the Matlab **Command Prompt**

```
x =   [0,4,7,0,-1,2];
y =   [1,2,8,0,-4,6];
z =   x | y
```

Matlab produces the output

```
z =
    1  1  1  0  1  1
```

Matlab evaluates the expression x|y and assigns the results to the vector z.

3.2.2.3   NOT "~" Logical Operator

The NOT "~" logical operator has one operand, and it produces true if its operand
has a zero value, while it produces false if its operand has a nonzero value. For
example, type at the Matlab **Command Prompt**

```
x =   [0,4,7,0,-1,2];
w =   ~x
```

Matlab responds with

```
w =
    1  0  0  1  0  0
```

Exercise 2[1]

Given the two different vectors shown below:

    $x = [2,4,7,9,-1,2]$,   and $y = [-1,4,8,1,-4,6]$,

explain the operation of the following Matlab commands:

1. $z = x \& (\sim y)$
2. $z = (\sim x) \& y$
3. $z = x \& y \mid x$
4. $z = x \& y \mid \sim x$

3.2.3 Combining Logical and Relational Operators

Logical and relational operators can be combined. For example, type at the Matlab
Command Prompt

```
x =   [0,4,7,0,-1,2];
y =   [1,2,8,0,-4,6];
z =   (x<3)&(y<0)
```

Matlab responds with

```
z =
    0   0   0   0   1   0
```

Exercise 3[1]

Given the following two different vectors:

    $x = [2,4,7,9,-1,2]$,   and $y = [-1,4,8,1,-4,6]$,

explain the operation of the following Matlab commands:

1. $z = (x>y) \mid (y<x)$
2. $z = (x>y) \& (y<x)$

Lesson 3.3 Accessing Elements in Vectors

Objectives
- To learn how to access elements in vectors depending on their indices.
- To learn how to access elements in vectors depending on their values.
- To learn how to access elements in vectors using relational and logical operators.

(cont'd)

Topics

3.3.1 Accessing an Individual Element in a Vector Using its Index
3.3.2 Accessing a Group of Elements in a Vector Using Their Indices
3.3.3 Accessing Elements in a Vector Using Their Values
3.3.4 Accessing Elements in a Vector Using the Relational and Logical Operators

---

3.3.1   Accessing an Individual Element in a Vector Using its Index

Once you have created a vector, you can access an individual element within that vector. To illustrate this process, first create the vector $x = [3, 6, 9, 12, 15, 18]$ as follows:

```
>> x = 3:3:18
```

Matlab responds with

```
x =
   3   6   9   12   15   18
```

The table below shows the indices of x versus their values.

Index	1	2	3	4	5	6
Value	3	6	9	12	15	18

To access the first element in the vector, or in other words the element that has the *index* = 1, type at the Matlab **Command Prompt**

```
>> x(1)
```

Herein, 1 refers to the index of the element, not the value that is stored there.

Note that in some languages, for example, the C programming language, the first element of a vector may be referred to as element 0. However, in Matlab the first element of a vector is always referred to as element 1.

Matlab responds with

```
ans =
   3
```

This command prints out the first entry in the vector. Note that a new special variable called ans has been created. Any time you perform an action that does not include a specific assignment, Matlab saves the result in the special variable ans.

To access the third element in the vector x, type at Matlab **Command Prompt**

```
>> r = x(3)
```

Matlab responds with

```
r =
    9
```

This command saves the third element of the vector in the scalar variable r.
To access the last element in the vector, type at the Matlab **Command Prompt**

```
>> s = x(end);
```

Where end here is used to represent the last index in any indexing expression.
Or use the command

```
>> s = x(6);
```

This command saves the last element of the vector in the variable s. To display
the value of the variable s, type at the Matlab **Command Prompt**

```
>> s
```

Matlab responds with

```
s =
    18
```

Let us try to access the seventh element in the vector x as follows:

```
>> x(7)
```

Matlab responds with the error message

```
??? Index exceeds matrix dimensions.
```

Exercise 1[1]

Explain the operation and the output of the Matlab commands

```
x = 2:10;
y = x(length(x));
```

3.3.2   Accessing a Group of Elements in a Vector Using Their Indices

Once you have created a vector, you can access a group of elements within that
vector. To illustrate this process, create a vector y as follows:

```
>> y = 2:3:18
```

Matlab responds with

```
y =
    2   5   8   11   14   17
```

To access the first three elements of the vector y

```
>> a = y(1:3);
```

To access the last three elements of the vector y

```
>> b = y(end – 2:end);
```

To access the second, third, and the fourth elements of the vector y

```
>> c = y(2:4);
```

or

```
>> c = y([2,3, 4]);
```

To access the second, fourth, and the sixth elements of the vector y

```
>> d = y(2:2:6);
```

or

```
>> d = y([2,4, 6]);
```

To access the sixth, fourth, and the second elements of the vector y

```
>> e = y(6: – 2:2);
```

or

```
>> e = y([6,4, 2]);
```

To access the first, second, and the fourth elements of the vector y

```
>> f = y([1,2, 4]);
```

Exercise 2[1]

create the vector **x** with elements **x** = [0, 2, 4, 6, 8, 10, 12, 14, 16, 18, 20].

Exercise 3[1]

For the vector **x** that was just created in Exercise 2, write a Matlab command to do the following:

1. Access the first four elements in the vector **x**.
2. Access the last four elements in the vector **x**.
3. Access the first, fourth, and last elements in the vector **x**.
4. Access the first, third, fifth, and seventh elements in the vector **x**.
5. Access the elements with the odd indices in the vector **x**, that is, first, third, fifth, etc.
6. Access the elements with the even indices in the vector **x**, that is, second, fourth, sixth, etc.

Exercise 4[1]

Ensure the Matlab commands in Exercise 3 work correctly irrespective of the vector length. For example, the Matlab command x(11) accesses the last element of the vector x, since the length of this vector is 11. But suppose that we add a new element to the vector x, then the command x(11) is no longer suitable for accessing the last element of the vector. So it is more appropriate to write the command as x(end) instead of x(11) in order to access the last element of the vector x.

Exercise 5[2]

Write a Matlab command to flip the vector x and assign the result to the new vector variable z. The value of z should therefore be

z = [20,18,16,14,12,10,8,6,4,2,0].

Ensure that the Matlab commands in this exercise work correctly irrespective of the length of the vector x.

3.3.3   Accessing Elements in a Vector Using Their Values

Matlab enables you to easily search for an individual element, or a group of elements, in a vector, depending on their values. To illustrate this process, first create the vector y, as follows:

```
>> y = [2,3,5,5,7,10,12];
```

To find the *indices* of the elements whose values are equal to 5, type at the Matlab **Command Prompt**

```
>> a = find(y == 5)
```

Note that the double equals sign " = = " does not mean that you are assigning the value 5 to the vector y. This sign instead means that you are checking whether the values of the elements in the vector y are equal to 5. After executing this command, Matlab responds with

```
a =
    3  4
```

This means that the third and fourth elements of the vector y have the value 5.

To find the *indices* of the elements in the vector y whose values are greater than 7, type at the Matlab **Command Prompt**

```
>> b = find(y > 7)
```

Matlab responds with

```
b =
    6  7
```

To find the *indices* of the elements whose values are less than or equal to 9, type at the Matlab **Command Prompt**

```
>> c = find(y <= 9)
```

Matlab responds with

```
c =
    1  2  3  4  5
```

Another command can be used in combination with the preceding command to find the *values* of the elements in the vector y that are less than, or equal to, 9; type at the Matlab **Command Prompt**

```
>> d = y(c)
```

Matlab responds with

```
d =
    2  3  5  5  7
```

Exercise 6[1]

Explain the operation and the output of the following Matlab commands:

1. x = 2:20;
   a = find(x > 2, 4);
   b = x(a);

2. c = find(x >= 10, 4, 'first');
   d = x(c);
3. e = find(x ~= 2, 12, 'last');
   f = x(e);

   Hint: In Matlab, the " ~= " sign means "is not equal to."

Exercise 7[3]

Given a vector x = [3, 11, -9, -13, -1, 1, -11, 9, -6, -2], write the Matlab command(s) that will do the following. Hint: Use the find Matlab function.

1. Set values of x that are multiples of 3 to the value 3. Hint: Use the Matlab function rem.
2. Multiply the values of x that are even by 5.
3. Extract the values of x that are greater than 10 into a vector called y.
4. Set the values in x that are less than the mean of x to 0.
5. Set the values in x that are above the mean to their difference from the mean.
6. Set the values of x that are positive to −1.

3.3.4   Accessing Elements in a Vector Using the Relational and Logical Operators

Matlab has an interesting way of using the relational and logical operations to access elements in vectors. For example, type at the Matlab **Command Prompt**

    x = [0,4,7,0, -1,2];
    y = [1,3,8,0, -4,6];
    x > 3

Matlab responds with

    ans =
         0 1 1 0 0 0

Now type at the Matlab **Command Prompt**

    >> r = y(x > 3)

Matlab responds with

    r =
        3 8

The command $y(x>3)$ here outputs the elements of the vector y that are in the same elemental positions as those elements of the vector x which have a value that is greater than 3; that is, those elements of y that correspond to the same positions where x is greater than 3. In this example, the second and the third elements in the vector x are the only elements in this vector that have values which are greater than 3. The command $y(x>3)$ therefore chooses the second and the third elements of the vector y and assigns both of these elements to the new vector r.

Exercise 8[2]

Given the following two vectors:

```
x = [2,4,7,9, −1,2],  and
y = [−1,4,8,1, −4,6],
```

find the output that is produced using these commands. Do this first without using Matlab, then check your answer using Matlab.

1. $x(y<0)$
2. $y(x<0)$
3. $x(x<0)$
4. $x((x<2)\mid(x>=8))$
5. $x((x<2)\&(\sim(x>=8)))$

Exercise 9[3]

Given the following vector:

```
x = [3,11, −9, −13, −1,1, −11,9, −6, −2],
```

write the command(s) that perform the following. Do not use the `find` Matlab function.

1. Set values of x that are multiples of 3 to the value 3. Hint: use the Matlab function `rem`.
2. Multiply the values of x that are even by 5.
3. Extract the values of x that are greater than 10 into a vector called y.
4. Set the values in x that are less than the mean of x to 0.
5. Set the values in x that are above the mean to their difference from the mean.
6. Set the values of x that are positive to −1.

Lesson 3.4 Arithmetical Operations on Vectors

Objectives
- To learn how to add, subtract, multiply, and divide vectors using Matlab.
- To differentiate between element-by-element and matrix arithmetical operations in Matlab.

Topics
3.4.1 Vector Addition and Subtraction
    3.4.1.1 Vector Addition
    3.4.1.2 Vector Subtraction
    3.4.1.3 Adding a Number to a Vector
    3.4.1.4 Subtracting a Number from a Vector
3.4.2 Matrix and Element-by-Element Arithmetical Operations for Vectors
3.4.3 Vector Multiplication
    3.4.3.1 Element-by-Element Multiplication for Vectors
    3.4.3.2 Matrix Multiplication for Vectors
        3.4.3.2.1. Mathematical Background
        3.4.3.2.2. Matrix Multiplication for Vectors
    3.4.3.3 Multiplying a Vector by a Number
3.4.4 Vector Division
    3.4.4.1 Element-by-Element Division for Vectors
    3.4.4.2 Matrix Division for Vectors
    3.4.4.3 Dividing a Vector by a Number

3.4.1 Vector Addition and Subtraction

3.4.1.1 Vector Addition

To illustrate how to add vectors using Matlab, let us start by creating the two vectors x and y and then adding them. Type at the Matlab **Command Prompt**

```
x = [1,2,3];
y = [4,5,6];
```

To add the two vectors and save the result in a new vector z, type at the Matlab **Command Prompt**

```
>> z = x + y
```

Matlab automatically creates the vector z and saves the results of this addition process in this vector. Matlab responds to the above command with

```
z =
    5   7   9
```

Note that the addition of the two vectors is performed on an element-by-element basis. This means that the value of the first element in the vector z is calculated by adding the first element of the vector x to the first element of the vector y. The value of the second element of the vector z is calculated by adding the second element of the vector x to the second element of the vector y and so on for the rest of elements.

Remember that the dimensions of the vectors x and y must be equal, that is, the number of rows and the number of columns in both vectors must be the same. If this is not the case, then Matlab will give you an error message.

3.4.1.2 Vector Subtraction

To subtract y from x and save the result in a new vector s, type at the Matlab **Command Prompt**

```
>> s = x - y
```

Matlab creates the vector s and saves the results of this subtraction process in this vector. Matlab responds to the above command with

```
s =
    -3   -3   -3
```

The subtraction here is once again performed on an element-by-element basis, that is, the value of s(1) is calculated by subtracting y(1) from x(1). The value of s(2) is calculated by subtracting y(2) from x(2). And so on for the rest of the elements of s.

Remember again that the dimensions of the vectors x and y must be equal.

3.4.1.3 Adding a Number to a Vector

Matlab also enables you to add a number to a vector. Suppose that we would like to add 10 to all of the elements in the vector x and then save the result in a new vector named s. Type at the Matlab **Command Prompt**

```
x = [1,2,3];
s = x + 10
```

Matlab responds with

```
s =
    11   12   13
```

3.4.1.4 Subtracting a Number from a Vector

Matlab also enables you to subtract a number from a vector in a similar manner. Suppose that we would like to subtract 2 from all the elements in the vector x and then save the results in a new vector named t.

```
x = [1,2,3];
t = x - 2
```

Matlab responds with

```
t =
    -1   0   1
```

Exercise 1[1]

Explain the operation and the output of the Matlab commands

1. x = [1, 2, 3, 4];
   y = [5, 6, 7, 8];
   z = x - y;
2. x = [1, 2, 3, 4];
   y = [5, 6, 7, 8];
   s = y - x;

Exercise 2[1]

Explain why Matlab flags up an error when executing these commands.

1. x = [1, 2];
   y = [4, 5]';
   z = x + y;
2. a = [1, 2];
   b = [4, 5, 6];
   z = a + b;

Exercise 3[1]

Explain the operation and the output of the Matlab commands.

1. x = [1, 2, 3];
   y = 4;
   z = x + y;

2. x = [1, 2, 3];
   y = 4;
   z = x − y;

3.4.2 Matrix and Element-by-Element Arithmetical Operations for Vectors

As you have learned before, Matlab is matrix-based software. A scalar is considered by Matlab to actually be a 1×1 matrix. A vector is considered by Matlab to be a matrix with either one row or alternatively one column. Arithmetical operations that are performed on vectors using Matlab can be divided into *element-by-element* and *matrix* operations. Let us illustrate this concept using the following example.

Suppose that we have the vectors **x** = [1, 2, 3] and **y** = [4, 5, 6]. Let us perform element-by-element multiplication of the vectors **x** and **y** and save the results in **z**. This produces the vector **z** = $[1 \times 4, 2 \times 5, 3 \times 6]$ = [4, 10, 18].

Suppose that we have the vectors **a** = [1, 2, 3] and **b** = [4, 5, 6]^T. Let us perform matrix multiplication on the vectors **a** and **b** and save the results in *c*. This produces the single value scalar variable $c = 1 \times 4 + 2 \times 5 + 3 \times 6 = 32$.

It should be obvious from the above example that element-by-element and matrix operations are very different and produce different results of differing dimensions. It is therefore very important to differentiate between element-by-element operations and matrix operations when performing arithmetical operations upon vectors.

3.4.3 Vector Multiplication

There are two ways to multiply vectors: element-by-element multiplication and matrix multiplication.

3.4.3.1 Element-by-Element Multiplication for Vectors

To illustrate how to multiply two vectors using Matlab, let us start by creating the two vectors x and y. Type at the Matlab **Command Prompt**

```
x = [1,2,3];
y = [4,5,6];
```

To multiply the two vectors x and y on an element-by-element basis and then save the result in a new vector z,

```
>> z = x.*y
```

Note the dot character (.) is added before the asterisk (*). This informs Matlab to perform the multiplication operation on an element-by-element basis. Matlab responds with

```
z =
   4  10  18
```

Remember that the vectors x and y must once again have the same dimensions here.

3.4.3.2 Matrix Multiplication for Vectors

3.4.3.2.1 Mathematical Background

Suppose that we would like to multiply the two vectors **x** and **y** together in terms of matrix multiplication and save the result in **z**, that is, **z** = **xy**. Here **x** is called the multiplier, **y** is called the multiplicand, and **z** is called the product. To perform matrix multiplication upon vectors correctly, the number of columns in the vector **x** must be equal to the number of rows in the vector **y**. The variable **z** will have a number of rows that is equal to the number of rows in the vector **x** and a number of columns that is equal to the number of columns in the vector **y**, in this case 1×1.

The following figure shows the case of multiplying the row vector **x** by the column vector **y** (**z** = **xy**). The number of columns in **x** must be similar to the number of rows in **y**. It can be seen that the multiplication process here produces a single value scalar number z.

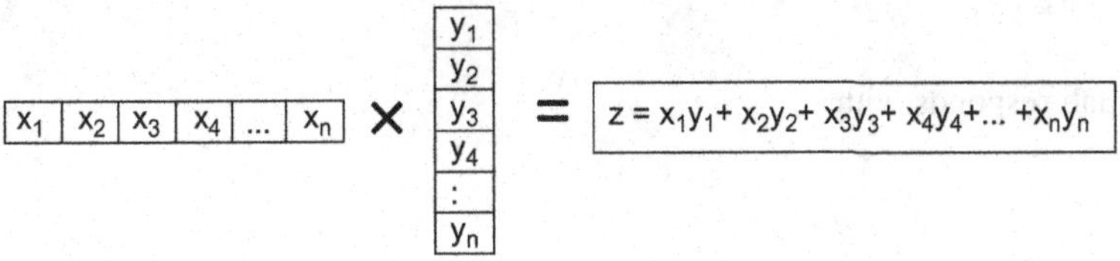

$$\boxed{x_1\ |\ x_2\ |\ x_3\ |\ x_4\ |\ \ldots\ |\ x_n} \quad \times \quad \boxed{\begin{matrix} y_1 \\ y_2 \\ y_3 \\ y_4 \\ : \\ y_n \end{matrix}} \quad = \quad \boxed{z = x_1 y_1 + x_2 y_2 + x_3 y_3 + x_4 y_4 + \ldots + x_n y_n}$$

The following figure shows the case of multiplying two vectors the other way around, that is, the column vector **y** by the row vector **x** (**z** = **yx**). The number of columns in **y** must be equal to the number of rows in **x**. The multiplication process is very different and this time produces a **square** matrix.

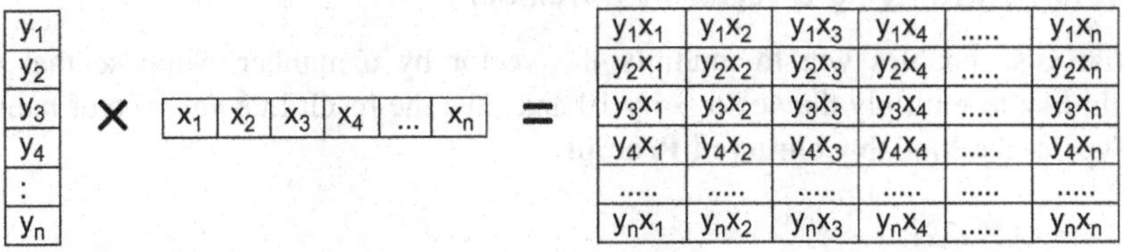

$$\boxed{\begin{matrix} y_1 \\ y_2 \\ y_3 \\ y_4 \\ : \\ y_n \end{matrix}} \quad \times \quad \boxed{x_1\ |\ x_2\ |\ x_3\ |\ x_4\ |\ \ldots\ |\ x_n} \quad = \quad \boxed{\begin{matrix} y_1 x_1 & y_1 x_2 & y_1 x_3 & y_1 x_4 & \ldots & y_1 x_n \\ y_2 x_1 & y_2 x_2 & y_2 x_3 & y_2 x_4 & \ldots & y_2 x_n \\ y_3 x_1 & y_3 x_2 & y_3 x_3 & y_3 x_4 & \ldots & y_3 x_n \\ y_4 x_1 & y_4 x_2 & y_4 x_3 & y_4 x_4 & \ldots & y_4 x_n \\ \ldots & \ldots & \ldots & \ldots & \ldots & \ldots \\ y_n x_1 & y_n x_2 & y_n x_3 & y_n x_4 & \ldots & y_n x_n \end{matrix}}$$

Remember: It is important to realize that in matrix multiplication $\mathbf{xy} \neq \mathbf{yx}$.

3.4.3.2.2   Matrix Multiplication for Vectors

To illustrate how to multiply two vectors together using Matlab, let us start by creating the vectors x and y. Type at the Matlab **Command Prompt**

```
x = [1,2,3];
y = [4;5;6];
```

Note that here x is a 1×3 row vector whose elements are separated by commas and that y is a 3×1 column vector whose elements are separated by semicolons. The following command multiplies the two vectors together via matrix multiplication and saves the scalar result in a variable z,

```
>> z = x*y
```

Note here that this time the dot character (.) **has not** been added before the asterisk (*). This informs Matlab to perform matrix multiplication instead of element-by-element multiplication. Matlab responds with

```
z =
    32
```

Note that this matrix multiplication process produces the number $1 \times 4 + 2 \times 5 + 3 \times 6 = 32$.

Now let us perform the multiplication the other way around, as R = y*x using Matlab.

```
>> R = y*x
```

Matlab responds with

```
R =
    4    8   12
    5   10   15
    6   12   18
```

Note that this time the vector multiplication process produces a 3×3 matrix.

3.4.3.3   Multiplying a Vector by a Number

Matlab also enables you to multiply the vector by a number. Suppose that we would like to multiply the vector x by 10 and save the result in a new vector named s. Type at the Matlab **Command Prompt**

```
x = [1,2,3];
s = x*10
```

Matlab responds with

```
s =
   10   20   30
```

Exercise 4[1]

Explain the operation and the output of the following Matlab commands:

1. x = [1, 2, 3];
   y = [4, 5, 6, 7];
   z = x.*y(1:3);
2. x = [1, 2, 3];
   y = [4, 5, 6, 7];
   z = x*(y(2:4))';
3. x = [1, 2, 3];
   y = [4, 5, 6, 7];
   z = y(2:4)*x';
4. x = [1, 2, 3];
   y = [4, 5, 6, 7];
   z = y(2)*x';
5. x = [1, 2, 3];
   y = [4, 5, 6, 7];
   z = y(2)*x;

Exercise 5[1]

Explain why Matlab flags up an error when executing these commands:

1. x = [1, 2, 3];
   y = [4, 5, 6];
   z = x*y;
2. x = [1, 2, 3];
   y = [4; 5; 6];
   z = y*x';
3. x = [1, 2, 3];
   y = [4; 5; 6];
   z = y'*x;

Exercise 6[1]

Write Matlab commands that compute the value of the vector **r** as shown below.

r = 0.2**x** + 0.3**y** + 0.4**z**, where
x = [1, 2, 3, 4, 5],

y = [2, 4, 6, 8, 10], and
z = [10, 20, 30, 40, 50]

3.4.4   Vector Division

3.4.4.1   *Element-by-Element Division for Vectors*

To illustrate the process of dividing two vectors using Matlab, let us start by creating the vectors x and y. Type at the Matlab **Command Prompt**

```
x = [1,2,3];
y = [4,5,6];
```

The following command divides the vector x by the vector y on an element-by-element basis and saves the result in a new vector z,

```
>> z = x./y
```

Note the dot character (.) is added before the division sign (/). This informs Matlab to perform the division operation here on an element-by-element basis. Matlab responds with

```
z =
    0.2500   0.4000   0.5000
```

Remember that the two vectors x and y here must have the same dimensions.

Exercise 7[2]

Let a vector x = [1, 2, 3, 4, 5, 6, 7, 8, 9, 10].
  Write Matlab command(s) to do the following:

1. Add 10 to each element in x. Assign the result to a new vector m.
2. Add 3 to only the odd-index elements of x, that is, the result should now be equal to [4, 2, 6, 4, 8, 6, 10, 8, 12, 10]. Assign the result to a new vector r.
3. Compute the square root of each element in x. Assign the result to a new vector s.
4. Compute the square of each element in x. Assign the result to a new vector t.

Exercise 8[2]

Let the column vectors x = [1; 2; 3; 4] and y = [5; 6; 7; 8]. Write Matlab command (s) to do the following:

1. Add the sum of the elements in x to the vector y (use the sum function). Assign the result to a new vector m.

2. Raise each element of x to the power specified by the corresponding element in y. Assign the result to the vector s.
3. Divide each element of y by the corresponding element in x. Assign the result to a new vector z.
4. Multiply each element in x by the corresponding element in y. Assign the result to a new vector r.
5. Find the sum of the vector x and assign the result to a variable called t.
6. Compute x'*y − t.

Exercise 9[2]

Given a vector, t = 1:0.2:2, write down the Matlab expressions that compute the following:

1. $\ln(2 + t + t^2)$. Use the Matlab function log.
2. $\log(2 + t + t^2)$. Use the Matlab function log10.
3. $\exp(1 + \cos(3t))$. Use the Matlab function exp.
4. $\cos^2(t) + \sin^2(t)$.
5. $\tan^{-1}(t)$. This is the inverse tangent function. Use the Matlab function atan.
6. $\cot(t)$.
7. $\sec^2(t) + \cot(t) - 1$.

3.4.4.2   Matrix Division for Vectors

Matrix division for vectors will not be discussed here because it does not have any mathematical meaning.

3.4.4.3   Dividing a Vector by a Number

Matlab also enables you to divide a vector by a number. Suppose that we would like to divide the vector x by 10 and save the result in a new vector named w. Type at the Matlab **Command Prompt**

```
x = [1,2,3];
w = x/10
```

Matlab responds with

```
w =
    0.1   0.2   0.3
```

Lesson 3.5   Plotting Vectors

Objective
* To learn how to plot vectors using Matlab.

Topics

3.5.1   Plotting Vectors

Matlab is an excellent software package for performing 2D graphics. Plotting vectors in Matlab is easy, as you will see. For example, let us plot the function $y = x^2$, where x is in the range of $[-3, 3]$. To plot this function let us initially create a vector to represent x.

```
>>x = - 3:1:3
```

Matlab produces the vector x as follows:

```
x =
   -3  -2  -1  0  1  2  3
```

The next step is to compute y as follows:

```
>>y = x.^2
```

Matlab produces the vector y as follows:

```
y =
   9  4  1  0  1  4  9
```

To plot the vector x versus the vector y, type at the Matlab **Command Prompt**

```
>>plot(x,y)
```

This produces the following figure. The `plot` function draws seven points, which are the number of elements in the vector x, and then connects the points together using straight lines. This is the reason why the function appears in the form of connected line segments.

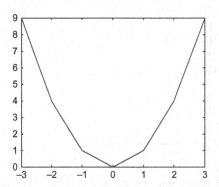

3.5.2   Increasing the Resolution of a Plot

To improve the resolution of the plot, you need to increase the number of points for the x vector, then recompute the y vector, and then once again plot the x vector versus the y vector. These steps are shown below.

```
x = -3:0.1:3;
y = x.^2;
plot(x,y)
```

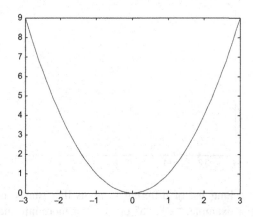

The number of points in the x vector has now been increased from 7 to 61.

3.5.3   Changing the Color of a Plot

You can change the color of the curve that represents the function $y = x^2$. For example, to change the color of the curve to red, type at the Matlab **Command Prompt**

```
>>plot(x,y,'r')
```

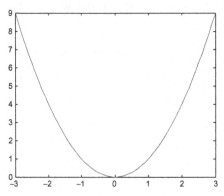

Matlab support the colors red "r", green "g", blue "b", cyan "c", magenta "m", yellow "y", white "w" and black "b".

3.5.4   Draw a Function as Points

You can plot the function $y = x^2$ in the form of unconnected points only, as shown below. Here we represent each point as an asterisk "*".

```
>>plot(x,y,'*')
```

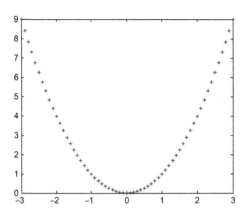

Matlab supports a long list of different symbols that can be used to represent points in a curve. For example, "+", "o" or "x". For more information, type at the Matlab **Command Prompt**

```
>>help plot
```

3.5.5   Labeling the x and y Axes

Matlab enables you to label the x and y axes. For example, to label the x and y axes, type the following Matlab commands

```
xlabel('Input data')
ylabel('System output')
```

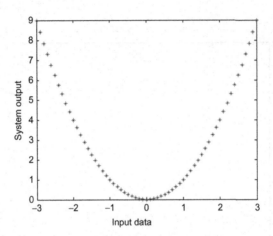

3.5.6   Adding a Title to a Figure

You can add a title for a figure. For example,

```
>>title('y=x^2')
```

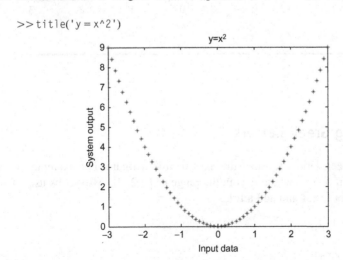

Note that Matlab enables you to format the text. Here we have used the symbol "^" in order to make the 2 in the expression x squared appear as a superscript.

Exercise 1[2]

Plot the function $y = \sin(x)$, where x is in the range of $[-\pi,\pi]$ to appear as the figure on the right.

Hint: Consider using the Matlab command

```
axis tight.
```

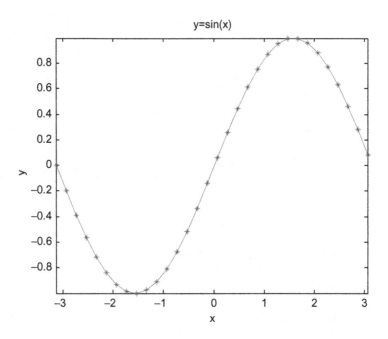

3.5.7 Using Greek Letters

You can use Greek letters to label the axes or title a figure. For example, let us draw the function $\beta = \alpha^3$ where α is in the range of $[-2, 2]$. Also let us use Greek letters to label both axes and add a title.

```
alpha = -2:0.1:2;
beta = alpha.^3;
plot(alpha, beta)
xlabel('\alpha')
ylabel('\beta')
title('\beta = \alpha^3')
```

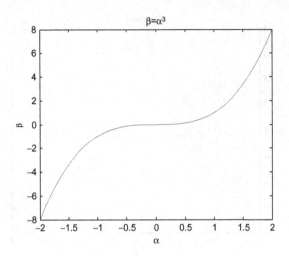

3.5.8   Adding a Grid to a Figure

Adding grid lines to a figure is very easy. You only need to give Matlab the following command:

```
>>grid on
```

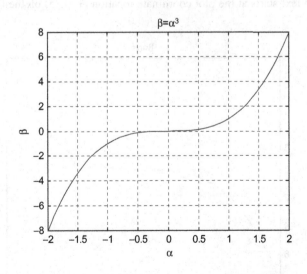

To remove the grid lines, you need to use the `grid off` command.

```
>>grid off
```

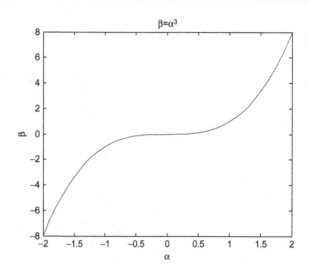

3.5.9   Adding a Text to a Figure

You can add a text anywhere to a figure using the `text` command as shown below.

```
>> text(1,0.75,'\beta = \alpha^3')
```

The added text starts at the plot coordinate location (1, 0.75) on the figure.

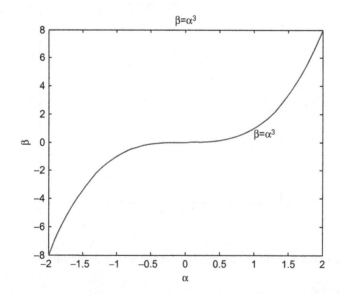

3.5.10   Changing the Font Size

You can change the font size for the axes labels, the figure title, and any text that you add to a figure. For example,

```
alpha = -2:0.1:2;
beta = alpha.^3;
plot(alpha, beta)
xlabel('\alpha','FontSize',24)
ylabel('\beta','FontSize',24)
title('\beta = \alpha^3','FontSize',17)
text(1,0.75, '\beta = \alpha^3','FontSize',18)
```

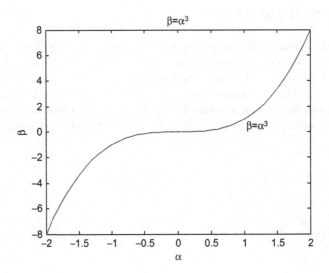

3.5.11   Changing the Line Width

Matlab enables you to change the line width of a curve. To illustrate this, let us plot the function $\beta = \alpha^3$ and increase the line width as shown in the following figure.

```
alpha = -2:0.1:2;
beta = alpha.^3;
plot(alpha, beta ,'LineWidth',3)
xlabel('\alpha','FontSize',24)
ylabel('\beta','FontSize',24)
title('\beta = \alpha^3','FontSize',17)
text(1,0.75, '\beta = \alpha^3','FontSize',18)
```

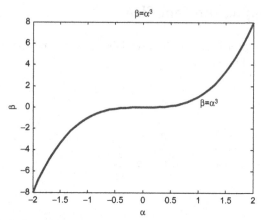

3.5.12   Multiple Plots

Matlab enables you to plot more than one function on the same figure. For example, let us plot two functions on the same figure. The first function is $y = x^2$, where x is in the range of $[-3, 3]$. The second function is $\beta = \alpha^3$ where α is in the range of $[-2, 2]$. The Matlab command `hold on` is used to hold the first figure, so as to plot the second function on it (which is done using the "r" keyword to plot the second function in red). The Matlab command `hold off` is used to release the figure.

```
x = -3:0.1:3;
y = x.^2;
plot(x,y, 'bo-')
hold on
alpha = -2:0.1:2;
beta = alpha.^3;
plot(alpha, beta,'rx-')
hold off
```

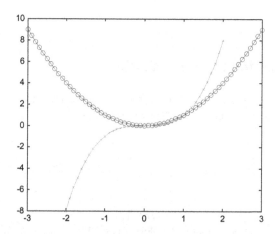

3.5.13   Adding a Legend to a Plot

You can add a legend to your figure as follows:

```
>> legend('y = x^2','\beta = \alpha^3')
```

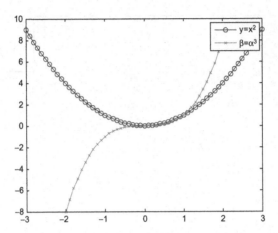

As you can see from the following figure, the legend is located on the curves. To solve this problem, we can change the location of the legend as follows:

```
>> legend('y = x^2','\beta = \alpha^3','Location','SouthEast')
```

Here we have changed the location of the legend so that it appears in the bottom right-hand corner of the figure.

Matlab enables you to change the location of the legend to be outside the figure. For more explanation, type at the Matlab **Command Prompt**

```
>> help legend
```

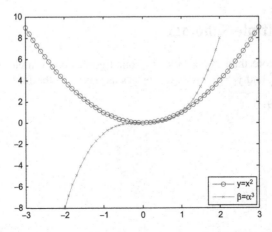

Exercise 2[2]

Write the Matlab commands that produce the following figure.

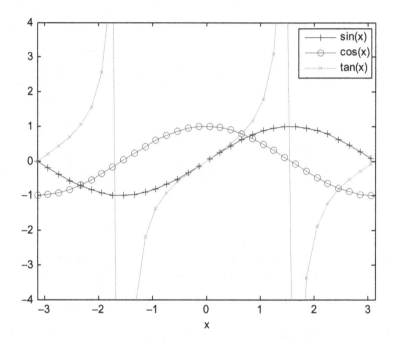

Hint: Use the Matlab command `axis` to scale the horizontal and vertical axis of the figure.

3.5.14   Multiple Subplots

You can have more than one subplot in your figure. For example, let us draw the functions $y_1 = x_1^2$ and $y_2 = x_2^3$ on two subplots as shown in the following figure.

```
x1 = -3:0.1:3;
y1 = x1.^2;
subplot(2,1,1)
plot(x1,y1)
x2 = -2:0.1:2;
y2 = x2.^3;
subplot(2,1,2)
plot(x2,y2)
```

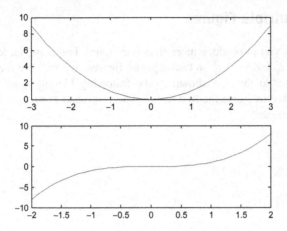

The subplot(m,n,p) command breaks the figure window down into an m × n matrix of smaller axes and selects the pth axis to display the current plot. For example,

The subplot(2,1,1) command breaks the figure window down into a matrix consisting of two rows and one column and selects the upper subplot in which to draw the function $y_1 = x_1^2$. The subplot(2,1,2) command breaks the figure window down into a matrix of two rows and one column and selects the lower subplot in which to draw the function $y_2 = x_2^3$.

Exercise 3[2]

Write the Matlab commands that produce the following figure.

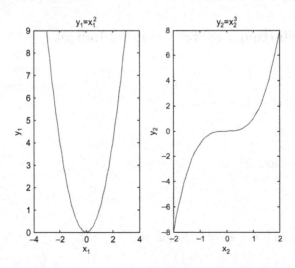

3.5.15   Multiple Figures

Matlab enables you to produce more than one figure. For example, let us draw the
functions $y_1 = x_1^2$ and $y_2 = x_2^3$ on two separate figures. We will use the Matlab command `figure` to do this. As shown in the following Matlab code, the command
`figure(1)` is used to create the first figure. The command `figure(2)` is used to create the second figure.

```
x1 = -3:0.1:3;
y1 = x1.^2;
figure(1)
plot(x1,y1)
x2 = -2:0.1:2;
y2 = x2.^3;
figure(2)
plot(x2,y2)
```

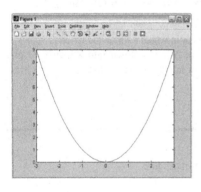
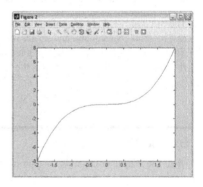

3.5.16   Plotting a Vector Using its Indices

Matlab enables you to plot a vector using its indices. For example, let us plot the
function $y = x^2$, where x is in the range of $[-3, 3]$. To plot this function let us initially create a vector to represent x.

```
>> x = - 3:1:3
```

Matlab produces the vector x as follows:

```
x =
     -3   -2   -1   0   1   2   3
```

The next step is to compute y as follows:

```
>> y = x.^2
```

Matlab produces the vector *y* as follows:

```
y =
    9  4  1  0  1  4  9
```

The values of the elements in the vector *y* versus their indices are shown in the following table.

indices	1	2	3	4	5	6	7
y	9	4	1	0	1	4	9

To plot the vector *y* versus its indices type at the Matlab **Command Prompt**

```
>> plot(y)
```

This produces the figure that is shown on the right. The plot function draws seven points, which are the number of elements in the vector *y*, and then it connects the points using straight lines. This is the reason why the function appears as a series of connected line segments.

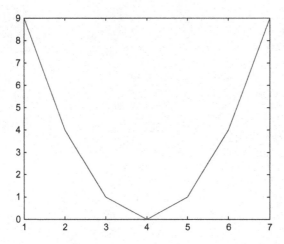

Answers to Selected Exercises

Lesson 3.1

Exercise 1

1. » x = [1, 2, 3, 4, 5]
2. » y = [1; 2; 3; 4; 5]

Exercise 2

1. » length(x)
2. » length(y)

Exercise 4

1. » x = −5:5 or
    » x = −5:1:5
2. » y = 5:−1:−5
3. » z = 10:−2:−4

Exercise 6

```
>> x = 10:2:20;
```

Exercise 7

```
>> x = 11:2:21;
```

Exercise 9

1. » x = linspace(−5,5,11)
2. » y = linspace(5,−5,11)
3. » z = linspace(10,−4,8)
4. » r = 1./ linspace(2,8,4)
5. » s = linspace(0,4,5)./ linspace(1,5,5)

Exercise 10

```
>> x = linspace(10,20,6)
```

Exercise 11

```
>> x = linspace(11,21,6)
```

Exercise 12

```
>>x = logspace(log10(1),log10(10),10)
```

Exercise 13

Type at the Matlab **Command Prompt**

```
>> help logspace
```

Matlab responds with

```
LOGSPACE Logarithmically spaced vector.
LOGSPACE(X1, X2) generates a row vector of 50 logarithmically equally
spaced points between decades 10^X1 and 10^X2. If X2 is pi, then the points
are between 10^X1 and pi.
```

For example, the Matlab command

```
>>x = logspace(log10(1),pi,5)
```

Produces the output

```
x =
     1.0000   1.3313   1.7725   2.3597   3.1416
```

Exercise 20

1. » x = (-5:-1) + i*(5:-1:1)
2. » y = 1./(2:2:10) + i*(0:4)./(1:5)

Exercise 21

1. » x = linspace(-5+5i, -1+i,5)
2. » y = 1./linspace(2,10,5) + i*linspace(0,4,5)./linspace(1,5,5)

Lesson 3.3

Exercise 2

```
>>x = [0,2,4,6,8,10,12,14,16,18,20]
```

Exercise 3

1. » x(1:4)
2. » x(8:11)
3. » x([1, 4, 11])
4. » x([1, 3, 5, 7])
5. » x(1:2:11)
6. » x(2:2:10)

Exercise 4

1. » x(1:4)
2. » x(end-3:end)
3. » x([1, 4, end])
4. » x([1, 3, 5, 7])
5. » x(1:2:end)
6. » x(2:2:end)

Exercise 5

```
>>z =   x(end:-1:1)  or
>>z =       fliplr(x)
```

Exercise 7

1. » x(find(rem(x,3) = =0)) = 3
2. » x(find(rem(x,2) = =0)) = x(find(rem(x,2) = =0))*5
3. » y = x(find(x>10))
4. » x(find(x<mean(x))) = 0
5. » x(find(x>mean(x))) = x(find(x>mean(x))) - mean(x)
6. » x(find(x>0)) = −1

Exercise 9

1. » x(rem(x,3) = =0) = 3
2. » x(rem(x,2) = =0) = x(rem(x,2) = =0)*5
3. » y = x(x>10)
4. » x(x<mean(x)) = 0
5. » x(x>mean(x)) = x(x>mean(x)) - mean(x)
6. » x(x>0) = −1

Lesson 3.4

Exercise 6

```
x =    [1,2,3,4,5];
y =    [2,4,6,8,10];
z = [10,20,30,40,50];
r = 0.2*x + 0.3*y + 0.4*z;
```

Exercise 7

1. » m = x + 10;
2. » r = x; r(1:2:end) = x(1:2:end) + 3
3. » s = sqrt(x)
4. » t = x.^2

Exercise 8

1. » m = y + sum(x)
2. » s = y.^ x
3. » z = y./ x
4. » r = y.* x
5. » t = sum(x)
6. » x'*y − t

```
ans =
        160
```

Exercise 9

1. » log(2 + t + t.^2)
2. » log10(2 + t + t.^2)
3. » exp(1 + cos(3*t))
4. » cos(t).^2 + sin(t).^2
5. » atan(t)
6. » cot(t)
7. » sec(t).^2 + cot(t) − 1

Lesson 3.5

Exercise 1

```
x = -pi:0.2:pi;
y = sin(x);
```

```
plot(x,y, 'r*-')
xlabel('x')
ylabel('y')
title('y = sin(x)')
axis tight
```

Exercise 2

```
clear; clc; close all
x = -pi:0.2:pi;
y1 = sin(x);
plot(x,y1,'b+-')
y2 = cos(x);
hold on
plot(x, y2, 'ro-')
y3 = tan(x);
plot(x,y3,'gx-')
axis([-pi pi -4 4])
legend('sin(x)','cos(x)','tan(x)')
xlabel('x')
hold off
```

Exercise 3

```
x1 = -3:0.1:3;
y1 = x1.^2;
subplot(1,2,1)
plot(x1,y1)
xlabel('x_1')
ylabel('y_1')
title('y_1 = x_1^2')
x2 = -2:0.1:2;
y2 = x2.^3;
subplot(1,2,2)
plot(x2,y2)
xlabel('x_2')
ylabel('y_2')
title('y_2 = x_2^3')
```

4 Arrays in Matlab

Chapter Outline

Lesson 4.1 Creating Arrays

Objectives
- To learn how to create arrays in Matlab manually.
- To learn how to create arrays in Matlab automatically.

Topics

4.1.1 Introduction

4.1.2 Creating Arrays Manually

    4.1.2.1 Creating Arrays Manually: Row-By-Row

    4.1.2.2 Creating Arrays Manually: Column-By-Column

4.1.3 Creating Arrays Using the `repmat` Function

4.1.4 Transpose an Array

4.1.5 Changing Array Dimensions Using the `reshape` Function

4.1.6 Finding the Size of an Array

4.1.7 Converting an Array to a Column Vector

4.1.8 Arrays Concatenation

4.1.9 Creating Complex Arrays

    4.1.9.1 Creating Complex Arrays Manually

    4.1.9.2 Creating Complex Arrays Automatically

Matlab by Example. DOI: http://dx.doi.org/10.1016/B978-0-12-405212-3.00004-9

4.1.1   Introduction

As you have learned in the previous lessons, Matlab can create scalars and vectors. Additionally, Matlab can create arrays. In the case of relatively small arrays, as shown below, you can use Matlab to generate these manually.

$$X = \begin{bmatrix} 1 & 2 & 4 \\ 7 & 3 & 5 \end{bmatrix}, \quad Y = \begin{bmatrix} 1 & 8 \\ 3 & 6 \\ 6 & 4 \end{bmatrix}, \quad Z = \begin{bmatrix} 1 & 2 & 5 \\ 8 & 3 & 4 \\ 9 & 6 & 7 \end{bmatrix}, \quad R = \begin{bmatrix} 3 & 5 \\ 9 & 7 \end{bmatrix}$$

When it comes to larger arrays, it will probably be more convenient to generate them automatically. Otherwise, you will have to manually type in very large sets of numbers. For example, you can use Matlab to automatically generate the large arrays shown below.

$$A = \begin{bmatrix} 1 & 2 & 3 & 4 & 5 & 6 \\ 1 & 2 & 3 & 4 & 5 & 6 \\ 1 & 2 & 3 & 4 & 5 & 6 \\ 1 & 2 & 3 & 4 & 5 & 6 \\ 1 & 2 & 3 & 4 & 5 & 6 \end{bmatrix}, \quad B = \begin{bmatrix} 1 & 1 & 1 & 1 & 1 \\ 2 & 2 & 2 & 2 & 2 \\ 3 & 3 & 3 & 3 & 3 \\ 4 & 4 & 4 & 4 & 4 \\ 5 & 5 & 5 & 5 & 5 \end{bmatrix}$$

$$R = \begin{bmatrix} 1 & 6 & 11 & 16 & 21 & 26 \\ 2 & 7 & 12 & 17 & 22 & 27 \\ 3 & 8 & 13 & 18 & 23 & 28 \\ 4 & 9 & 14 & 19 & 24 & 29 \\ 5 & 10 & 15 & 20 & 25 & 30 \end{bmatrix}, \quad S = \begin{bmatrix} 1 & 2 & 3 & 4 & 5 \\ 6 & 7 & 8 & 9 & 10 \\ 11 & 12 & 13 & 14 & 15 \\ 16 & 17 & 18 & 19 & 20 \\ 21 & 22 & 23 & 24 & 25 \end{bmatrix}$$

Remember: We will use bold uppercase letters to represent arrays in this book.

4.1.2   Creating Arrays Manually

4.1.2.1   Creating Arrays Manually: Row-By-Row

Now we will demonstrate how to create arrays manually by showing some examples. To create the array

$$X = \begin{bmatrix} 1 & 2 & 4 \\ 7 & 3 & 5 \end{bmatrix}$$

by using the row-by-row manual method, type at the Matlab **Command Prompt**

```
>> X = [1,2,4;7,3,5];
```

Note here that a comma (,) is used to separate elements in the same row. A semicolon (;) is used to separate rows.

To get some information about the array X, type at the Matlab **Command Prompt**

```
>>whos X
```

Matlab responds with

```
Name  Size  Bytes  Class   Attributes
X     2×3   48     double
```

Matlab informs you that X is an array that contains two rows and three columns. The array has a data class of double (8 bytes) and Matlab has therefore used 48 bytes (6 × 8) of your computer memory to save the array X.

To create the array

$$\mathbf{Y} = \begin{bmatrix} 1 & 8 \\ 3 & 6 \\ 6 & 4 \end{bmatrix}$$

by using the row-by-row manual method , type at the Matlab **Command Prompt**

```
>>Y = [1,8;3,6;6,4];
```

Exercise 1[1]

Create the following arrays using the row-by-row manual method.

$$\mathbf{Z} = \begin{bmatrix} 1 & 2 & 5 \\ 8 & 3 & 4 \\ 9 & 6 & 7 \end{bmatrix}, \quad \mathbf{R} = \begin{bmatrix} 3 & 5 \\ 9 & 7 \end{bmatrix}$$

4.1.2.2 Creating Arrays Manually: Column-By-Column

To create the array

$$\mathbf{X} = \begin{bmatrix} 1 & 2 & 4 \\ 7 & 3 & 5 \end{bmatrix}$$

by using the column-by-column manual method, type at the Matlab **Command Prompt**

```
>>X = [[1;7],[2;3],[4;5]];
```

[1;7] creates the first column in the array X.
[2;3] creates the second column.
[4;5] creates the third column.
The three columns are combined together (concatenated) using commas.
To create the array

$$Y = \begin{bmatrix} 1 & 8 \\ 3 & 6 \\ 6 & 4 \end{bmatrix}$$

by using the column-by-column manual method, type at the Matlab **Command Prompt**

```
>> Y = [[1;3;6],[8;6;4]];
```

Exercise 2[1]

Create the following arrays using the column-by-column manual method.

$$Z = \begin{bmatrix} 1 & 2 & 5 \\ 8 & 3 & 4 \\ 9 & 6 & 7 \end{bmatrix}, \quad R = \begin{bmatrix} 3 & 5 \\ 9 & 7 \end{bmatrix}$$

4.1.3   Creating Arrays Using the repmat Function

The repmat function is an abbreviation of "**rep**eat **mat**rix," and it has the syntax $B = repmat(A,M,N)$. This function creates a large matrix B consisting of an $M \times N$ tiling of copies of A. This function has the following three arguments:

1. A is the source array.
2. M is the number of times A is repeated in the vertical direction.
3. N is the number of times A is repeated in the horizontal direction.

Example 1

Suppose that you have the following array **A**:

$$A = \begin{bmatrix} 1 & 2 & 3 & 4 & 5 & 6 \\ 1 & 2 & 3 & 4 & 5 & 6 \\ 1 & 2 & 3 & 4 & 5 & 6 \\ 1 & 2 & 3 & 4 & 5 & 6 \\ 1 & 2 & 3 & 4 & 5 & 6 \end{bmatrix}$$

Answer

You can create this array manually as explained before, but this necessitates the tedious typing of many numbers. Alternatively, you can create this array automatically by using the repmat function. The array is created by repeating the first row five times. Let us create a vector that is similar to the first row in **A** and then repeat it vertically five times over, as follows:

```
>>a = [1,2,3,4,5,6];
>>A = repmat(a,5,1)
```

Example 2

Let us create the following array using Matlab. In this array, the first column is repeated six times.

$$B = \begin{bmatrix} 1 & 1 & 1 & 1 & 1 \\ 2 & 2 & 2 & 2 & 2 \\ 3 & 3 & 3 & 3 & 3 \\ 4 & 4 & 4 & 4 & 4 \\ 5 & 5 & 5 & 5 & 5 \end{bmatrix}$$

Answer

In this array, the first column is repeated horizontally six times. To create **B** using Matlab, type at the **Command Prompt**

```
>>b = [1;2;3;4;5];
>>B = repmat(b,1,5)
```

Example 3

Create the array below using the repmat function.

$$C = \begin{bmatrix} 1 & 2 & 1 & 2 \\ 3 & 4 & 3 & 4 \\ 1 & 2 & 1 & 2 \\ 3 & 4 & 3 & 4 \end{bmatrix}$$

Answer

```
>>C1 = [1,2;3,4];
>>C = repmat(C1,2,2);
```

4.1.4   Transpose an Array

This operation means changing the rows in an array into columns and changing the
columns into rows. Mathematically, if we refer to an array as **X**, then we refer to
the transpose of **X** as $\mathbf{X}^\mathbf{T}$. For example,

$$if \quad \mathbf{X} = \begin{bmatrix} 1 & 2 & 4 \\ 7 & 3 & 5 \end{bmatrix}, \quad \mathbf{X}^\mathbf{T} = \begin{bmatrix} 1 & 7 \\ 2 & 3 \\ 4 & 5 \end{bmatrix}$$

Create the array **X** using Matlab as follows:

```
>> X = [1,2,4;7,3,5]
```

Matlab responds with

```
X =
    1   2   4
    7   3   5
```

To transpose the array X, type at the **Command Prompt**

```
>> XT = X'
```

where (') refers to the transpose operation and we have stored the transposed array
as a new array variable called XT
Matlab responds with

```
XT =
    1   7
    2   3
    4   5
```

4.1.5   Changing Array Dimensions Using the reshape Function

The reshape function has the syntax B = reshape(X,M,N). This function changes
the dimensions of the array X to the new size of M × N. The elements are taken from
the source array X in a column-by-column fashion. The arguments for the reshape
function are

1. X is the source array.
2. M is the number of rows in the destination array B.
3. N is the number of columns in the destination array B.

Example 4

Using Matlab, change the dimensions of the 2 × 3 array

$$X = \begin{bmatrix} 1 & 2 & 4 \\ 7 & 3 & 5 \end{bmatrix}$$

to 3 × 2.

Answer

```
>> X = [1,2,4;7,3,5]
>> B = reshape(X,3,2)
```

Matlab responds with

```
B =
    1   3
    7   4
    2   5
```

Remember: The elements are taken from the source array X in a column-by-column fashion. We have a 2 × 3 array and need to make a 3 × 2 array from it by reshaping it, so the first column of X and also the first element of the second column of X together form the first column of B. The second column of B is formed from the second element of the second column of X and the third column of X, respectively.

Example 5

Create the array **B** using the reshape function.

$$B = \begin{bmatrix} 1 & 6 & 11 & 16 & 21 & 26 \\ 2 & 7 & 12 & 17 & 22 & 27 \\ 3 & 8 & 13 & 18 & 23 & 28 \\ 4 & 9 & 14 & 19 & 24 & 29 \\ 5 & 10 & 15 & 20 & 25 & 30 \end{bmatrix}$$

Answer

```
>> b = 1:1:30;
>> B = reshape(b,5,6)
```

Example 6

Create the following array **S** using the `reshape` function.

$$S = \begin{bmatrix} 1 & 2 & 3 & 4 & 5 \\ 6 & 7 & 8 & 9 & 10 \\ 11 & 12 & 13 & 14 & 15 \\ 16 & 17 & 18 & 19 & 20 \\ 21 & 22 & 23 & 24 & 25 \end{bmatrix}$$

Answer

```
>> s = 1:1:25;
>> S = reshape(s,5,5);
>> S = S';
```

Remember: Case sensitivity applies, so s and S are different variables!

Example 7

Create the following arrays using Matlab. The dimensions of **F** are 3×4.

$$F = \begin{bmatrix} 1 & 3 & 2 & 5 \\ 6 & 7 & 8 & 9 \\ 10 & 12 & 4 & 11 \end{bmatrix}$$

Change the dimensions of **F** to 4×3.

Answer

```
>> F = [1,3,2,5;6,7,8,9;10,12,4,11];
>> K = reshape(F,4,3)
```

Matlab responds with

```
K =
     1    7    4
     6   12    5
    10    2    9
     3    8   11
```

Remember: The elements that make up K are taken from F in a column-by-column fashion.

4.1.6 Finding the Size of an Array

Matlab enables you to determine the number of rows and columns in an array. For example, let us create the following array in Matlab.

$$\mathbf{X} = \begin{bmatrix} 1 & 2 & 4 \\ 7 & 3 & 5 \end{bmatrix}$$

```
>> X = [1,2,4;7,3,5];
```

To find the number of rows in X, type at the Matlab **Command Prompt**

```
>> m = size(X,1)
```

Matlab responds with

```
m =
    2
```

Here the "1" keyword in the size function indicates that we wish to know the first dimension of the array X, that is, the number of rows.

To find the number of columns in X, type at the Matlab **Command Prompt**

```
>> n = size(X,2)
```

Matlab responds with

```
n =
    3
```

Here the "2" keyword in the size function indicates that we wish to know the second dimension of the array X, that is, the number of columns.

To find the total number of elements in the array X, type at the Matlab **Command Prompt**

```
>> r = numel(X)
```

Matlab responds with

```
r =
    6
```

4.1.7 Converting an Array to a Column Vector

You can convert an array to a column vector using the colon (:) operator. For example, to convert the array

$$X = \begin{bmatrix} 1 & 2 & 4 \\ 7 & 3 & 5 \end{bmatrix}$$

to a column vector, type at the Matlab **Command Prompt**

```
>> X = [1,2,4;7,3,5]
>> x = X(:)
```

Matlab responds with

```
X =
    1  2  4
    7  3  5
```

and

```
x =
    1
    7
    2
    3
    4
    5
```

Note that the elements have been extracted from the array X, in a column-by-column fashion.

The array

$$X = \begin{bmatrix} 1 & 2 & 4 \\ 7 & 3 & 5 \end{bmatrix}$$

is actually saved in Matlab memory in the following order:

1	7	2	3	4	5

4.1.8 Arrays Concatenation

Arrays can be concatenated (combined) together to produce larger arrays.

Example 8

Concatenate the two arrays

$$X = \begin{bmatrix} 1 & 2 & 4 \\ 7 & 3 & 5 \end{bmatrix} \quad \text{and} \quad Z = \begin{bmatrix} 1 & 2 & 5 \\ 8 & 3 & 4 \\ 9 & 6 & 7 \end{bmatrix}$$

to produce the array

$$F = \begin{bmatrix} 1 & 2 & 5 \\ 8 & 3 & 4 \\ 9 & 6 & 7 \\ 1 & 2 & 4 \\ 7 & 3 & 5 \end{bmatrix} = \begin{bmatrix} X \\ Z \end{bmatrix}$$

Answer

```
>> X = [1,2,5;8,3,4;9,6,7];
>> Z = [1,2,4;7,3,5];
>> F = [X;Z];
```

Note that here we have used the semicolon (;) to combine X and Z arrays in the vertical direction.

Example 9

Concatenate the arrays

$$X = \begin{bmatrix} 1 & 2 & 4 \\ 7 & 3 & 5 \end{bmatrix} \quad \text{and} \quad R = \begin{bmatrix} 3 & 5 \\ 9 & 7 \end{bmatrix}$$

to produce the array

$$S = \begin{bmatrix} 1 & 2 & 4 & 3 & 5 \\ 7 & 3 & 5 & 9 & 7 \end{bmatrix} = \begin{bmatrix} X & R \end{bmatrix}$$

Answer

```
>> X = [1,2,4;7,3,5];
>> R = [3,5;9,7];
>> S = [X,R];
```

Note that here we have used the comma (,) to combine X and R arrays in the horizontal direction.

4.1.9   Creating Complex Arrays

Matlab can be used to create complex arrays, either manually or automatically.

4.1.9.1   Creating Complex Arrays Manually

To create the complex array,

$$G = \begin{bmatrix} 3 + i2 & i5 \\ 9 - i & 7 \end{bmatrix}$$

type at the Matlab **Command Prompt**

```
>>G=[3+2i,5i;9-i,7]
```

Matlab responds with

```
G =
    3.0000 + 2.0000i   0 + 5.0000i
    9.0000 - 1.0000i   7.0000
```

4.1.9.2   Creating Complex Arrays Automatically

To create the complex array,

$$A = \begin{bmatrix} 1 + 2i & 2 + 4i & 3 + 6i & 4 + 8i & 5 + 10i \\ 1 + 2i & 2 + 4i & 3 + 6i & 4 + 8i & 5 + 10i \\ 1 + 2i & 2 + 4i & 3 + 6i & 4 + 8i & 5 + 10i \\ 1 + 2i & 2 + 4i & 3 + 6i & 4 + 8i & 5 + 10i \\ 1 + 2i & 2 + 4i & 3 + 6i & 4 + 8i & 5 + 10i \end{bmatrix}$$

type at the Matlab **Command Prompt**

```
>>a=(1:1:5)+i*(2:2:10)
>>A=repmat(a,5,1)
```

Matlab responds with

```
A =
  1.0000+2.0000i   2.0000+4.0000i   3.0000+6.0000i   4.0000+8.0000i   5.0000+10.0000i
  1.0000+2.0000i   2.0000+4.0000i   3.0000+6.0000i   4.0000+8.0000i   5.0000+10.0000i
  1.0000+2.0000i   2.0000+4.0000i   3.0000+6.0000i   4.0000+8.0000i   5.0000+10.0000i
  1.0000+2.0000i   2.0000+4.0000i   3.0000+6.0000i   4.0000+8.0000i   5.0000+10.0000i
  1.0000+2.0000i   2.0000+4.0000i   3.0000+6.0000i   4.0000+8.0000i   5.0000+10.0000i
```

Lesson 4.2   Relational and Logical Operations on Arrays

Objectives
- To learn the main six relational operators on arrays.
- To learn the main three logical operators on arrays.
- To learn the `logical` class in Matlab.

Topics
4.2.1 Relational Operators on Vectors
4.2.2 Logical Operators on Vectors
    4.2.2.1 AND "&" Logical Operator
    4.2.2.2 OR "|" Logical Operator
    4.2.2.3 NOT "~" Logical Operator
4.2.3 Combining Logical and Relational Operations on Arrays

4.2.1   Relational Operations on Vectors

As you learned in Lesson 2.4, Matlab has six relational operators, which are

1. Greater than "$>$"
2. Less than "$<$"
3. Greater than or equal to "$>=$"
4. Less than or equal to "$<=$"
5. Equal to "$==$"
6. Not equal to "$\sim=$"

Here we will explain the use of these relational operators for arrays, again by using examples. Create the arrays

$$\mathbf{X} = \begin{bmatrix} 1 & 2 & -4 \\ 7 & 0 & 5 \end{bmatrix} \quad \text{and} \quad \mathbf{Y} = \begin{bmatrix} -3 & 5 & 1 \\ 9 & 7 & 0 \end{bmatrix}$$

using Matlab as follows:

```
>>X=[1,2,-4;7,0,5];
>>Y=[-3,5,1;9,7,0];
```

The following Matlab command determines whether the value of each element in the array X is greater than the corresponding element in the array Y. The results of this comparison are saved in the array Z.

```
>>Z=X>Y
```

Matlab responds and displays the value of Z as

```
Z =
   1   0   0
   0   0   1
```

The value of the first element of X(1,1) is 1. The value of the first element of Y(1,1) is −3. The execution of the command Z = X > Y is equivalent to asking Matlab the following question: "Are the elements in the array X greater than the elements in the array Y?" The answer is true(1) for the first elements in the X and Y arrays, since 1 is greater than −3. So Matlab assigns the first element of Z to a value of 1, which is equivalent to true.

To determine the value of the element Z(2,1) in Z, Matlab compares the value of the element of X(2,1) with the element of Y(2,1) to evaluate the logical expression X > Y. The value of the element X(2,1) is 7, and the value of the element Y(2,1) is 9. Since 7 is less than 9, the evaluation of the logical expression X(2,1) > Y(2,1) is false. So Matlab assigns the value of Z(2,1) to 0, which is equivalent to false.

The same operation is repeated for the rest of the elements in both the vectors X and Y.

The class of the array Z is logical. The values of a logical class can be either 1 or 0 and are represented by a byte of computer memory. Since Z is a six-element logical array, Matlab therefore uses 6 bytes of your computer memory to save Z. To check the class of Z, type at the Matlab **Command Prompt**

```
>>whos Z
```

Matlab responds with

```
Name  Size  Bytes  Class     Attributes
Z     2x3   6      logical
```

Exercise 1[1]

Given the following two arrays:

```
X = [1,2,−4;7,0,5], and
Y = [−3,5,1;9,7,0],
```

explain the operation of the following Matlab commands

1. Z = X < Y
2. Z = X == Y
3. Z = Y < X
4. Z = X <= Y
5. Z = Y >= X

4.2.2   Logical Operations on Vectors

As you learned in Lesson 2.4, Matlab has three logical operators, which are

1. AND "&"
2. OR "|"
3. NOT "~"

4.2.2.1   AND "&" Logical Operator

The AND logical operator "&" produces true if both of its operands are true. For example, create the two arrays

$$X = \begin{bmatrix} 1 & 2 & -4 \\ 7 & 0 & 5 \end{bmatrix} \quad \text{and} \quad Y = \begin{bmatrix} -3 & 5 & 1 \\ 9 & 7 & 0 \end{bmatrix}$$

using Matlab as follows:

```
>>X = [1,2, -4;7,0,5];
>>Y = [-3,5,1;9,7,0];
```

Type at the Matlab **Command Prompt**

```
>>Z = X & Y
```

Matlab produces the output

```
Z =
    1  1  1
    1  0  0
```

Matlab evaluates the expression X&Y and assigns the results to the array Z.

The first element in the array Z is evaluated as follows. The first element in the array X is 1, and it is considered to be true. The first element in the array Y is −3, and it is also considered to be true. Evaluating the "&" logical operation true&true produces true, since both operands for the "&" logical operator are true. A logical value of 1, which is equivalent to true, is therefore assigned to the first element of the vector Z.

Remember: An operand to logical operators is considered to be true if it has any nonzero value. Also, note that an operand with a negative value is therefore considered to be true. Any operand with a 0 value is considered to be false.

4.2.2.2   OR "|" Logical Operator

The OR logical operator "|" produces an output of true if one of its operands is true. For example, create the two arrays

$$\mathbf{X} = \begin{bmatrix} 1 & 2 & -4 \\ 7 & 0 & 0 \end{bmatrix} \quad \text{and} \quad \mathbf{Y} = \begin{bmatrix} -3 & 5 & 1 \\ 9 & 7 & 0 \end{bmatrix}$$

using Matlab as follows:

```
>>X = [1,2,-4;7,0,0];
>>Y = [-3,5,1;9,7,0];
```

Type at the Matlab **Command Prompt**

```
>>Z = X|Y
```

Matlab produces the output

```
Z =
   1  1  1
   1  1  0
```

Matlab evaluates the expression X|Y and assigns the results to the new array Z.

4.2.2.3 NOT "~" Logical Operator

The NOT "~" logical operator has only one operand and it produces an output of true if its operand has a value of zero. Also, the "~"operator produces an output of false if its operand has any nonzero value. For example, type at the Matlab **Command Prompt**

```
>>X = [1,2,-4;7,0,0]
>>W = ~X
```

Matlab responds with

```
X =
   1  2  -4
   7  0   0

W =
   0  0  0
   0  1  1
```

Exercise 2[1]

Given the following two arrays:

X = [1,2,-4;7,0,5], and Y = [-3,5,1;9,7,0],

explain the operation of the following Matlab commands

1. Z = X & (~Y)
2. Z = (~X) & Y
3. Z = X & Y | X
4. Z = X & Y | ~X

4.2.3   Combining Logical and Rational Operators

Logical and relational operators can be combined. For example, create the two arrays

$$\mathbf{X} = \begin{bmatrix} 1 & 2 & -4 \\ 7 & 0 & 0 \end{bmatrix} \quad \text{and} \quad \mathbf{Y} = \begin{bmatrix} -3 & 5 & 1 \\ 9 & 7 & 0 \end{bmatrix}$$

using Matlab as follows:

```
>>X=[1,2,-4;7,0,0];
>>Y=[-3,5,1;9,7,0];
```

Type at the Matlab **Command Prompt**

```
>>Z=(X<3)&(Y<0)
```

Matlab responds with

```
Z =
    1  0  0
    0  0  0
```

Exercise 3[1]

Given the following two arrays:

```
X=[1,2,-4;7,0,5], and Y=[-3,5,1;9,7,0],
```

explain the operation of the following Matlab commands:

1. Z = (X > Y) | (Y < X)
2. Z = (X > Y) & (Y < X)

Lesson 4.3   Accessing Elements in Arrays

4.3.1   Accessing an Individual Element in an Array Using its Index

There are two methods that are available to access the elements within an array. The first method is by row-and-column indexing. The second method is by linear indexing.

4.3.1.1 Row-and-Column Indexing Method

Once you have created an array, you can access an individual element within that array. Let us illustrate this using the following 3×4 array

$$\mathbf{X} = \begin{bmatrix} 3 & 4 & 8 & 12 \\ 2 & 5 & 7 & 11 \\ 1 & 6 & 9 & 10 \end{bmatrix}$$

The *row-and-column* indices of the elements of $\mathbf{X}$ are

$$\begin{bmatrix} X_{1,1} & X_{1,2} & X_{1,3} & X_{1,4} \\ X_{2,1} & X_{2,2} & X_{2,3} & X_{2,4} \\ X_{3,1} & X_{3,2} & X_{3,3} & X_{3,4} \end{bmatrix}$$

We refer to an element in the array $\mathbf{X}$ as $X_{m,n}$, where m refers to the row number and n refers to the column number. An element is identified using its row and column numbers. For example, the element $X_{1,1}$ has a value of 3 in the example given above. The element $X_{2,3}$ has a value of 7, and so on.

To create the array **X** using Matlab, type at the Matlab **Command Prompt**

```
>> X = [3,4,8,12;2,5,7,11;1,6,9,10];
```

To access the element $X_{1,1}$, type at the Matlab **Command Prompt**

```
>> X(1,1)
```

Make sure you use round brackets ( ) here!!!

Remember: Use square brackets [ ] to create the array, but round brackets ( ) to access the elements.

Matlab responds with

```
ans =
     3
```

This command prints out the individual array element $X_{1,1}$. Note that a new special variable called ans has been created. Matlab saves the result in the ans special variable.

To access the element $X_{2,3}$, type at the Matlab **Command Prompt**

```
>> f = X(2,3)
```

Matlab responds with

```
f =
    7
```

This command saves the value that is stored in the individual array element X(2,3) in the new scalar variable f.

To access the last element in the first row of X, type at the Matlab **Command Prompt**

```
>> s = X(1,end);
```

Or alternatively use the command

```
>> s = X(1,4);
```

which does the same thing.

This command saves the last element of the first row of X in the variable s. To display the value of the variable s, type at the Matlab **Command Prompt**

```
>> s
```

Matlab responds with

```
s =
    12
```

To access the last element in the third column of X, type at the Matlab **Command Prompt**

```
>> t = X(end,3);
```

Or use the alternative command

```
>> t = X(3,3);
```

to do the same thing. This command saves the last element of the third column of X in the variable t. To display the value of the variable t, type at the Matlab **Command Prompt**

```
>> t
```

Matlab responds with

```
t =
    9
```

Let us try to access the element $X_{1,5}$ as follows:

```
>> X(1,5)
```

Matlab responds with the error message
??? Index exceeds matrix dimensions.
This is because there is no fifth column in the array X!

Exercise 1[1]
Explain the operation and the output of the following Matlab commands:

```
>> X = [3,4,8,12;2,5,7,11;1,6,9,10];
>> y = X(size(X,1),size(X,2))
```

Exercise 2[1]
Explain the operation and the output of the following Matlab commands:

```
>> X = [3,4,8,12;2,5,7,11;1,6,9,10];
>> y = X(end,end)
```

4.3.1.2 Linear-Indexing Method

Let us illustrate this method using the following 3×4 array:

$$\mathbf{X} = \begin{bmatrix} 3 & 4 & 8 & 12 \\ 2 & 5 & 9 & 11 \\ 1 & 6 & 7 & 10 \end{bmatrix}$$

The linear indices of the elements of $\mathbf{X}$ are

$$\begin{bmatrix} X_1 & X_4 & X_7 & X_{10} \\ X_2 & X_5 & X_8 & X_{11} \\ X_3 & X_6 & X_9 & X_{12} \end{bmatrix}$$

Remember that in Lesson 4.1, Topic 4.1.7, we learned that arrays are actually stored in Matlab memory in the form of a linear series of the elements, stored in a column-by-column order. This method uses this approach to index the array elements. In the example above, the element X_1 has the value of 3. The element X_{10} has the value of 12, and so on.

To create the 3x4 array $\mathbf{X}$ using Matlab, type at the Matlab **Command Prompt**

```
>>X = [3,4,8,12;2,5,9,11;1,6,7,10];
```

To access the element X_1, type at the Matlab **Command Prompt**

```
>>a = X(1)
```

Matlab responds with

```
a =
  3
```

4.3.2 Accessing Rows in an Array

You can use the colon operator (:) to access a row in an array. For example, create the array

$$\mathbf{X} = \begin{bmatrix} 3 & 4 & 8 & 12 \\ 2 & 5 & 7 & 11 \\ 1 & 6 & 9 & 10 \end{bmatrix}$$

using Matlab as follows:

```
>>X = [3,4,8,12;2,5,7,11;1,6,9,10];
```

To access the first row, type at the Matlab **Command Prompt**

```
>> a = X(1, :)
```

Matlab responds with

```
a =
   3  4  8  12
```

To access the last row, type at the Matlab **Command Prompt**

```
>> b = X(end, :)
```

Matlab responds with

```
b =
   1  6  9  10
```

To access the last two rows, type at the Matlab **Command Prompt**

```
>> B = X(end - 1 : end, :)
```

Matlab responds with

```
B =
   2  5  7  11
   1  6  9  10
```

To access the first and the third rows, type at the Matlab **Command Prompt**

```
>> C = X([1, 3], :)
```

Matlab responds with

```
C =
   3  4  8  12
   1  6  9  10
```

4.3.3   Accessing Columns in an Array

You can use the colon operator (:) to access a column in an array. For example, create the array

$$X = \begin{bmatrix} 3 & 4 & 8 & 12 \\ 2 & 5 & 7 & 11 \\ 1 & 6 & 9 & 10 \end{bmatrix}$$

using Matlab as follows:

>> X = [3,4,8,12;2,5,7,11;1,6,9,10];

To access the first column, type at the Matlab **Command Prompt**

>> a = X(:,1)

Matlab responds with

    a =
        3
        2
        1

To access the last column, type at the Matlab **Command Prompt**

>> b = X(:,end)

Matlab responds with

    b =
        12
        11
        10

To access the first and second columns, type at the Matlab **Command Prompt**

>> C = X(:,[1, 2])

Matlab responds with

    C =
        3 4
        2 5
        1 6

4.3.4   Accessing a Group of Elements in an Array Using Their Indices

Once you have created an array, you can access a group of elements within that array. For example, to access the elements that are encircled by the oval in the array **X** below,

$$X = \begin{bmatrix} 3 & 4 & 8 & 12 \\ 2 & 5 & 7 & 11 \\ 1 & 6 & 9 & 10 \end{bmatrix}$$

type at the Matlab **Command Prompt**

```
>> X = [3,4,8,12;2,5,7,11;1,6,9,10];
>> r = X([1,2],3)
```

The last command means that you are asking Matlab to extract the first and second rows of the third column. Matlab responds with

```
r =
     8
     7
```

To access the elements that are encircled by the oval in the array **X** below,

$$X = \begin{bmatrix} 3 & 4 & 8 & 12 \\ 2 & 5 & 7 & 11 \\ 1 & 6 & 9 & 10 \end{bmatrix}$$

type at the Matlab **Command Prompt**

```
>> e = X(2,[2,3,4])
```

This command means that you are asking Matlab to extract the second, third, and fourth columns of the second row. Matlab responds with

```
e =
     5   7   11
```

To access the elements that are encircled by the rectangular area in the array **X** below,

$$X = \begin{bmatrix} 3 & 4 & 8 & 12 \\ 2 & 5 & 7 & 11 \\ 1 & 6 & 9 & 10 \end{bmatrix}$$

type at the Matlab **Command Prompt**

```
>> G = X([2,3],[2,3,4])
```

This command means asking Matlab to extract the second and third rows of the second, third, and fourth columns. Matlab responds with

```
G =
     5   7   11
     6   9   10
```

Exercise 3[1]

Create the array **Y** below. Then access the elements of **Y** that are encircled by the oval as shown, and assign them to a new vector named **r**.

$$Y = \begin{bmatrix} 1 & 2 & 16 & 31 & 22 \\ 2 & 8 & 12 & 21 & 23 \\ 4 & 9 & 11 & 14 & 25 \\ 3 & 6 & 10 & 16 & 34 \end{bmatrix}$$

Exercise 4[1]

Create the array **Z** below. Access the elements of **Z** that are encircled by the rectangle as shown, and assign them to a new array named **R**.

$$Z = \begin{bmatrix} 1 & 2 & 16 & 31 & 22 \\ 2 & 8 & 12 & 21 & 23 \\ 4 & 9 & 11 & 14 & 25 \\ 3 & 6 & 10 & 16 & 34 \end{bmatrix}$$

Exercise 5[1]

Explain the operation of the Matlab commands

```
>> X = [3,4,8,12;2,5,7,11;1,6,9,10];
>> A = X(1:2,1:2)
```

Exercise 6[1]

Explain the operation of the Matlab commands

```
>> X = [3,4,8,12;2,5,7,11;1,6,9,10];
>> b = X(1:2,end)
```

Exercise 7[1]

Explain the operation of the Matlab commands

```
>> X = [3,4,8,12;2,5,7,11;1,6,9,10];
>> c = X(end,1:2)
```

Exercise 8[1]

Explain the operation of the Matlab commands

```
>> X = [3,4,8,12;2,5,7,11;1,6,9,10];
>> D = X(1:end,1:end)
```

Exercise 9[1]

Explain the operation of the Matlab commands

```
>> X = [3,4,8,12;2,5,7,11;1,6,9,10];
>> e = X(end - 2:end,end - 1:end)
```

Exercise 10[2]

Explain the operation of the Matlab commands

```
>> X = [3,4,8,12;2,5,7,11;1,6,9,10];
>> F = X(end: - 1:end - 2,end: - 1:end - 2)
```

Exercise 11[2]

Explain the operation of the Matlab commands

```
>> X = [3,4,8,12;2,5,7,11;1,6,9,10];
>> f = X(1:5);
```

Exercise 12[1]

Explain why Matlab cannot run the following Matlab commands:

```
>> X = [3,4,8,12;2,5,7,11;1,6,9,10];
>> G = X(1:2,3:5)
```

Exercise 13[1]

Explain why Matlab cannot run the following commands:

```
>> X = [3,4,8,12;2,5,7,11;1,6,9,10];
>> h = X(0,0)
```

Exercise 14[3]

Write a Matlab command to flip the array

$$A = \begin{bmatrix} 1 & 2 & 3 \\ 4 & 5 & 6 \\ 7 & 8 & 9 \end{bmatrix} \text{ horizontally as follows } B = \begin{bmatrix} 3 & 2 & 1 \\ 6 & 5 & 4 \\ 9 & 8 & 7 \end{bmatrix}$$

The command should also assign the result to the variable **B**. Ensure the Matlab commands in this exercise work correctly irrespective of the size of the array **A**.

Exercise 15[3]

Write a Matlab command to flip the array

$$C = \begin{bmatrix} 1 & 2 & 3 \\ 4 & 5 & 6 \\ 7 & 8 & 9 \end{bmatrix} \text{ vertically as follows } D = \begin{bmatrix} 7 & 8 & 9 \\ 4 & 5 & 6 \\ 1 & 2 & 3 \end{bmatrix}$$

The command should also assign the result to the variable **D**. Ensure the Matlab commands in this exercise work correctly irrespective of the size of the array **C**.

4.3.5   Accessing Elements in an Array Using Their Values

Matlab enables you to search easily for an element or a group of elements in an array depending on their values. To illustrate this, create the array

$$E = \begin{bmatrix} 7 & 3 & 9 \\ 1 & 0 & 2 \\ 5 & 8 & 4 \end{bmatrix}$$

using Matlab as follows:

```
>> E = [7,3,9;1,0,2;5,8,4];
```

To find the *indices* of the elements whose values is greater than 7, type at the Matlab **Command Prompt**

```
>>[a,b] = find(E > 7);
>>[a,b]
```

After executing both commands, Matlab responds with

```
ans =
    3  2
    1  3
```

The output of Matlab means that the elements E(3,2) and E(1,3) are greater than 7.

To find the *indices* of the elements in the array E whose value is less than 3, type at the Matlab **Command Prompt**

```
>>[c,d] = find(E < 3);
>>[c,d]
```

Matlab responds with

```
ans =
    2  1
    2  2
    2  3
```

The output of Matlab means that the elements E(2,1), E(2,2) and E(2,3) are less than 3.

To find the *values* of the elements in E that have values that are less than 3, type at the Matlab **Command Prompt**

```
>>f = find(E < 3);
>>r = E(f)
```

Matlab responds with

```
r =
    1
    0
    2
```

Exercise 16[1]

Explain the operation and the output of the following Matlab commands:

1. E = [7, 3, 9; 1, 0, 2; 5, 8, 4];
   a = find(E > 2, 4);
   b = E(a);

2. E = [7, 3, 9; 1, 0, 2; 5, 8, 4];
   c = find(E >= 1, 3, 'first');
   d = E(c);
3. E = [7, 3, 9; 1, 0, 2; 5, 8, 4];
   E = find(E ~= 2, 1, 'last');
   f = E(e);

4.3.6 Accessing Elements in an Array Using Relational and Logical Operators

Matlab has an interesting way of using relational and logical operations to access elements in arrays. For example, create the following two arrays:

$$\mathbf{X} = \begin{bmatrix} 1 & 2 & -4 \\ 7 & 0 & 5 \end{bmatrix} \quad \text{and} \quad \mathbf{Y} = \begin{bmatrix} -3 & 5 & 1 \\ 9 & 7 & 0 \end{bmatrix}$$

using Matlab as follows:

```
>> X = [1,2, - 4;7,0,5];
>> Y = [ - 3,5,1;9,7,0];
```

Find the elements in X whose values are greater than 3.

```
>> X > 3
```

Matlab responds with

```
ans =
    0   0   0
    1   0   1
```

Note that ans is a logical array.
Now type at the Matlab **Command Prompt**

```
>> r = Y(X > 3)
```

Matlab responds with

```
r =
    9
    0
```

The command Y(X > 3) outputs the elements of Y which have the corresponding elemental positions within the array to locations in the array X where X is greater than 3. Here the elements X(2,1) and X(2,3) have values that are greater than 3.

The command Y(X>3) chooses the corresponding positions in the array Y, namely elements Y(2,1)and Y(2,3), and assigns both of these elements to the new variable r.

Exercise 17[2]

Given the following two arrays:

```
X =  [1,2,-4;7,0,5], and
Y =  [-3,5,1;9,7,0].
```

find the output that will be produced using the following commands, first without using Matlab. Then check your answer using Matlab.

1. X(Y < 0)
2. Y(X < 0)
3. X((X < 2) | (X >= 8))
4. Y((X < 2) & (~(X >= 8)))

Exercise 18[2]

Given the array A = [2, 4, 1; 6, 7, 2; 3, 5, 9], provide Matlab commands to do the following:

1. Assign the first row of A to a vector called x1.
2. Assign the last 2 rows of A to an array called Y.
3. Compute the sum over the columns of A.
4. Compute the sum over the rows of A.
5. Compute the standard deviation of each column of A.
6. Compute the mean of each column of A.

Exercise 19[2]

Given the vectors x = [1, 4, 8], y = [2, 1, 5] and the array
A = [3, 1, 6; 5, 2, 7], determine which of the following statements will correctly execute, and for those that will execute correctly, provide the result. If the command will not correctly execute, state why it will not do so.

1. x + y
2. x + A
3. x' + y
4. A - [x', y']
5. [x ; y']
6. [x ; y]
7. A - 3

Exercise 20[2]

Given the array $A = [2, 7, 9, 7; 3, 1, 5, 6; 8, 1, 2, 5]$, provide the Matlab command that will

1. Assign the even-numbered columns of A to an array called B.
2. Assign the odd-numbered rows to an array called C.
3. Convert A into a 4×3 array.
4. Compute the reciprocal of each element of A.
5. Compute the square-root of each element of A.

Lesson 4.4   Arithmetical Operations on Arrays

Objectives
- To learn how to add, subtract, multiply, and divide arrays using Matlab.
- To differentiate between element-by-element and matrix arithmetical operations in Matlab.

Topics
4.4.1 Array Addition and Subtraction
    4.4.1.1 Array Addition
    4.4.1.2 Array Subtraction
    4.4.1.3 Adding a Number to an Array
    4.4.1.4 Subtracting a Number from an Array
4.4.2 Matrix and Element-By-Element Arithmetical Operations
4.4.3 Array Multiplication
    4.4.3.1 Element-By-Element Multiplication for Arrays
    4.4.3.2 Matrix Multiplication for Arrays
        4.4.3.2.1 Mathematical Background
        4.4.3.2.2 Matrix Multiplication for Arrays
        4.4.3.2.3 Multiplying an Array by a Number
4.4.4 Array Division
    4.4.4.1 Element-By-Element Division for Arrays
    4.4.4.2 Matrix Division for Arrays
    4.4.4.3 Dividing an Array by a Number

4.4.1   Array Addition and Subtraction

4.4.1.1   Array Addition

To illustrate how to add arrays together using Matlab, let us start by creating the two arrays **X** and **Y** and then add them together.

$$X = \begin{bmatrix} 1 & 2 & -4 \\ 7 & 0 & 5 \end{bmatrix}, \quad Y = \begin{bmatrix} -6 & 12 & -5 \\ -2 & 16 & 15 \end{bmatrix}$$

```
>> X = [1,2, -4;7,0,5];
>> Y = [-6,12,-5;-2,16,15];
```

To add the two arrays and save the result in the new array Z, type at the Matlab **Command Prompt**

```
>> Z = X + Y
```

Matlab creates the new array Z and saves the results of the addition process in this array. Matlab responds to the above command with

```
Z =
   -5   14   -9
    5   16   20
```

The value of Z(1,1) is calculated by adding X(1,1) to Y(1,1). The value of Z (2,1) is calculated by adding X(2,1) to Y(2,1) and so on for the rest of the elements of Z. Remember that the dimensions of the arrays X and Y must once again be equal here, that is, the number of rows and the number of columns in both arrays must be the same.

4.4.1.2 Array Subtraction

To subtract Y from X and save the result in the new array S, type at the Matlab **Command Prompt**

```
>> S = X - Y
```

Matlab creates the array S and saves the result of the subtraction process in this array. Matlab responds to the above command with

```
S =
    7   -10    1
    9   -16   -10
```

The value of S(1,1) is calculated by subtracting Y(1,1) from X(1,1). The value of S(2,1) is calculated by subtracting Y(2,1) from X(2,1) and so on for the rest of the elements of the array S. Remember that the dimensions of the arrays X and Y must be equal here.

4.4.1.3 Adding a Number to an Array

Matlab also enables you to add a number to an array. Suppose that we would like to add the number 10 to all the elements to the array

$$X = \begin{bmatrix} 1 & 2 & -4 \\ 7 & 0 & 5 \end{bmatrix},$$

and save the result in a new array named A.

```
>> X = [1,2, -4;7,0,5];
>> A = X + 10
```

Matlab responds with

```
A =
   11  12  6
   17  10  15
```

4.4.1.4 Subtracting a Number from an Array

Matlab also enables you to simply subtract a number from an array. Suppose that we would like to subtract the number 1 from all the elements in the following array:

$$X = \begin{bmatrix} 1 & 2 & -4 \\ 7 & 0 & 5 \end{bmatrix},$$

and save the result in a new array named B.

```
>> X =  [1,2, -4;7,0,5];
>> B    X - 1
```

Matlab responds with

```
B =
    0   1  -5
    6  -1   4
```

Exercise 1[1]

Explain why Matlab flags up an error when executing these commands.

```
C =  [1,3;4,7];
D =  [4,6,7;2,4,6];
E =  C + D
```

4.4.2   Matrix and Element-By-Element Arithmetical Operations

Arithmetical operations performed on arrays using Matlab can be divided into *element-by-element* and *matrix* operations. Let us illustrate this concept using the following example.

Suppose that we have the arrays

$$\mathbf{X} = \begin{bmatrix} 1 & 2 & -4 \\ 7 & 0 & 5 \end{bmatrix}, \quad \mathbf{Y} = \begin{bmatrix} -6 & 12 & -5 \\ -2 & 16 & 15 \end{bmatrix}, \quad \text{and} \quad \mathbf{Z} = \begin{bmatrix} 3 & 8 \\ 4 & 9 \\ 6 & -1 \end{bmatrix}$$

Let us perform *element-by-element* multiplication of the arrays $\mathbf{X}$ and $\mathbf{Y}$ and save the results in a new array $\mathbf{R}$. This produces the array

$$\mathbf{R} = \begin{bmatrix} 1 \times (-6) & 2 \times 12 & -4 \times (-5) \\ 7 \times (-2) & 0 \times 16 & 5 \times 15 \end{bmatrix} = \begin{bmatrix} -6 & 24 & 20 \\ -14 & 0 & 75 \end{bmatrix}$$

Let us now perform *matrix* multiplication of the arrays $\mathbf{X}$ and $\mathbf{Z}$ and save the results in a new array $\mathbf{S}$. This produces the array

$$\mathbf{S} = \begin{bmatrix} 1 \times 3 + 2 \times 4 + (-4) \times 6 & 1 \times 8 + 2 \times 9 + (-4) \times (-1) \\ 7 \times 3 + 0 \times 4 + 5 \times 6 & 7 \times 8 + 0 \times 9 + 5 \times (-1) \end{bmatrix} = \begin{bmatrix} -13 & 30 \\ 51 & 51 \end{bmatrix}$$

4.4.3   Array Multiplication

There are two different ways to multiply arrays, namely by either *element-by-element* multiplication or by *matrix* multiplication.

4.4.3.1   Element-By-Element Multiplication for Arrays

To illustrate how to multiply two arrays together on an element-by-element basis using Matlab, first create the two arrays X and Y.

$$\mathbf{X} = \begin{bmatrix} 1 & 2 & -4 \\ 7 & 0 & 5 \end{bmatrix}, \quad \mathbf{Y} = \begin{bmatrix} -6 & 12 & -5 \\ -2 & 16 & 15 \end{bmatrix}$$

```
>> X = [1,2, -4;7,0,5];
>> Y = [-6,12, -5; -2,16,15];
```

The following command multiplies the two arrays X and Y together on an element-by-element basis and saves the result in the new array R.

```
>> R = X.*Y
```

Matlab responds to the above command with

```
R =
   -6   24   20
  -14    0   75
```

The value of R(1,1) is calculated by multiplying X(1,1) by Y(1,1). The value of R(2,1) is calculated by multiplying X(2,1) by Y(2,1) and so on for the rest of the elements of the array Z. Remember that the dimensions of the arrays X and Y must be equal here.

4.4.3.2 Matrix Multiplication

4.4.3.2.1 Mathematical Background

Suppose that we would like to perform matrix multiplication for the two arrays $\mathbf{X}$ and $\mathbf{Y}$ and save the results in a new array $\mathbf{Z}$, that is, $\mathbf{Z} = \mathbf{XY}$. Here $\mathbf{X}$ is called the multiplier, $\mathbf{Y}$ is called the multiplicand, and $\mathbf{Z}$ is called the product.

To do the matrix multiplication correctly, the number of columns in array $\mathbf{X}$ must be equal to the number of rows in array $\mathbf{Y}$. Matrix multiplication produces the new array $\mathbf{Z}$. The number of rows in $\mathbf{Z}$ is equal to the number of rows in $\mathbf{X}$. However, the number of columns in $\mathbf{Z}$ is equal to the number of columns in $\mathbf{Y}$.

The following figure shows matrix multiplication process for two arrays, firstly array $\mathbf{X}$ with a size of m × n, and secondly array $\mathbf{Y}$ with a size of n × s. The number of columns in $\mathbf{X}$ is n. The number of rows in $\mathbf{Y}$ is also n. The product array $\mathbf{Z}$ has the size of m × s.

$$(m \times [n]) x ([n] \times s) = m \times s$$

An element in the product array $Z_{i,j}$ is calculated by multiplying the elements in the row i of $\mathbf{X}$ by the elements in the column j of $\mathbf{Y}$. For example,

$$Z_{1,2} = X_{1,1}Y_{1,2} + X_{1,2}Y_{2,2} + X_{1,3}Y_{3,2} + \ldots + X_{1,n}Y_{n,2} \quad \text{or}$$
$$Z_{2,3} = X_{2,1}Y_{1,3} + X_{2,2}Y_{2,3} + \ldots + X_{2,n}Y_{n,3}$$

$Y_{1,1}$	$Y_{1,2}$	$Y_{1,3}$	......	$Y_{1,s}$
$Y_{2,1}$	$Y_{2,2}$	$Y_{2,3}$	......	$Y_{2,s}$
......	......	......	......	......
$Y_{n,1}$	$Y_{n,2}$	$Y_{n,3}$	......	$Y_{n,s}$

$X_{1,1}$	$X_{1,2}$	......	$X_{1,n}$
$X_{2,1}$	$X_{2,2}$	......	$X_{2,n}$
$X_{3,1}$	$X_{3,2}$	......	$X_{3,n}$
......	......	......	......
$X_{m,1}$	$X_{m,2}$	......	$X_{m,n}$

$Z_{1,1}$	$Z_{1,2}$	$Z_{1,3}$	......	$Z_{1,s}$
$Z_{2,1}$	$Z_{2,2}$	$Z_{2,3}$	......	$Z_{2,s}$
$Z_{3,1}$	$Z_{3,2}$	$Z_{3,3}$	......	$Z_{3,s}$
......	......	......	......	......
$Z_{m,1}$	$Z_{m,2}$	$Z_{m,3}$	......	$Z_{m,s}$

$$Z_{2,3} = X_{2,1}Y_{1,3} + X_{2,2}Y_{2,3} + \ldots + X_{2,n}Y_{n,3}$$

Remember: In matrix multiplication $\mathbf{XY} \neq \mathbf{YX}$

4.4.3.2.2   Matrix Multiplication for Arrays

Let us multiply the arrays

$$\mathbf{X} = \begin{bmatrix} 1 & 2 & -4 \\ 7 & 0 & 5 \end{bmatrix} \quad \text{and} \quad \mathbf{Z} = \begin{bmatrix} 3 & 8 \\ 4 & 9 \\ 6 & -1 \end{bmatrix}$$

Here we are using Matlab to perform *matrix* multiplication. First, let us create the arrays X and Y using Matlab.

```
>> X = [1,2, - 4;7,0,5];
>> Z = [3,8;4,9;6, - 1];
```

The following command multiplies the two arrays via matrix multiplication and saves the result in a new array S,

```
>> S = X*Z
```

Note that here the dot character (.) **has not** been added before the asterisk (*). This informs Matlab to perform matrix multiplication instead of multiplying in element-by-element mode. Matlab responds with

```
S =
    - 13   30
      51   51
```

Now using Matlab. Let us perform the matrix multiplication the other way around, that is, Z*X rather than Z*X and store the result in a new array T, T = Z*X

```
>> T = Z*X
```

Matlab responds with

```
T =
     59    6    28
     67    8    29
     -1   12   -29
```

4.4.3.2.3   Multiplying an Array by a Number

Suppose that we would like to multiply the following array X by the number 10

$$X = \begin{bmatrix} 1 & 2 & -4 \\ 7 & 0 & 5 \end{bmatrix}$$

and save the result in a new array named S.

```
>>X =  [1,2, - 4;7,0,5];
>>S =  X*10
```

Matlab responds with

```
S =
   10  20  - 40
   70   0    50
```

4.4.4 Array Division

There are two ways to divide arrays: *element-by-element* and *matrix* division.

4.4.4.1 Element-By-Element Division for Arrays

To illustrate how to divide two arrays on an element-by-element basis using Matlab, first create the two arrays **X** and **Y**.

$$\mathbf{X} = \begin{bmatrix} 1 & 2 & -4 \\ 7 & 0 & 5 \end{bmatrix}, \quad \mathbf{Y} = \begin{bmatrix} -6 & 12 & -5 \\ -2 & 16 & 15 \end{bmatrix}$$

```
>>X = [1,2, - 4;7,0,5];
>>Y = [-6,12, - 5; - 2,16,15];
```

The following command divides the two arrays on an element-by-element basis and then saves the result in a new array Z.

```
>>Z = X./Y
```

Matlab responds to the above command with

```
Z =
   - 0.1667  0.1667  0.8000
   - 3.5000  0       0.3333
```

The value of $Z(1,1)$ is calculated by dividing $X(1,1)$ by $Y(1,1)$. The value of $Z(2,1)$ is calculated by dividing $X(2,1)$ by $Y(2,1)$ and so on for the rest of the elements of Z. Remember that the dimensions of the arrays X and Y must once again be equal here.

4.4.4.2   Matrix Division for Arrays

Let us divide the array

$$\mathbf{X} = \begin{bmatrix} 1 & 2 \\ 3 & 4 \end{bmatrix} \quad by \quad \mathbf{Y} = \begin{bmatrix} 5 & 6 \\ 7 & 8 \end{bmatrix}$$

using Matlab by way of *matrix* division. First, let us create the arrays X and Y using Matlab.

```
>> X = [1,2;3,4];
>> Y = [5,6;7,8];
```

The following command divides the array X by the array Y via *matrix* division and saves the result in a new array Z,

```
>> Z = X/Y
```

Note here that the dot character (.) **has not** been added before the slash (/). This informs Matlab to perform matrix division, rather than performing the division on an element-by-element basis. Matlab responds with

```
Z =
     3.0000   -2.0000
     2.0000   -1.0000
```

Exercise 2[2]

Given the array A = [2, 7, 9, 7; 3, 1, 5, 6; 8, 1, 2, 5], explain the results of the following commands:

1. A'
2. A(:,[1,4])
3. A([2,3],[3,1])
4. reshape(A,2,6)
5. A(:)
6. flipud(A)
7. fliplr(A)
8. [A; A(end,:)]
9. A(1:3,:)
10. [A; A(1:2,:)]
11. sum(A)
12. sum(A')
13. sum(A,2)
14. [[A; sum(A)] [sum(A,2); sum(A(:))]]

Lesson 4.5 Plotting Arrays

4.5.1 Mathematical Background for 3D Plotting of Arrays

Matlab is an excellent software package for producing three-dimensional (3D) graphics. Plotting arrays in Matlab is easy, as you will soon see. For example, let us plot the function $Z = X^2 - Y^2$, where X is in the range of $[-2, 2]$ and Y is in the range of $[-3, 3]$. To plot this function let us initially create two arrays to represent X and Y as follows:

$$\mathbf{X} = \begin{bmatrix} -2 & -1 & 0 & 1 & 2 \\ -2 & -1 & 0 & 1 & 2 \\ -2 & -1 & 0 & 1 & 2 \\ -2 & -1 & 0 & 1 & 2 \\ -2 & -1 & 0 & 1 & 2 \\ -2 & -1 & 0 & 1 & 2 \\ -2 & -1 & 0 & 1 & 2 \end{bmatrix} \quad \text{and} \quad \mathbf{Y} = \begin{bmatrix} -3 & -3 & -3 & -3 & -3 \\ -2 & -2 & -2 & -2 & -2 \\ -1 & -1 & -1 & -1 & -1 \\ 0 & 0 & 0 & 0 & 0 \\ 1 & 1 & 1 & 1 & 1 \\ 2 & 2 & 2 & 2 & 2 \\ 3 & 3 & 3 & 3 & 3 \end{bmatrix}$$

Let us use the arrays X and Y to build the grid

$$(\mathbf{X}, \mathbf{Y}) = \begin{bmatrix} (-2,-3) & (-1,-3) & (0,-3) & (1,-3) & (2,-3) \\ (-2,-2) & (-1,-2) & (0,-2) & (1,-2) & (2,-2) \\ (-2,-1) & (-1,-1) & (0,-1) & (1,-1) & (2,-1) \\ (-2,0) & (-1,0) & (0,0) & (1,0) & (2,0) \\ (-2,1) & (-1,1) & (0,1) & (1,1) & (2,1) \\ (-2,2) & (-1,2) & (0,2) & (1,2) & (2,2) \\ (-2,3) & (-1,3) & (0,3) & (1,3) & (2,3) \end{bmatrix}$$

The grid is shown below graphically.

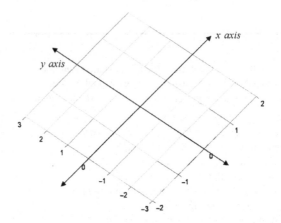

You can calculate **Z** using the equation $\mathbf{Z} = \mathbf{X}^2 - \mathbf{Y}^2$. For example,

$$Z_{1,1} = X_{1,1}^2 - Y_{1,1}^2 = (-2)^2 - (-3^2) = 4 - 9 = -5$$

Z is shown below both as an array of numbers and also as a graph.

$$\mathbf{Z} = \begin{bmatrix} -5 & -8 & -9 & -8 & -5 \\ 0 & -3 & -4 & -3 & 0 \\ 3 & 0 & -1 & 0 & 3 \\ 4 & 1 & 0 & 1 & 4 \\ 3 & 0 & -1 & 0 & 3 \\ 0 & -3 & -4 & -3 & 0 \\ -5 & -8 & -9 & -8 & -5 \end{bmatrix}$$

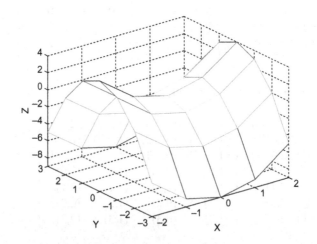

4.5.2   3D Plot an Array with the mesh Function

Let us plot the function $Z = X^2 - Y^2$, where X is in the range of $[-2, 2]$ and Y is in the range of $[-3, 3]$. To plot this function using Matlab, first we need to create two arrays to represent X and Y. We can use the meshgrid function as follows:

```
x = -2:1:2;
y = -3:1:3;
[X,Y] = meshgrid(x,y);
```

Matlab produces the vectors x and y as follows:

```
x =
    -2  -1   0   1   2
```

```
y =
    -3  -2  -1   0   1   2   3
```

Also, Matlab produces the arrays X and Y as follows:

```
X =
    -2  -1   0   1   2
    -2  -1   0   1   2
    -2  -1   0   1   2
    -2  -1   0   1   2
    -2  -1   0   1   2
    -2  -1   0   1   2
    -2  -1   0   1   2
```

```
Y =
    -3  -3  -3  -3  -3
    -2  -2  -2  -2  -2
    -1  -1  -1  -1  -1
     0   0   0   0   0
     1   1   1   1   1
     2   2   2   2   2
     3   3   3   3   3
```

To evaluate Z using Matlab, type at the **Command Prompt**

```
Z = X.^2 - Y.^2
```

Matlab responds with

```
Z =
    -5  -8  -9  -8  -5
     0  -3  -4  -3   0
     3   0  -1   0   3
     4   1   0   1   4
     3   0  -1   0   3
     0  -3  -4  -3   0
    -5  -8  -9  -8  -5
```

To plot the array Z versus X and Y, type at the **Command Prompt**

```
mesh(X,Y,Z)
```

This produces the following figure. This plot function draws 35 points, which are the number of elements in the X array, and then connects the points using straight lines. This is the reason that the function appears as a low-resolution mesh.

The complete code to perform this is shown below. This code also labels the X, Y, and Z axes.

```
clear; clc; close all
x = -2:1:2;
y = -3:1:3;
[X,Y]=meshgrid(x,y);
Z = X.^2-Y.^2;
mesh(X,Y,Z)
xlabel('X')
ylabel('Y')
zlabel('Z')
```

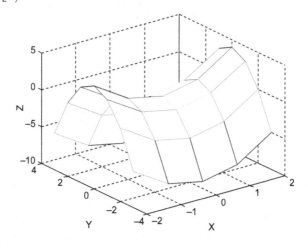

4.5.3   Increasing the Resolution of a 3D Plot

To improve the resolution of the 3D plot, you need to increase the number of points within the X and Y arrays, and then recompute the Z array. These steps are shown below. The change in the code is shown here in bold font.

```
clear; clc; close all
x = -2:0.1:2;
y = -3:0.1:3;
[X,Y] = meshgrid(x,y);
Z = X.^2 - Y.^2;
mesh(X,Y,Z)
xlabel('X')
```

```
ylabel('Y')
zlabel('Z')
```

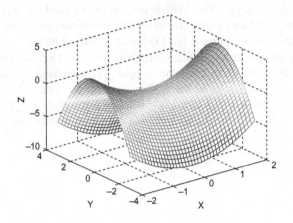

4.5.4   3D Plot an Array with the surf Function

The surf function plots an array as a surface as shown below. This surface consists of quadrilaterals. Neighboring sets of four points in the Z array are used to form the quadrilaterals. The Z array has a size of 5×7. Then the surface consists of $4 \times 6 = 24$ quadrilaterals.

```
clear; clc; close all
x = -2:1:2;
y = -3:1:3;
[X,Y] = meshgrid(x,y);
Z = X.^2-Y.^2;
surf(X,Y,Z)
xlabel('X')
ylabel('Y')
zlabel('Z')
```

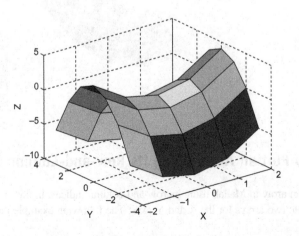

This book is printed in monochrome color; whereas the online version is in full color. Some of the figures produced by Matlab are in full color and are printed in this book in monochrome. The Matlab commands to produce these figures are given for all these colour figures. To follow the discussion presented in this book, you can reproduce these figures using Matlab as explained below.

Matlab plots each quadrilateral using a specific color. The values of the four points that construct the quadrilateral determine its color. The command `colorbar` shows the relationship between the color in the surface plot and the value of Z. For example, low values in Z are given a dark blue color, whereas high values are given a red color. The same code as above, with the addition of a `colorbar`, is shown below.

```
clear; clc; close all
x = -2:1:2;
y = -3:1:3;
[X,Y] = meshgrid(x,y);
Z = X.^2-Y.^2;
surf(X,Y,Z)
xlabel('X')
ylabel('Y')
zlabel('Z')
colorbar
```

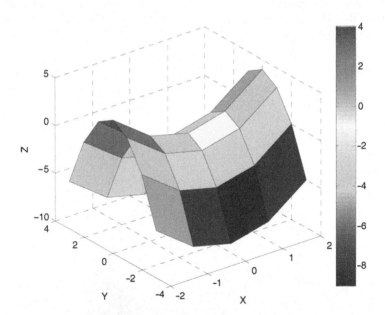

4.5.5   3D Plot an Array Using its Row-and-Column Indices

You can plot an array in Matlab using its row-and-column indices. In this case, you do not need to generate two arrays for the X and Y axes. The following example illustrates this.

Example 1

Use Matlab to plot the array

$$B = \begin{bmatrix} 1 & 6 & 11 & 16 & 21 & 26 \\ 2 & 7 & 12 & 17 & 22 & 27 \\ 3 & 8 & 13 & 18 & 23 & 28 \\ 4 & 9 & 14 & 19 & 24 & 29 \\ 5 & 10 & 15 & 20 & 25 & 30 \end{bmatrix}$$

Answer

```
b = 1:1:30;
B = reshape(b, 5, 6);
surf(B)
```

Matlab generates the grid automatically to plot the array B.

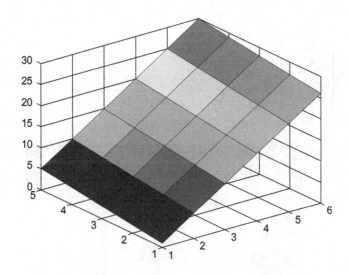

4.5.6   Background for 2D Plotting of Arrays

Let us explain how to plot an array as a two-dimensional (2D) plot using an example.

Example 1

Plot the function $Z = X^2 - Y^2$, where X is in the range of $[-2, 2]$ and Y is in the range of $[-3, 3]$ as a 2D plot.

Answer
To plot this function let us initially create two arrays to represent **X** and **Y** as follows, and use both **X** and **Y** arrays to build the grid

$$(\mathbf{X,Y}) = \begin{bmatrix} (-2,-3) & (-1,-3) & (0,-3) & (1,-3) & (2,-3) \\ (-2,-2) & (-1,-2) & (0,-2) & (1,-2) & (2,-2) \\ (-2,-1) & (-1,-1) & (0,-1) & (1,-1) & (2,-1) \\ (-2,0) & (-1,0) & (0,0) & (1,0) & (2,0) \\ (-2,1) & (-1,1) & (0,1) & (1,1) & (2,1) \\ (-2,2) & (-1,2) & (0,2) & (1,2) & (2,2) \\ (-2,3) & (-1,3) & (0,3) & (1,3) & (2,3) \end{bmatrix}$$

You can calculate **Z** using the equation $\mathbf{Z} = \mathbf{X}^2 - \mathbf{Y}^2$. **Z** is shown below both as an array of numbers and also as a 2D graph.

$$\mathbf{Z} = \begin{bmatrix} -5 & -8 & -9 & -8 & -5 \\ 0 & -3 & -4 & -3 & 0 \\ 3 & 0 & -1 & 0 & 3 \\ 4 & 1 & 0 & 1 & 4 \\ 3 & 0 & -1 & 0 & 3 \\ 0 & -3 & -4 & -3 & 0 \\ -5 & -8 & -9 & -8 & -5 \end{bmatrix}$$

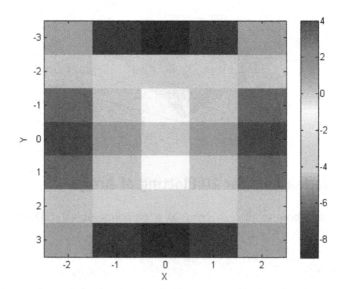

As you have probably noted, there is a relationship between the values of **Z**, the color bar, and the color of the 2D graph. For example, the value of $\mathbf{Z}(0, -1) = -1$. From the color bar, the value of -1 corresponds to the color yellow. The color at the point $(0, -1)$ on the 2D graph is also yellow.

4.5.7   2D Plot an Array with the imagesc Function

Let us plot the function $\mathbf{Z} = \mathbf{X}^2 - \mathbf{Y}^2$ as a 2D plot using Matlab. Here **X** is in the range of $[-2,2]$ and **Y** is in the range of $[-3, 3]$. To plot this function using Matlab, first we need to create the x and y vectors as follows:

```
x =    -2:1:2;
y =    -3:1:3;
```

Matlab produces the vectors x and y as follows:

```
x =
     -2  -1  0  1  2

y =
     -3  -2  -1  0  1  2  3
```

To evaluate Z using Matlab, type at the **Command Prompt**

```
[X,Y] =   meshgrid(x,y);
Z =       X.^2 - Y.^2;
```

To plot the array Z versus x and y, type at the Matlab **Command Prompt**

```
imagesc(x,y,Z)
```

This produces the following figure. This plot function draws 35 points, which are the number of elements in the array Z. Each point is given a color depending on its value. This is the reason that the function appears as a low-resolution 2D graph. The complete code to perform this is shown below. This code also labels the X, Y and Z axes.

```
x = -2:1:2;
y = -3:1:3;
[X,Y] = meshgrid(x,y);
Z = X.^2 - Y.^2;
imagesc(x,y,Z)
xlabel('x')
ylabel('y')
colorbar
```

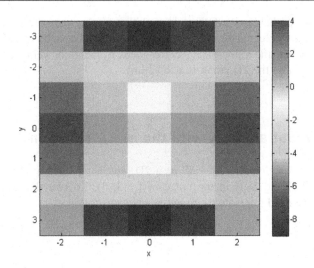

Answers to Selected Exercises

Lesson 4.3

Exercise 14

```
A = [1, 2, 3; 4, 5, 6; 7, 8, 9]
B = A(:, end: - 1:1)
```

Exercise 15

```
C = [1, 2, 3; 4, 5, 6; 7, 8, 9]
D = C(end:-1:1,:)
```

Exercise 18

1. `x1 = A(1,:)`
2. `Y = A(end - 1:end,:)`
3. `sum(A)`
4. `sum(A,2)`
5. `std(A)`
6. `mean(A)`

Exercise 20

1. `B = A(:,2:2:end)`
2. `C = A(1:2:end,:)`
3. `reshape(A,4,3)`
4. `1./A`
5. `sqrt(A)`

5 Matlab Functions

Chapter Outline

Lesson 5.1   Introduction to Functions

Objectives
- To learn about functions in Matlab.
- To understand the purpose of a function.
- To learn how to call a function.

Topics

5.1.1 What Is a Function?
5.1.2 The Purpose of a Function
   5.1.2.1 Improves Code Readability
   5.1.2.2 Improves Code Reusability
   5.1.2.3 Modifying Code
5.1.3 Calling a Matlab Function

5.1.1   What Is a Function?

A Matlab function is a collection of commands that does a specific task and must have a unique name. The function accepts one or more Matlab variables as input arguments, operates on them in some way, and then returns one or more Matlab variables as outputs. This is indicated in the following figure.

Matlab by Example. DOI: http://dx.doi.org/10.1016/B978-0-12-405212-3.00005-0

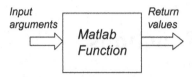

The first example of a Matlab function that we will show you here is in the rectangle.

```
function a = add2(b,c)
a = b + c;
end
```

The name of this function is `add2`.
This function has two input arguments `b` and `c`.
The collection of commands in this function is `a = b + c;`
This function returns one value `a`, which is the sum of `b` and `c`.

A second example of a Matlab function is shown below:

```
function [r,theta] = Cartesian2polar(x,y)
r = sqrt(x^2 + y^2);
theta = atan2(y,x);
end
```

The name of this function is `Cartesian2polar`.
This function has two input arguments `x` and `y`.
The collection of commands in this function is

```
r = sqrt(x^2 + y^2);
theta = atan2(y,x);
```

This function returns two values `r` and `theta` and converts Cartesian to polar coordinates.

5.1.2   The Purpose of a Function

5.1.2.1   Improves Code Readability

It is good programming/engineering practice to produce Matlab programs that are readable. Research has shown that programmers spend most of their time reading code rather than writing code. This makes it important to learn how to write Matlab programs that are easy to understand both for you and for others. There are five techniques to improve the readability of your programs:

1. Use proper names for variables
2. Comment your code
3. Use functions
4. Use consistent code indentation
5. Peer-review of code.

We have explained the first two techniques in Lesson 1.2. We will explain here the use of functions to improve code readability. Consistent code indentation will be explained in Lesson 8.5.

Peer review is considered to be the best practice for ensuring the readability of your code. Show your code to a colleague and ask him/her to review your code. Explain your code for the colleague in less than five minutes. Then ask your colleague if he/she understands the code. If he/she cannot, then it is likely that your code is not very easily readable and you may need to rewrite your programs.

The following example shows how to improve your code readability using functions.

Example 1

A mathematical function is given by

$$y(x) = 3x^4 + 1.5x^3 + \sqrt{x}$$

Write a Matlab program to calculate the value of z

$$z = y(2) + y(7) + y(6) + y(5)$$

Answer

You can solve this problem using two different ways as follows:

In the first method, you can type Matlab commands to calculate z in a script file without using functions as follows.

```
x1 = 2;
x2 = 7;
x3 = 6;
x4 = 5;
y1 = 3*x1^4 + 1.5*x1^3 + sqrt(x1);
y2 = 3*x2^4 + 1.5*x2^3 + sqrt(x2);
y3 = 3*x3^4 + 1.5*x3^3 + sqrt(x3);
y4 = 3*x4^4 + 1.5*x4^3 + sqrt(x4);
z = y1 + y1 + y3 + y4;
```

In the second method, you can divide the various Matlab commands between a script file and a function as follows.

```
x1 = 2;
x2 = 7;
x3 = 6;
x4 = 5;
z = y(x1) + y(x2) + y(x3) + y(x4);
function f = y(x)
f = 3*x^4 + 1.5*x^3 + sqrt(x);
end
```

As you can readily note here, the use of functions has improved the readability of the program and has also reduced the code size. Code size means the total number of characters in a program.

5.1.2.2 Improves Code Reusability

"A piece of code should be typed only once and then used as many times as required."

Suppose that you have written a program that contains a piece of code. Also, suppose that you need to use this piece of code on several different occasions. You have two options to do this.

1. Type out the piece of code over again each time you need to use it.
2. Place the piece of code in a function and call this function as required.

Let us clarify this by the following example.

Example 2

A mathematical function is given by

$$y(x) = 3x^4 + 1.5x^3 + \sin(x)$$

Write a Matlab program to calculate the value of z.

$$z = y(2) + y(7) + y(6) + y(5)$$

Answer
You can solve this problem by following two different approaches as follows.

In the <u>first</u> method, you can type the Matlab commands to calculate $y(x)$ four times over. In this case, you need to type the piece of code $y = 3*x^4 + 1.5*x^3 + sin(x);$ four times.

```
x1 = 2;
x2 = 7;
x3 = 6;
x4 = 5;
y1 = 3*x1^4 + 1.5*x1^3 + sin(x1);
y2 = 3*x2^4 + 1.5*x2^3 + sin(x2);
y3 = 3*x3^4 + 1.5*x3^3 + sin(x3);
y4 = 3*x4^4 + 1.5*x4^3 + sin(x4);
z = y1 + y1 + y3 + y4;
```

In the second method, you need to type in the Matlab commands to calculate $y(x)$ only once, place the commands in a function, and call this function whenever required.

```
x1 = 2;
x2 = 7;
x3 = 6;
x4 = 5;
```

```
z = y(x1) + y(x2) + y(x3) + y(x4);
function f = y(x)
f = 3*x^4 + 1.5*x^3 + sin(x);
end
```

As you can see in the example given, the use of functions here has significantly improved the code reusability.

5.1.2.3 Modifying Code

Suppose that you have written a program that contains a specific piece of code. Also, suppose that you then need to use this piece of code over and over again on a thousand different occasions. After a while, you then decide to modify the specific piece of code. In this case, you need to search within your program for every single occurrence of this piece of code and then modify it. This takes a long time to do, and it is easy to make mistakes. Suppose that you instead place this piece of code within a function. Now if you need to modify this segment of code, you only need to do this once, not a thousand times!

Example 3

Modify the code in Example 1 and use it to evaluate z as follows:

$z = y(2) + y(7) + y(6) + y(5)$ where

$y(x) = 3x^4 + 1.5x^2 + \cos(x)$

Answer
You can solve this problem via the use of two different approaches as follows.
In the first method, you can modify the code in the script file to calculate z. In this case, you need to modify the code four times.

```
x1 = 2;
x2 = 7;
x3 = 6;
x4 = 5;
y1 = 3*x1^4 + 1.5*x1^3 + cos(x1);
y2 = 3*x2^4 + 1.5*x2^3 + cos(x2);
y3 = 3*x3^4 + 1.5*x3^3 + cos(x3);
y4 = 3*x4^4 + 1.5*x4^3 + cos(x4);
z = y1 + y1 + y3 + y4;
```

In the second method, you can modify the code in the function f( ) that calculates z. In this case, you only need to modify the code once.

```
x1 = 2;
x2 = 7;
x3 = 6;
x4 = 5;
z = y(x1) + y(x2) + y(x3) + y(x4);
```

```
function f = y(x)
f = 3*x^4 + 1.5*x^3 + cos(x);
end
```

Which method is easier to modify?

5.1.3   Calling a Matlab Function

You can call a Matlab function from a script file, from the **Command Window**, or from another function. This is shown in the following figure and will be explained in detail in the next lesson.

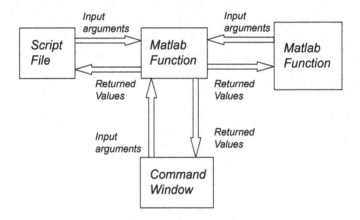

Lesson 5.2   Creating Functions

Objectives
- To learn how to create a function.
- To learn how to name a function.
- To learn how to save a function.
- To learn how to call a function.

Topics
5.2.1 Creating a Matlab Function
5.2.2 Naming a Matlab Function
5.2.3 Saving a Matlab Function
5.2.4 Calling a Matlab Function
    5.2.4.1 Calling a Matlab Function from the **Command Window**
    5.2.4.2 Calling a Matlab Function from a Script File
    5.2.4.3 Calling a Matlab Function from Another Function
5.2.5 A Matlab Function Returning Two Values

5.2.1 Creating a Matlab Function

A Matlab function can have one or more input arguments, which are to be supplied to it. Also the function returns output values, which it produces and then it passes them back to the program that has called this function. This is shown in the schematic diagram below. The variables that are created by the function are not displayed in the **Workspace** window, and they vanish as soon as the execution of the function terminates, that is, variables defined in a function will be deleted when Matlab returns from this function.

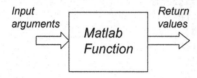

Create a new folder and name it **MyFunctions**.

Make **MyFunctions** the current folder of Matlab.

Refer to Lesson 1.2, to see how to make a folder as the current folder of Matlab.

5.2.2 Naming a Matlab Function

Choosing the name of a function is a similar process to that of choosing the name of a script file and involves similar restrictions which must be taken into consideration.

- The function name must not contain spaces or hyphens (-).
- The function name must start with an alphabetical character (a–z or A–Z).
- The file name **must** contain only alphabetical characters (a–z or A–Z), numbers (1–9), or underscores (_).
- Punctuation characters such as commas (,) or apostrophes (') are not allowed, because many of them have special meanings in Matlab.
- The function name must be neither a **Matlab variable** nor an existing **Matlab script file**.
- The use of a **Matlab reserved word** as a function name is not allowed. A list of **Matlab reserved words** follows.

```
'name'                'across_variable'
'node'                'build'
'output'              'description'
'parameter'           'descriptor'
'setup'               'element'
'signal'              'input'
'source'              'interface_input'
'terminal'            'interface_node'
'through_variable'    'interface_output'
```

```
'variable'                  'item_type'
                            'local_variable'
```

- The use of a **Matlab keyword** as a function name is not allowed. A list of **Matlab keywords** follows.

```
'break'        'global'
'case'         'if'
'catch'        'otherwise'
'classdef'     'parfor'
'continue'     'persistent'
'else'         'return'
'elseif'       'spmd'
'end'          'switch'
'for'          'try'
'function'     'while'
```

Suppose that we would like to write a function that adds two numbers together and returns the result of their addition. This function takes two arguments and returns one value. Suppose that we are considering the possibility of naming our new function add. To check that the add function is not a **Matlab keyword** or an existing **Matlab function**, type at the **Command Prompt**

> > help add

Matlab informs you that there is already a function present in a file called **add. m**. So we should choose another name that is not restricted.

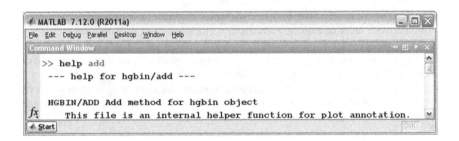

Let us try another name: add2. Type at the **Command Prompt**

> > help add2

Matlab informs you that there is no such file called **add2.m** and it produces the following.

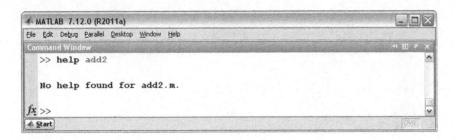

Therefore we can safely name our function add2.

To create the add2 function, go to **Menu→File→New→Function**. The **Matlab Editor** pops up. Delete everything in the **Editor** and type the following code in the **Editor**:

```
function z = add2(x, y)
%This function adds the numbers x and y
% and returns the value z which is the result of
% the addition of the two numbers
z = x + y;
end
```

5.2.3   Saving a Matlab Function

Save the add2 function using the name *add2.m*. The name of the file **MUST** be exactly the same as the name of the function and must be followed by the *.m* extension.

Here the function name is add2. This is the name which appears directly before the brackets () in the function declaration line.

```
function z = add2(x, y)
```

The input arguments to this function are x and y. The return value is z. The % character at the beginning of a line signifies the beginning of a comment and directs Matlab to ignore all the text that appears after it on that line only.

Note that the Matlab **Editor** uses different colored text to simplify the programming process.

Keywords have a blue color.
Comments have a green color.
Code appears in a black color.

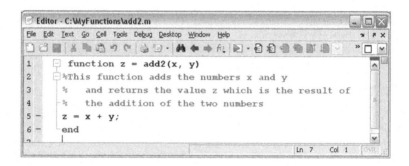

Exercise 1[3]

Give two reasons why naming the function below **power.m** would be wrong.

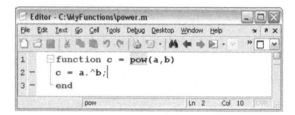

5.2.4   Calling a Matlab Function

5.2.4.1   *Calling a Matlab Function from the Command Window*

You can call a function from the **Command Window.** To call the function `add2` from the **Command Window**, at the **Command Prompt** type

> > a = add2 (3, 5);

Note that you must give the correct number of input arguments (within the brackets) that the function expects or you will get an error. Matlab executes the `add2` function, and the result that is returned from this function is assigned to the variable a. Note the change in the **Workspace** window after executing the `add2` function. A new variable a is created and its value is 8.

Note that the function arguments `x`, `y` and the returned value `z` that is created by the `add2` function do not actually appear in the **Workspace** window and they do not exist in Matlab memory, as they were only temporary function variables.

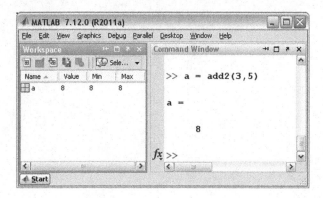

At the **Command Prompt** type

```
>>help add2
```

Matlab prints out the comments that you added at the beginning of the add2 function. It should be obvious then that it is important to comment functions both clearly and with a full functional description.

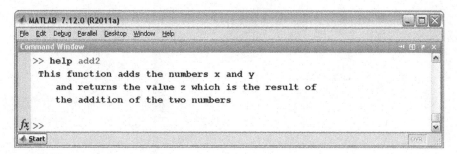

5.2.4.2 Calling a Matlab Function from a Script File

You can call a function from a script file. The following example shows you how to do this.

Example 1

Create the following script file:

```
a = 1;
b = 2;
c = add2(a,b)
```

Name the script file **call_add2.m.** The script file calls the add2() function to add the variables a and b and assigns the result of their addition to a variable called c. Note the changes that occur in the **Workspace** window.

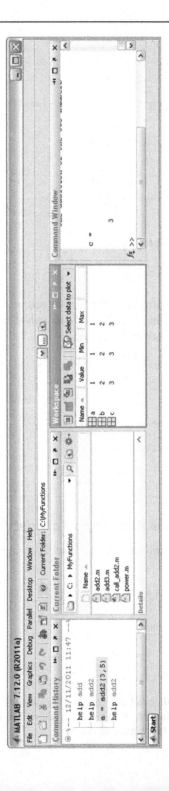

Note the following:

1. The local variables x, y, and z of the add2( ) function do not exist in the **Workspace**.

The *call_add2.m* script file is located in the same directory as the add2( ) function.

5.2.4.3 Calling a Matlab Function from Another Function

You can call a function from another function. The following example shows you how to call the add2 function from another function.

Example 2

Write a Matlab function that has three input arguments and returns one value. This function calculates the addition of the values of its input arguments and returns the result of their addition. This function must use the add2 function to perform the addition process. Name this function add3.

Answer

```
function d = add3(a, b, c)
e = add2(a,b);
d = add2(e, c);
end
```

To call this function, at the **Command Prompt** type

> > z = add3 (1, 2, 3)

Matlab responds with

```
z =
    6
```

Exercise 2[1]

Write a Matlab function that has four input arguments and returns one value. This function calculates the addition of the values of its input arguments and returns the result of their addition. This function must use the add2 and add3 functions to perform the addition process. Name this function add4.

5.2.5 A Matlab Function Returning Two Values

A Matlab function can return more than one value. To show this property, let us write a function that has two input arguments and returns two values: the addition and subtraction of its input arguments. Let us call this function add_sub. The Matlab code for this function is shown below.

```
function [addition, subtraction] = add_sub(x,y)
addition = x + y;
subtraction = x - y;
end
```

To call this function, at the **Command Prompt** type

```
> >[r, s] = add_sub (5,3)
```

The result of calling this function is

```
r =
    8

s =
    2
```

Exercise 3[2]

It is possible that the function `add_sub` could be called from the **Command Window** using the following syntax.

```
> > t = add_sub(5,3);
```

Type the Matlab command that is shown above at the **Command Prompt** and press the **Enter** Key to run it. Determine the value of the variable t, and explain the results of running this command using this form of syntax for the function call.

Exercise 4[1]

Run the following code using Matlab. What is the value of z? Explain the operation of this code.

```
function c = multiply2(a, b)
c = a * b;
end
```

The following code calls the `multiply2` function.

```
x = 1;
y = 2;
z = multiply2(x, y);
```

Lesson 5.3   Scope of Matlab Variables in a Function

Objectives
- To learn about the scope of variables in a function.
- To learn about local variables.

Topic
5.3.1 The Scope of a Variable in a Matlab Function

5.3.1   The Scope of a Variable in a Matlab Function

A variable that is created within a function has a limited scope. This means that this variable can be only accessed or modified by this function. This variable is called a *local* variable. Let us illustrate this principle by using examples.

Example 1

Create a function that raises its input argument to the power $r = 2$.

Answer
The function is shown below:

```
function c = pow(a)
r = 2;
c = a.^r;
end
```

Save this function in a file ***pow.m***. To call this function, type at the **Command Prompt**

```
> > f = pow(3)
```

Matlab executes the function pow and calculates the value of $f = a^r = 3^2 = 9$.

```
f =
    9
```

The variables a, r, and c are *local variables* to the function pow and can only be accessed by this function. To check this for the variable r, type at the **Command Prompt**

```
> > r
```

Matlab responds with

> ??? Undefined function or variable 'r'.

To check for the scope of the variable a, type at the **Command Prompt**

> >>a

Matlab responds with

> ??? Undefined function or variable 'a'.

To check for the scope of the variable c, type at the **Command Prompt**

> >>c

Matlab responds with

> ??? Undefined function or variable 'c'.

Only the variable f is defined here, which was created in the **Command Window** to store the returned value of the function and is external to it.

Example 2

A variable created in the **Command Window** cannot be accessed by a function. To illustrate this principle, modify the pow function, shown in Example 1, as follows and save it.

```
function c = pow(a)
c = a.^r;
end
```

Call this function from the **Command Window** as follows:

```
» r = 2;
» f = pow(2)
```

Matlab responds with

> ???Undefined function or variable'r'.

```
Error in ==> pow at 2
c = a.^r;
```

Even though we have created the variable r in the **Command Window,** the pow function cannot access this variable.

Example 3

Similarly, a variable that is created in a script file cannot be accessed by a function. To illustrate this principle, open the **Editor** and type the following Matlab commands. Save the Matlab script file as *example4.m*.

```
r = 2;
f = pow(a)
```

Run the *example4.m* script file. Matlab responds with

```
??? Undefined function or variable 'r'.
Error in ==> pow at 2
c = a.^r;
Error in ==> example4 at 2
f = pow(2)
```

Even though we have created the variable r in the script file, the pow function cannot access this variable.

Exercise 1[2]

Find the value of r that Matlab displays after running the following code.

```
>> r = sub2(2, 2)

function c = sub2(a,b)
a = 1;
c = a - b;
end
```

Exercise 2[2]

Find the values of r and c that Matlab displays after running the following code:

```
» r = 1;
» c = foo(1,2);
» r
» c
function c = foo(a,b)
r = 3;
c = r*(a + b);
end
```

Example 4

The foo6 function has two input arguments and returns one value.

```
function c = foo6(a,b)
a = a + 1;
b = b.^2;
c = a + 2*b;
end
```

This function can be called from the **Command Window** as follows:

```
» a = 1;
» b = 2;
» c = foo6(a,b)
```

Here it must be noted that the a and b variables in the foo6 function are different from the a and b variables that have been created in the **Workspace**. Changing the values of the a and b variables in the function will not change the values of the a and b variables in the **Workspace**. Let us use Matlab to check the value of a.

```
> >a
```

Matlab responds with

```
a =
    1
```

To check the value of b.

```
> >b
```

Matlab responds with

```
b =
    2
```

Exercise 3[2]

Find the values of r and c that Matlab displays after running the following code:

```
» clear
» c = foo(1,2);
» r
» c
function c = foo(a,b)
r = 3;
c = r*(a + b);
end
```

Exercise 4[2]

Find the value of c that Matlab displays after running the following code:

```
» c = foo1(1,2);
» c
```

```
function c = foo1(a,b)      function c = foo2(e)
c = 2*a + foo2(b);          c = e^2;
end                         end
```

Exercise 5[2]

Explain why the following code does not run correctly in Matlab.

```
» clear
» r = 1;
» c = foo3(1,2);
function c = foo3(a,b)
c = r*(a + b);
end
```

Exercise 6[2]

Explain why the following code does not run correctly in Matlab.

```
» c = foo4(1,2);
» c
function c = foo4(a,b)
clear
r = 3;
c = r*(a + b);
end
```

Exercise 7[2]

Find the value of c that Matlab displays after running the following code.

```
» c = 1
» foo5();
» c
function c = foo5()
c = 2;
c = c + 1;
end
```

Answers to Selected Exercises

Lesson 5.2

Exercise 1

1. Matlab already has a built-in function with the name of power.
2. The name of the file must be identical to the name of the function. We should save this file with the name **pow.m**.

Exercise 2

```
function g = add4(a, b, c, d)
e = add3(a,b,c);
g = add2(e,d);
end
```

Exercise 3

The function add_sub can be incorrectly called from the **Command Window** using the following syntax.

```
>>t = add_sub(5,3);
```

The add_sub function actually has two return values, but only a single scalar value has been provided here for its return values; therefore, the first return value (the sum, 8) is assigned to the single scalar variable t that has been provided. The second return value is just discarded.

Exercise 4

This code contains the function

```
function c = multiply2(a, b)
c = a * b;
end
```

This function must be saved in a file called **multiply2.m**. This function can be called from the Matlab **Command Window** as shown. The value of z = 2.

```
» x = 1;
» y = 2;
» z = multiply2(x, y);
```

Lesson 5.3

Exercise 1

The value of r that Matlab displays is -1. This is because the value of a has been changed inside the function sub2.

Exercise 2

The values of r and c are 1 and 9, respectively.

Exercise 3

The value of c is 9. When typing the Matlab command at the **Command Prompt**

```
>>r
```

Matlab responds with

```
??? Undefined function or variable 'r'.
```

Exercise 4

The value of c that Matlab displays is 6.

Exercise 5

Explain why the following code does not run correctly in Matlab.
```
» clear
» r = 1;
» c = foo3(1,2);
function c = foo3(a,b)
c = r*(a+b);
end
```
The value for r is not available within the function foo3. This could be corrected in two different potential ways by either

1. Passing the value for r as a parameter to the function, or
2. Defining r inside the function.

Exercise 6

```
> >??? Reference to a cleared variable a.
```

The Matlab command clear deletes all current variables in memory. This means that neither the "a" or "b" variables actually exist after the variables have been cleared. As a side note: Clearing all Matlab variables inside a function is deemed to be particularly bad practice, so do not do it.

Remember: Using the `clear` command inside a function clears all Matlab variables, even variables created by other functions or script files.

Exercise 7

We can consider that the `foo5()` function does nothing, since this function does not take any arguments and it does not return any value. The local variable c inside the `foo5()` function is different from the variable c that you typed inside the **Command Window**. Calling the `foo5()` function will not change the value of c in the workspace. The value of c stays equal to 1 both before and after running the `foo5()` function and is completely unchanged by it.

6 Conditional Statements in Matlab

Chapter Outline

Lesson 6.1   The Construction of an if Statement

Objectives
- To learn how to exchange the values of two variables.
- To learn how to construct an if statement.
- To learn how to improve the readability of Matlab functions.

Topics
6.1.1 Swap the Values of Two Variables
6.1.2 if Statement
6.1.3 Improving the Readability of Matlab Functions
6.1.4 Examples for if Statements

6.1.1 Swap the Values of Two Variables

The figure below shows three glasses. Glass X is filled with green liquid. Glass Y is filled with blue liquid. Suppose we want to swap the contents of glass X with the contents of glass Y. To do this, we need an empty glass for temporary use. Let us call the empty glass *temp*.

Matlab by Example. DOI: http://dx.doi.org/10.1016/B978-0-12-405212-3.00006-2

X Y *temp*

The steps to swap the content of glass X with the content of glass Y are

1. Pour the content of glass X into glass *temp*. Now glass X is empty.
2. Pour the content of glass Y into glass X. Now glass Y is empty.
3. Pour the content of glass *temp* into glass Y.

Now glass *temp* is empty and we do not need it anymore.

To swap the values of two variables, you will use the same steps that were performed for swapping the contents of the two glasses. Suppose that we have the variables x and y as follows:

```
>> x = 1;
>> y = 2;
```

Let us swap the values of x and y. Initially we need to save the value of x in a temporary variable. As you know, a variable needs a name. We will name the temporary variable temp. The three steps to swap the contents of x and y are

1. Save the value of x in temp.

```
>> temp = x;
```

2. Save the value of y in x.

```
>> x = y;
```

3. Save the value of temp in y.

```
>> y = temp;
```

The temp variable is not required anymore, so you can clear it as follows:

```
>> clear temp;
```

Example 1

Write a Matlab function that has two input arguments and returns two values. This function swaps the values of its input arguments. Name this function swap().

Answer

```
function[y,x] = swap(x,y)
end
```

Save the function as **swap.m**.
You can test the operation of the swap()function as follows.

6.1.2 if **Statement**

The syntax for an if statement is
```
if (expression)
    commands are evaluated if expression is true
end
```
Let us explain the if statement for you, using examples.

Example 2

Find the value of r in the program

```
x = 1
r = 1
if(x > 0)
        r = 2
end
```

Answer

The initial value for r is 1. The expression x > 0 is true. Hence the command r = 2 is evaluated. Therefore, as a result this sets the value of r to 2.

Example 3

Find the values of r and b in the program

```
x = 1;
y = -4;
r = 1;
b = 0
if (x > 0 y < 3)
  r = 3;
  b = b - 1;
end
```

Answer

The initial values for r and b are 1 and 0, respectively. The condition x > 0 is true. The condition is y < 3 is true. The logical operation true&true produces true. Hence the commands r = 3 and b = b−1 are evaluated. This sets the value of r and b to 3 and −1, respectively.

Example 4

Write a Matlab program to change the value of the variable x as follows:

• If the value of x is greater than 0, set the value of x to 10.

Answer

Initially, the variable x is created and a number is assigned to it, for example, here we have chosen a value of 1. Then Matlab checks the value of x that we have just assigned. If it is greater than 0, Matlab then sets the value of x to 10. The Matlab program to do this is shown below:

```
x = 1;
if (x > 0)
    x = 10;
end
x
```

Running the program produces the result

```
x =
    10
```

because the value that we initially assigned to x was greater than 0.
Now test the program using x = −1:

```
x = −1;
if (x > 0)
    x = 10;
end
x
```

Running the program produces the result

```
x =
    −1
```

Because the initial value that we assigned was not greater than 0, its original value was not changed.

Example 5

Write a Matlab function that has one input argument and returns one value. Name this function change_it( ). This function operates as follows:

- If the value of the input argument is greater than 0, the function returns the value 10.
- If the value of the input argument is less than or equal to 0, the function returns the value of the input argument.

Answer
The following figure shows the code for the function change_it( ). Save this function as **change_it.m**.

```
function y = change_it(x)
if (x > 0)
    y = 10;
end
if (x <= 0)
    y = x;
end
end
```

This function may be tested using two values, $x = 1$ and $x = -9$, as shown in the following left and the right figures, respectively.

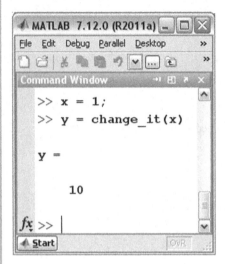 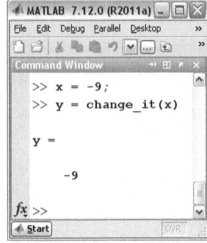

You can rewrite the function `change_it()` as follows to reduce the code size.

```
function y = change_it(x)
y = x;
if (x > 0)
   y = 10;
end
end
```

Exercise 1[1]

Write a Matlab program that changes the values of the x and y variables as follows:

• If the value of x is greater than y, exchange their values.

Example 6

John has got £40 and he would like to buy at least 10 kilograms of fruit. The price of 1 kilogram of apples is £3.20. The price of 1 kilogram of oranges is £5. Write a Matlab program that finds out which type of fruit John should buy and how many kilograms he can buy.

Answer
The Matlab program below is self-explanatory.

```
clear; clc; close all;
John_has_got_pounds = 40;
price_apple_per_kg = 3.2;
```

```
price_orange_per_kg = 5;
minimum_weight_John_wants_kg = 10;
maximum_price_John_should_pay = John_has_got_pounds /...
  minimum_weight_John_wants_kg;
if (price_apple_per_kg <= maximum_price_John_should_pay)
  weight_John_buy = John_has_got_pounds / price_apple_per_kg;
  disp('John can buy'); disp(weight_John_buy); disp('kg of apple');
end
if (price_orange_per_kg <= maximum_price_John_should_pay)
  weight_John_buy = John_has_got_pounds / price_orange_per_kg;
  disp('John can buy'); disp(weight_John_buy); disp('kg of orange');
end
```
Running this program produces the result

When writing a piece of Matlab code, you should place code readability as a top priority.

6.1.3 Improving the Readability of Matlab Functions

When writing a Matlab function you need to follow the stated programming style guidelines. These guidelines are designed to improve the readability of your Matlab functions.

1. Add comments that explain what the function does, the input arguments, and the return values.
2. Add comments that give an example of how to use the function.
3. The name of the person who has written the function.
4. The date that the function was written or last modified.
5. The function should automatically check that the size of the input arguments is ok.

For example, let us rewrite the add2() function, explained in Lesson 5.2, according to these guidelines. This function has two arguments and returns a value which is equal to the addition of both arguments.

```
function z = add2(x,y)
%This function adds "x" to "y" and returns their addition
%This example shows how to use this function
%a = 1;
%b = 2;
%c = add2(a,b);
%This function returns "3" which is a result of adding "1" and "2"
%This function was written by Dr. Munther Gdeisat on 25/10/2011
%ensure that the both input arguments are scalars (numbers)
if(~isscalar(x) || ~isscalar(y))
    disp('both input arguments must be scalars (numbers)')
    return
end
z = x + y;
end
```

This function checks whether both arguments are scalars. If both arguments are scalars, the function performs the addition; otherwise, it displays a warning message and returns without attempting to perform the addition. Depending on the complexity of a project, it may be worthwhile setting up standard error messages that are returned, so that, if possible, the function call can continue to run.

Let us test the add2() function using two numbers as shown in the following figure. As you can see from the figure, the function works properly.

Now let us test the add2() function using a number and a vector. The function does not work properly and displays an error message.

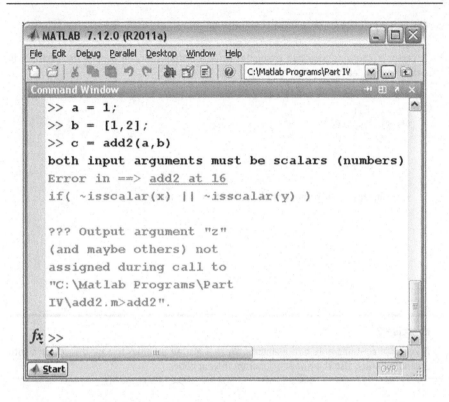

6.1.4 Examples for `if` Statements

Example 7

A vector s contains only two elements. Write a Matlab program to sort the vector s in ascending order (smallest values first).

Answer
In the following code segment, Matlab checks whether the value of s(1) is greater than the value of s(2). If it is greater, both elements of s are exchanged.

```
s = [2, 1];
if (s(1) > s(2))
  temp = s(1);
  s(1) = s(2);
  s(2) = temp;
end
s
```

Running this code segment produces the following result:

```
s =
     1   2
```

Example 8

A vector s contains only two elements. Write a Matlab program to sort the vector s in descending order (largest values first).

Answer
```
s = [1, 2];
if (s(1) < s(2))
  temp = s(1);
  s(1) = s(2);
  s(2) = temp;
end
```
Running this code segment produces the following result:

```
s =
    2   1
```

Exercise 2[1]

A vector s contains only two elements. Write a Matlab program to sort the vector s into ascending order. Use the swap() function in your code.

Exercise 3[1]

Write a Matlab function that sorts a two-element vector into ascending order.

Example 9

Write a Matlab function that has two scalar input arguments and returns the maximum value of its input arguments. Name this function max2.

Answer
```
function maximum = max2(x,y)
maximum = x;
if (x < y)
  maximum = y;
end
end
```
Examples for using the max2 function are shown below.

Exercise 4[1]

Rewrite the max2() function using the programming style guidelines that were given previously in Lesson 6.1, Topic 6.1.3.

Example 10

Write a Matlab function that has three input arguments and returns the maximum value of its input arguments. Name this function max3. Use the max2 function to help you in writing the code for the max3 function.

Answer
```
function d = max3(a,b,c)
e = max2(a,b);
d = max2(e,c);
end
```
An example for using the max3 function is shown below.

Exercise 5[1]

Write a Matlab function that has four input arguments and returns the maximum value of its input arguments. Name this function `max4`. Use the `max2` and `max3` functions to help you in writing the code for the `max4` function.

Exercise 6[1]

Write a Matlab function that has three input arguments and returns the maximum value of its input arguments. Name this function `max3a`. This function should not call any other functions.

Exercise 7[1]

Write a Matlab function that has four input arguments and returns the maximum value of its input arguments. Name this function `max4a`. This function should not call any other functions.

Lesson 6.2   The Construction of an `if else` Statement

Objectives
* To learn how to construct an `if else` statement.
Topic
6.2.1 `if else` Statement

6.2.1   `if else` Statement

The syntax for the Matlab `if else` statement is
```
if (expression)
        commands are evaluated if expression is true
else
        commands are evaluated if expression is false
end
```
Let us explain the `if else` statement by using some examples.

Example 1

Find the value of r in the program

```
x = 1;
r = 1;
if (x > 0)
    r = 2;
else
    r = 3;
end
```

Answer
The initial value for r is set to 1. The expression $x > 0$ is `true`. Hence the command $r = 2$ is evaluated. This sets the value of r to 2.

Example 2

Find the value of r in the program

```
x = 1;
r = 1;
if (x > 3)
    r = 2;
else
    r = 3;
end
```

Answer
The initial value for r is set to 1. The expression $x > 3$ is `false`. Hence the command $r = 3$ is evaluated. This sets the value of r to 3.

Example 3

Use the debug tools in Matlab to follow the execution of the following program on a step-by-step basis.

```
x = 1;
r = 1;
if (x > 0)
    r = 2;
else
    r = 3;
end
```

Answer

Step 1 Type the program above into the Matlab **Editor**. Save the program in a file with the name of, for example, **find_r.m**. Click on the ▬ symbol, as indicated by the arrow in the figure, below-left, in order to set a **Breakpoint** in the first line of the program.

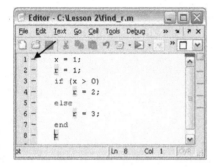 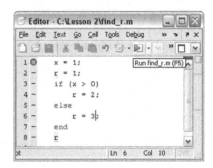

Step 2 Click on the icon to run the program. Matlab stops executing the program when it reaches the **Breakpoint**. Press **F10** to run the first line of the program.

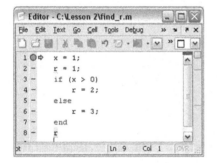 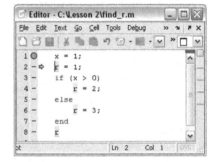

Step 3 Press **F10** twice to run the second and third lines of the program. Since the value of the expression $x > 0$ is true, Matlab goes to line 4.

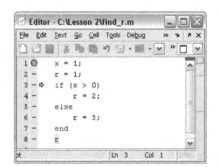 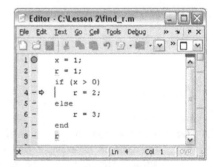

Step 4 Press **F10** to run the fourth line of the program. The value of r is now 2. Then Matlab jumps to line 8. The else command r = 3 is not executed.

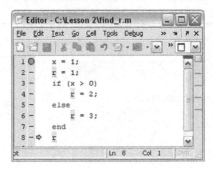

Step 5 Press **F10** to run the eighth line of the program. Matlab displays the value of r.

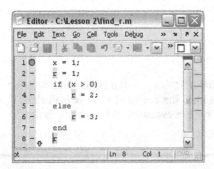

Example 4

Find the value of r in the program

```
a = 1;
b = 2;
r = 0;
if (a > 0)
    if (b > 10)
        r = 1;
    end
    r = 2;
else
    r = 3;
end
```

Answer

The initial value for r is set to 0. The expression a > 0 is true. The expression b > 10 is false. Hence the command r = 1 is not evaluated. The command r = 2 is evaluated. This sets the value of r to 2.

Exercise 1[1]

Use the debug tools in Matlab to follow the execution of the Example 4 Matlab program on a step-by-step basis.

Example 5

Find the value of r in the program
```
a = 1;
b = 2;
r = 0;
if (a > 0)
  if (b > 10)
    r = 1;
  else
    r = 2;
  end
  r = 3;
end
```

Answer

The initial value for r is 0. The expression $a > 0$ is true. The expression $b > 10$ is false. Hence the command $r = 1$ is not evaluated. The command $r = 2$ is evaluated. This sets the value of r to 2. Then the command $r = 3$ is evaluated. The value of r is now 3.

Exercise 2[1]

Use the debug tools in Matlab to follow the execution of the Example 5 Matlab program on a step-by-step basis.

Example 6

Write a Matlab program to change the value of the variable x as follows:

- If the value of x is greater than 1, set x to 10.
- If the above condition has not been satisfied, set x to the *absolute* value of x.

Answer

Initially, we create the variable x and assign a specific number to it; for example, here we set it to a value of 2. After that, Matlab checks the value of x. If x is greater than 1, Matlab then sets x to 10. If x is **not** greater than 1, Matlab sets x to the *absolute* value of x.

The initial value of x is 2. Therefore the expression $x > 1$ is true. Hence the value of x is set to be 10.

```
x = 2;
if (x > 1)
  x = 10;
else
  x = abs(x);
end
x
```
Running the program produces the result

```
x =
     10
```

Now let us test the program using $x = -1$. The expression $x > 1$ is false. Hence the value of x is set to abs(x). Therefore here the final value of x is set to be 1.

```
x = -1;
if (x > 1)
  x = 10;
else
  x = abs(x);
end
x
```
Running the program produces the result
```
x =
     1
```

Example 7

Write a Matlab function that has two input arguments and returns the maximum value of its input arguments. Name this function max2b. Use an if else statement in your code.

Answer
The following code shows the max2() function that you wrote in the previous lesson.
```
function maximum = max2(x,y)
maximum = x;
if (x < y)
  maximum = y;
end
end
```
The code for this function is rewritten, this time using the if else statement.
```
function maximum = max2b(x,y)
if (x < y)
  maximum = y;
else
  maximum = x;
end
end
```
Compare the readability of both functions. Which function is easier to understand?

Example 8

Use the debug tools in Matlab to follow the execution of the max2b() function on a step-by-step basis.

Answer

Step 1 Write a script file to test call the max2b() function. Name this script file *test.m*.

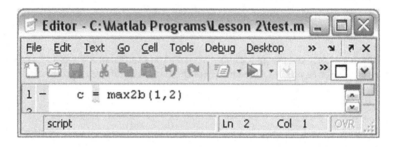

Step 2 Click on the ■ symbol to set a **Breakpoint** in the first line of the program.

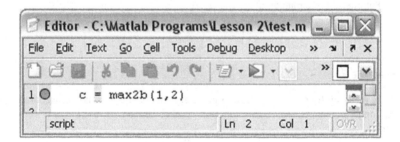

Step 3 Click on the icon ▶ to run the program. Matlab stops executing the program at the **Breakpoint**.

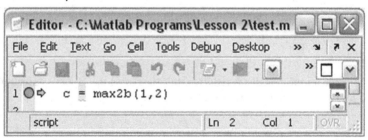

Step 4 Press **F11** to **Step In** the max2b() function. Matlab opens file *max2b.m* and stops executing the function at line 3.

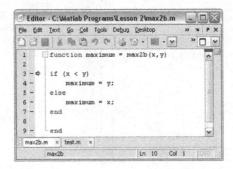

Step 5 Move the mouse over the x and y variables to check their values.

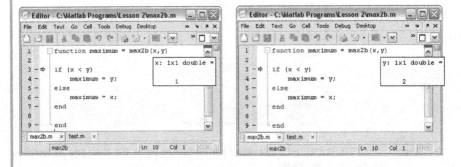

Step 6 Press **F10**. The condition $x < y$ is true. Hence Matlab steps to line 4.

Step 7 Press **F10**. Matlab executes line 4. The value of the maximum variable is 2. Then Matlab jumps to line 9. The command maximum = x is not executed.

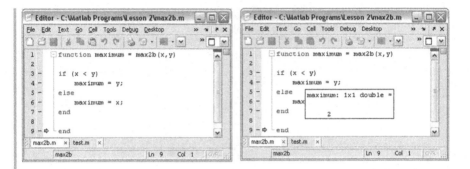

Step 8 Press **F10**. Matlab finishes running the function.

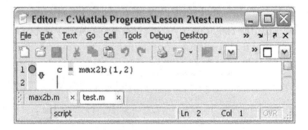

Step 9 Press **F10**. Matlab returns control to the *test.m* script file that originally called the `max2b()` function.

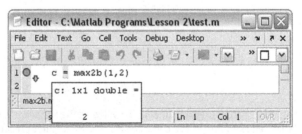

Step 10 Move the mouse over the `c` variable to check its value.

Step 11 Press **F10**. Matlab has finished running the **test.m** script file. The value of the c variable now is 2.

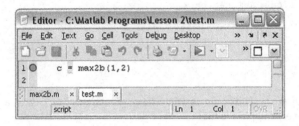

Lesson 6.3   Recursive Functions

Objective
* To learn about recursive functions in Matlab.

Topic
6.3.1 Recursive Functions

6.3.1   Recursive Functions

Example 9

A function that calls itself is called a *recursive* (iterative) function. The following code shows an example of a recursive function. Use the debug tools in Matlab to follow the execution of this function on a step-by-step basis. Test this function using x = 1:3.

```
function addition = sum_vector(x)
if (length(x) > 1)
  x = [x(1:end − 2), x(end − 1) + x(end)];
  addition = sum_vector(x);
else
  addition = x(1);
end
end
```

Answer

Step 1 Open the **Editor**. Go to **File→New→Function**. This creates a new file. Delete everything in the file.

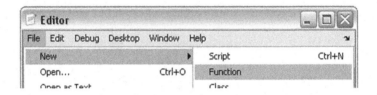

Step 2 Type the code for the sum_vector() function. Name this file *sum_vector.m.*

Step 3 Write a script file to call the sum_vector() function. Save this script file with the name of *test1.m*.

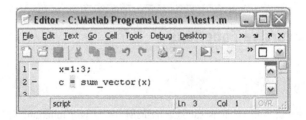

Step 4 Click on the ▬ symbol to set a **Breakpoint** in the first line of the program.

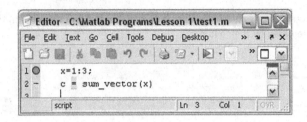

Step 5 Click on the icon ▶ to run the *test1.m* program. Matlab stops executing the program at the **Breakpoint**.

Step 6 Press **F10**. Matlab executes line 1.

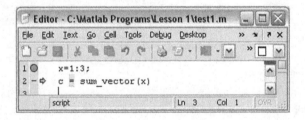

Step 7 Press **F11** to **Step In** the sum_vector() function. Matlab opens the *sum_vector.m* file and stops executing the function at line 3. Move the mouse over the x variable and check its value.

 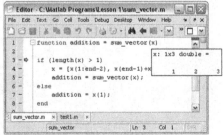

Step 8 The value of the expression length(x)>1 is true. Press **F10**. Matlab executes line 3. Press **F10** again and Matlab executes line 4. Move the mouse over the x

variable and check its value. Note that the last two elements in the vector x are replaced by their addition.

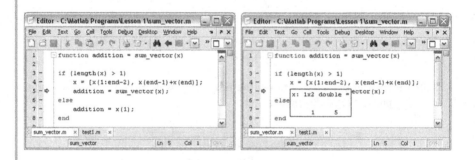

Step 9   Press **F11**. Note the white and green arrows as shown. This is because the function has called itself. Note that up to now the function sum_vector() has been called twice. Move the mouse over the x variable and check its value.

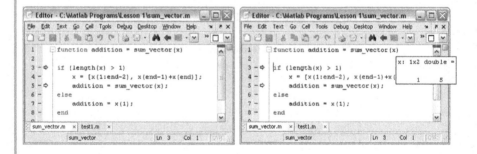

Step 10   Press **F10**. Since the vector x contains two elements, Matlab steps to line 4.

Step 11   Press **F10**. Matlab executes line 5. Move the mouse over the x variable and check its value. Note that the vector x contains one element only.

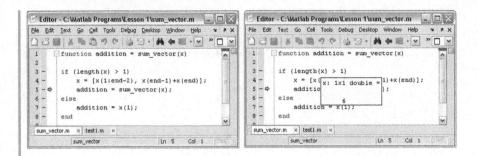

Step 12 Press **F11**. Matlab calls the `sum_vector()` function and stops executing at line 3.

Note that up to now the function `sum_vector()` has been called three times. Move the mouse over the x variable and check its value. Note that the vector x contains one element only.

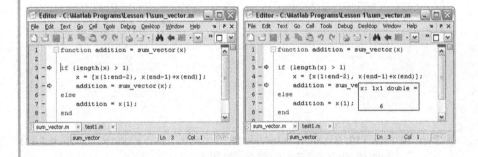

Step 13 Press **F10**. The variable x contains one element only. The expression `length (x) > 1` is `false`. Hence Matlab jumps to line 6.

Step 14 Press **F10**. Matlab steps to line 7.

Step 15 Press **F10**. Matlab executes line 7 and it will not call the function `sum_vector()` again. The variable `addition` has a value that is equal to 6.

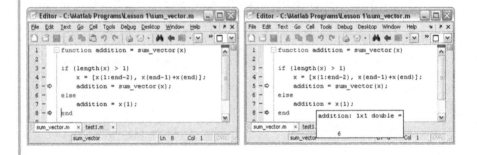

Step 16 Press **F10**. Matlab executes line 8. Press **F10**. Matlab executes line 10 and it is ready to return control to the calling function `sum_vector()`.

Step 17 Press **F10**. Matlab executes line 8. Press **F10**. Matlab executes line 10 and it is ready to return control to the calling function `sum_vector()`.

Step 18 Press **F10**. Matlab executes line 8. Press **F10**. Matlab executes line 10 and it is ready to return control to the calling function sum_vector().

Step 19 Press **F10**. Matlab returns control to the *test1.m* file. The value of c is 6.

Step 20 Press **F10**. This terminates the execution of the *test1.m* file.

Exercise 1[1]

Use the debug tools in Matlab to follow the execution of the function sum_vector(x) on a step-by-step basis. Test this function using $x = 1:4$.

Exercise 2[1]

Use the debug tools in Matlab to follow the execution of the function `factorial2(x)` on a step-by-step basis.

```
function fact = factorial2(x)
if (x>1)
    x = x - 1;
    fact = factorial2(x)*(x + 1);
else
    fact = x(1);
end
end
```

Test the operation of this function with the following code.

```
x = 3;
c = factorial2(x)
```

Lesson 6.4   The Construction of an `if elseif else` Statement

Objective
* To learn the construction of an `if elseif else` statement.

Topic
6.4.1 `if elseif else` Statement

6.4.1   `if elseif else` Statement

The syntax for the Matlab `if elseif else` statement is

```
if (expression 1)
        commands are evaluated if expression 1 is true. Then jump to end.
elseif (expression 2)
        commands are evaluated if expression 2 is true. Then jump to end.
        :
elseif (expression n)
        commands are evaluated if expression n is true. Then jump to end.
else
        commands are evaluated if all the expressions 1, 2,...n are false.
end
```

Let us explain the `if elseif else` statement for you by using examples.

Example 1

Find the value of `r` in the program

```
x = 1;
y = 3;
r = 1;
if (x > 0)
    r = 2;
elseif (y < -2)
    r = 3;
else
    r = 4;
end
```

Answer

The initial value for `r` is 1. The expression `x > 0` is `true`. Hence the command `r = 2` is evaluated. This sets the value of `r` to 2. Matlab then jumps to the `end` statement. Note that the condition $y < -2$ is `false`.

Example 2

Find the value of `r` in the program

```
x = 1;
y = -3;
r = 1;
if (x > 0)
    r = 2;
elseif (y < -2)
    r = 3;
else
    r = 4;
end
```

Answer

The initial value for `r` is 1. The expression `x > 0` is `true`. Hence the command `r = 2` is evaluated. This sets the value of `r` to 2. Matlab then jumps to the `end` statement. Note that even though the condition $y < -2$ is `true` here, the command `r = 3` is not executed.

Example 3

Find the value of `r` in the program

```
x = -1;
```

```
y = -3;
r = 1;
if (x > 0)
    r = 2;
elseif (y < -2)
    r = 3;
else
    r = 4;
end
```

Answer

The initial value for r is 1. The expression x > 0 is false. Hence the command r = 2 is not evaluated. The condition y < − 2 is true. Thus the command r = 3 is evaluated. This sets the value of r to 3. Matlab then jumps to the end statement.

Example 4

Find the value of r in the program

```
x = -1;
y = 3;
r = 1;
if (x > 0)
    r = 2;
elseif (y < -2)
    r = 3;
else
    r = 4;
end
```

Answer

The initial value for r is 1. The expression x > 0 is false. Hence the command r = 2 is not evaluated. The condition y < −2 is false. Thus the command r = 3 is not evaluated. Matlab evaluates the command r = 4. This sets the value of r to 4. Matlab then goes to the end statement.

Example 5

Find the value of r in the program

```
x = -1;
y = 3;
z = 1;
r = 1;
if (x > 0)
    r = 2;
elseif (y < -2)
    r = 3;
elseif (z ~ = 1)
```

```
    r = 5;
  else
    r = 4;
  end
```

Answer
The initial value for r is 1. The expression $x > 0$ is false. Hence the command $r = 2$ is not evaluated. The condition $y < -2$ is false. Thus the command $r = 3$ is not evaluated. The condition $z \sim = 1$ is false. Thus the command $r = 5$ is not evaluated. Matlab evaluates the command $r = 4$. This sets the value of r to 4. Matlab then goes to the end statement.

Exercise 1[2]
Explain why Matlab cannot run the following program.

```
x = -1;
if (x > 0)
  x = 2;
else if (x < -2)
  x = 3;
else
  x = 4;
end
```

Lesson 6.5 The Construction of a switch case Statement

Objective
• To learn the construction of a switch case statement.

Topic
6.5.1 switch case Statement

6.5.1 switch case Statement

The syntax for a switch case statement is

```
switch (expression)
        case {expression 1}
                commands 1 are evaluated if expression 1 is true. Then jump to end.
        case {expression 2}
                commands 2 are evaluated if expression 2 is true. Then jump to end.
```

```
                    :
                    :
                    :
        case {expression n}
            commands n are evaluated if expression n is true. Then jump to end.
        otherwise
            commands are evaluated if all the expressions 1, 2,...n are false.
        end
```

The term `expression` here must be either an integer scalar or a string character. Examples of integer scalars are −1 and 100. Examples of a string character are 'm', 'hello', and 'cars'.

Let us explain the `switch case` statement by using some examples.

Example 1

Write a Matlab program to convert a distance with units of either kilometers, meters, centimeters, or millimeters into meters.

Answer
Suppose that we could like to convert 10 centimeters to meters.

```
x = 10;
units = 'cm';
switch (units)
  case {'km'}
    y = 1000 * x
  case {'m'}
    y = x
  case {'cm'}
    y = x / 100
  case {'mm'}
    y = x / 1000
  otherwise
    disp(['Unknown Units: ', units])
end
```

`units` is a character string variable with the value of 'cm'.

The term `expression` in the `switch` statement is `units`.

`expression 1` in the first `case` statement is 'km' and it is not equal to the `units` string variable. Hence the command y = 1000 * x is not evaluated.

`expression 2` in the second `case` statement is 'm' and it is not equal to the `units` string variable. Hence the command y = x is not evaluated.

`expression 3` in the third `case` statement is 'cm' and it is equal to the `units` string variable. Hence the command y = x/ 100 is evaluated. The value of y is 10/100 = 0.1. Then Matlab jumps to the `end` statement.

The Matlab command disp(['Unknown Units: ', units]) in the `otherwise` statement is not evaluated. This is because one of the other case expressions, in this case `expression 3`, is true.

Running the above Matlab program produces the output

```
y =
    1
```

Exercise 1[1]

Rewrite the program in Example 1 using an if-elseif-else statement.

Exercise 2[1]

Use the debug tools in Matlab to follow the execution of the program given in Example 1 on a step-by-step basis.

Example 2

The code in Example 1 can be modified as follows.

Answer
```
x = 10;
  units = 'cm';
  switch (units)
    case {'km', 'kilometer'}
      y = 1000 * x;
    case {'m', 'meter'}
      y = x;
    case {'cm', 'centimeter'}
      y = x / 100;
    case {'mm', 'millimeter'}
      y = x / 1000;
    otherwise
      disp(['Unknown Units: ', units])
  end
  y
```

The expression case {'km', 'kilometer'} means that the command y = 1000*x; is evaluated when units variable is equal to either 'km' or 'kilometer'.

Exercise 3[1]

Rewrite the program in Example 2 using an if-elseif-else statement.

Example 3

Find the value of r in the following program.

```
x = 1;
r = 0;
switch (x)
  case {1}
    r = 1;
  case {2}
    r = r + 1;
  otherwise
    r = 3;
end
r
```

Answer

x is equal to 1.

The term expression in the switch statement is x.

expression 1 in the first case statement is 1 and it is equal to the x variable.
Hence the command r = 1 is evaluated.

expression 2 in the second case statement is 2 and it is not equal to the x variable.
Hence the command r = r + 1 is not evaluated.

The Matlab command r = 3 in the otherwise statement is not evaluated.

This is because expression 1 is true.

Running the above Matlab program produces the output

```
r =
    1
```

Exercise 4[1]

Find the value of r in the following program:

```
x = 4;
r = 0;
switch (x)
  case {1}
    r = 1;
  case {2}
    r = r + 1;
  otherwise
    r = 3;
end
r
```

Answers to Selected Exercises

Lesson 6.1

Exercise 1

```
clc; clear; close all
x = 2;
y = 1;
if (x > y)
    temp = x;
    x = y;
    y = temp;
end
x, y
```

Exercise 2

```
clear; clc; close all
s = [2, 1];
if (s(1) > s(2))
    [s(1), s(2)] = swap(s(1), s(2));
end
s
```

Exercise 3

```
function t = sort2(s)
%This function sorts a vector of two elements only
%if the input is not a vector
if (isvector(s) ~ = 1)
    disp('The input argument must be a vector');
    return
end
%if the input vector does not contain two elements
if (length(s) ~ = 2)
    disp('The input vector must contain two elements');
    return
end
if (s(1) > s(2))
    temp = s(1);
    s(1) = s(2);
    s(2) = temp;
end
t = s;
end
```
Save this function as *sort2.m*.

Exercise 4

```
function z = max2(x,y)
%This function returns the maximum of two input numbers
%This example shows how to use this function
%a = 1;
%b = 2;
%c = max2(a,b);
%This function returns "2" which is the maximum of "1" and "2"
%This function was written by Dr. Gdeisat on 25/10/2011%ensure that the
both input arguments are numbers
if( ~isscalar(x) || ~isscalar(y) )
    disp('both input arguments must be scalars (numbers)')
    return
end
maximum = x;
if (x < y)
    maximum = y;
end
end
```

Exercise 5

```
function e = max4(a,b,c,d)
f = max3(a,b,c);
e = max2(f,d);
end
```
Save this function as *max4.m*.

Exercise 6

```
function maximum = max3a(x,y,z)
maximum = x;
if (maximum < y)
    maximum = y;
end
if (maximum < z)
    maximum = z;
end
end
```
Save this function as *max3a.m*.

Exercise 7

```
function maximum = max4a(v,x,y,z)
maximum = v;
if (maximum < x)
    maximum = x;
```

```
end
if (maximum < y)
   maximum = y;
end
if (maximum < z)
   maximum = z;
end
end
```

Save this function as *max4a.m*.

Lesson 6.4

Exercise 1

elseif should appear as one word. The use here of else if as two words is incorrect and will produce an error.

Lesson 6.5

Exercise 1

```
x = 10;
units = 'cm';
if ( strcmp(units, 'km') )
        y = 1000 * x;
elseif ( strcmp(units, 'm') )
        y = x;
elseif ( strcmp(units, 'cm') )
        y = x / 100;
elseif ( strcmp(units, 'mm') )
        y = x / 1000;
else
        disp(['Unknown Units: ', units])
end
```

Exercise 3

```
x = 10;
units = 'cm';
if ( strcmp(units, 'km') || strcmp(units, 'kilometer') )
        y = 1000 * x;
elseif ( strcmp(units, 'm') || strcmp(units, 'meter') )
        y = x;
elseif ( strcmp(units, 'cm') || strcmp(units, 'centimeter') )
        y = x / 100;
```

```
elseif ( strcmp(units, 'mm') || strcmp(units, 'millimeter') )
      y = x/ 1000;
else
      disp(['Unknown Units: ', units])
end
```

7 Loop Statements in Matlab

Chapter Outline

Lesson 7.1   The Construction of a for Loop Statement

Objectives
- To learn how to construct a for statement.
- To learn how to construct a nested for statement.

Topics

7.1.1 The Need for Loops in Matlab

7.1.2 The Construction of a for Statement
     7.1.2.1 Introduction to for Loops
     7.1.2.2 for Loops for Scalars
     7.1.2.3 for Loops for Vectors

7.1.3 The Construction of a Nested for Statement
     7.1.3.1 Introduction to Nested for Loops
     7.1.3.2 Nested for Loops for Arrays

7.1.1 The Need for Loops in Matlab

One of the Matlab keywords that you will need and use most frequently is the for keyword. This keyword is used to run a piece of code for a specific number of times, as illustrated in the following example.

Matlab by Example. DOI: http://dx.doi.org/10.1016/B978-0-12-405212-3.00007-4

Example 1

Write a Matlab program to produce the first seven numbers of a Fibonacci series. By definition, the first two numbers in a Fibonacci series are 0 and 1, and each subsequent number is the sum of the previous two. In mathematical terms, the series F_n of Fibonacci numbers is defined by the equation

$$F_n = F_{n-1} + F_{n-2}$$

The first seven numbers of a Fibonacci series are

0, 1, 1, 2, 3, 5, 8

Answer
The following program produces the first seven numbers of a Fibonacci series. Here we have used a vector f to save the first seven numbers of a Fibonacci series.

```
f(1) = 0;
f(2) = 1;
f(3) = f(2) + f(1);
f(4) = f(3) + f(2);
f(5) = f(4) + f(3);
f(6) = f(5) + f(4);
f(7) = f(6) + f(5)
```

Now, if you would like to write a Matlab program to generate the first 1000 numbers of the Fibonacci series, what are you going to do? Would you like to write a 1000-line Matlab program to perform this simple task? Is there another way of writing this program? The answer is yes. You can use loops in Matlab to easily do this simple task, as indicated in the following example.

Example 2

Write a Matlab program to produce the first 1000 numbers of a Fibonacci series using Matlab's for keyword.

```
f(1) = 0;
f(2) = 1;
n = 1000;
for iNo = 3:n
    f(iNo) = f(iNo-1) + f(iNo-2);
end
```

7.1.2 The Construction of a for Statement

7.1.2.1 Introduction to for Loops

The syntax of a for statement is

```
for iteration Variable = initial value: increment: final value
   commands
end
```

$$\text{The number of iterations for the for loop} = \left\lfloor \frac{\text{final value} - \text{initial value}}{\text{increment}} \right\rfloor + 1$$

where $\lfloor \cdot \rfloor$ rounds down a real number toward the nearest lower integer. The loop stops executing the commands when the value of the iteration Variable is greater than or equal to the final value.

Example 3

In the following program

```
f(1) = 0;
f(2) = 1;
for iNo = 3:1:7
    f(iNo) = f(iNo-1) + f(iNo-2);
end
```

the iteration variable is iNo.
The initial value for the iteration variable is 3.
The increment for the iteration variable is 1.
The final value for the iteration variable is 7.
The command in the for statement is f(iNo) = f(iNo-1) + f(iNo-2);
The number of iterations for the for loop $= \lfloor \frac{7-3}{1} \rfloor + 1 = 5$.
The values of iNo are 3, 4, 5, 6, and 7.

Example 4

In the following program

```
f(1) = 0;
f(2) = 1;
for iNo = 3:7
    f(iNo) = f(iNo-1) + f(iNo-2);
end
```

The default increment for the iteration variable is 1.

Example 5

In the following program

```
x = 1;
for ix = 0:2:10
    x = 0.9 * x;
end
```

The iteration variable is ix.
The initial value for the iteration variable is 0.
The increment for the iteration variable is 2.
The final value for the iteration variable is 10.

The command in the for statement is x = 0.9 * x;
The number of iterations for the for loop = $\lfloor \frac{10-0}{2} \rfloor + 1 = 6$.
The values of ix are 0, 2, 4, 6, 8, and 10.

Example 6

In the following program

```
x = 1;
for ix = 1:2:10
    x = 0.9 * x;
end
```

The iteration variable is ix.
The initial value for the iteration variable is 1.
The increment for the iteration variable is 2.
The final value for the iteration variable is 10.
The command in the for statement is x = 0.9 * x;
The number of iterations for the for loop = $\lfloor \frac{10-1}{2} \rfloor + 1 = 4 + 1 = 5$.
The values of ix are 1, 3, 5, 7, and 9.

Example 7

In the following program

```
x = 1;
for ix = 1:2:1
    x = 0.9 * x;
end
```

The iteration variable is ix.
The initial value for the iteration variable is 1.
The increment for the iteration variable is 2.
The final value for the iteration variable is 1.
The command in the for statement is x = 0.9 * x;
The number of iterations for the for loop = $\lfloor \frac{1-1}{2} \rfloor + 1 = 0 + 1 = 1$.
The value of ix is 1.

Example 8

In the following program

```
x = 1;
for ix = 1:2:-3
    x = 0.9 * x
end
```

The iteration variable is ix.
The initial value for the iteration variable is 1.
The increment for the iteration variable is 2.

The final value for the iteration variable is -3.

The command in the for statement is $x = 0.9 * x$;

The number of iterations for the for loop $= \lfloor \frac{-3-1}{2} \rfloor + 1 = -2 + 1 = -1$. In this case, Matlab will not execute the commands inside the loop since the number of iterations is negative.

The value of ix is [].

Example 9

In the following program

```
x = 1;
for ix = 6:-2:-6
    x = 0.9 * x
end
```

The iteration variable is ix.

The initial value for the iteration variable is 6.

The increment for the iteration variable is -2.

The final value for the iteration variable is -6.

The command in the for statement is $x = 0.9 * x$;

The number of iterations for the for loop $= \lfloor \frac{6--6}{2} \rfloor + 1 = 6 + 1 = 7$.

The values of ix are 6, 4, 2, 0, -2, -4, and -6.

7.1.2.2 *for Loop for Scalars*

Example 10

Find the value of x produced by this program.

```
x = 1;
for ix = 1:2:10
    x = 0.9 * x*ix
end
```

Answer

The number of iterations is 5.

The initial value for x is 1.

In the first iteration,	ix = 1
	x = 0.9*1*1 = 0.9
In the second iteration,	ix = 3
	x = 0.9*0.9*3 = 2.43
In the third iteration,	ix = 5
	x = 0.9*2.43*5 = 10.9350
In the fourth iteration,	ix = 7
	x = 0.9*10.9350*7 = 68.8905
In the fifth iteration,	ix = 9
	x = 0.9*68.8905*9 = 558.0131

You can use tables to follow the execution of the program as follows:

Iteration	ix	x
First	1	$0.9 \times 1 \times 1 = 0.9$
Second	3	$0.9 \times 0.9 \times 3 = 2.43$
Third	5	$0.9 \times 2.43 \times 5 = 10.9350$
Fourth	7	$0.9 \times 10.9350 \times 7 = 68.8905$
Fifth	9	$0.9 \times 68.8905 \times 9 = 558.0131$

Example 11

Follow the execution of the following program on a step-by-step basis using the debug tools available in Matlab.

```
x = 1;
for ix = 1:2:10
    x = 0.9 * x*ix
end
```

Answer

Step 1 Type the preceding program into the Matlab **Editor**. Save the program in a file with the name of, for example, *ex8.m*. Click on the ▬ symbol indicated by the arrow in the following figure, below-left, in order to set a **Breakpoint** in the first line of the program.

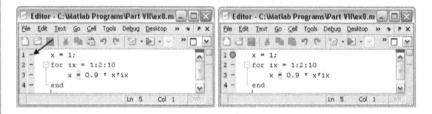

Step 2 Click on the icon to run the program. Matlab stops executing the program at the **Breakpoint**.

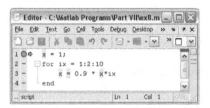

Step 3 Press **F10** to run the first line of the program. Move the mouse and position it over the variable x to find its value. The value of x is 1.

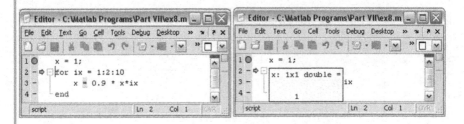

Step 4 Press **F10** to run the second line of the program. The value of ix is 1.

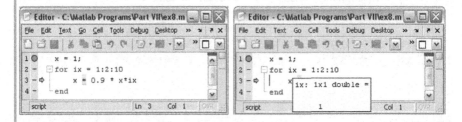

Step 5 Press **F10** to run the third line of the program. This is the first iteration of the for loop. The value of x is equal to $0.9 \times 1 \times 1 = 0.9$.

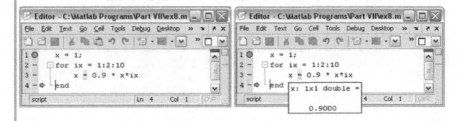

Step 6 Press **F10** twice to execute the second iteration of the for loop. The value of x is equal to $0.9 \times 0.9 \times 3 = 2.43$. The value of ix is 3.

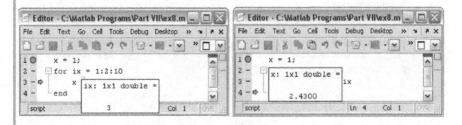

Step 7 Press **F10** twice to execute the third iteration of the `for` loop. The value of x is equal to $0.9 \times 2.43 \times 5 = 10.9350$. The value of `ix` is 5.

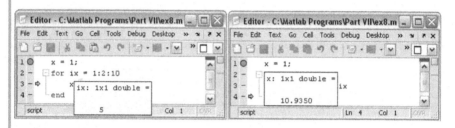

Step 8 Press **F10** twice to execute the fourth iteration of the `for` loop. The value of x is equal to $0.9 \times 10.9350 \times 7 = 68.8905$. The value of `ix` is 7.

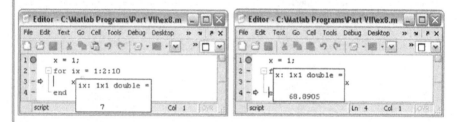

Step 9 Press **F10** twice to execute the fifth iteration of the `for` loop. The value of x is equal to $0.9 \times 68.8905 \times 5 = 558.0131$. The value of `ix` is 9.

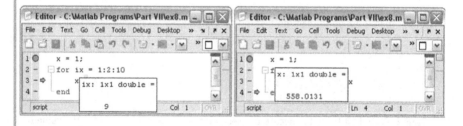

Step 10 Press **F10** and Matlab exists the `for` loop. Press **F10** and Matlab finishes running the program.

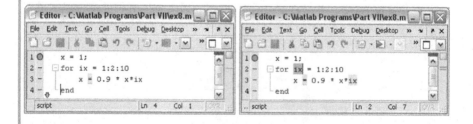

Exercise 1[1]

Follow the execution of the following program on a step-by-step basis by using the debug tools that are available in Matlab.

```
f(1) = 0;
f(2) = 1;
n = 7;
for iNo = 3:n
    f(iNo) = f(iNo-1) + f(iNo-2);
end
```

Example 12

Write a Matlab program to calculate the factorial of an integer number n. The factorial of a number n is defined as

$$n! = n \times (n-1) \times (n-2) \times (n-3)\ldots\ldots\ldots\ldots(3) \times (2) \times (1)$$

The factorial of the number 1 is 1 by definition.
The factorial of 2 is $2 \times 1 = 2$.
The factorial of 3 is $3 \times 2 \times 1 = 6$ and so on.
The factorial 4 is $4 \times 3 \times 2 \times 1 = 24$ and so on.

Answer
This program calculates the factorial of the number $n = 4$.

```
%This program calculates the factorial of n
n = 4;
%calculate the factorial of n
factorial_of_n = 1;
for in = 2:n
    factorial_of_n = factorial_of_n * in;
end
```

In the first iteration,	in = 2
	factorial_of_n = 1 * 2 = 2;
In the second iteration,	in = 3
	factorial_of_n = 2 * 3 = 6;
In the third iteration,	in = 4
	factorial_of_n = 6 * 4 = 24;

You can use tables to follow the execution of the program as follows:

Iteration	in	factorial_of_n
First	2	$1 \times 2 = 2$
Second	3	$2 \times 3 = 6$
Third	4	$6 \times 4 = 24$

Example 13

Write a Matlab function to calculate the factorial of an integer number n.

Answer
This function calculates the factorial of the number n.

```
%This function calculates the factorial of the number m
function fact_of_n = factorialN(n)
fact_of_n = 1;
for in = 2:n
    fact_of_n = fact_of_n * in;
end
end
```

Example 14

Write a Matlab program to calculate the binomial coefficient

$$\binom{n}{r} = \frac{r!}{n!(n-r)!}$$

where "!" represents the factorial of the integer number n. Use the factorialN (n) function.

Answer

```
%This program calculates the binomial coefficient of n and r
n = 5;
r = 3;
binomial_n_r = factorialN(r) / ( factorialN(n) * factorialN(n-r) )
```

Exercise 2[1]

Follow the execution of the program given in Example 13 on a step-by-step basis by using the debug tools available in Matlab. Use **F11** to **Step In** the factorialN function.

Example 15

The exponential function can be calculated using the series

$$e^x = 1 + x + \frac{x^2}{2} + \frac{x^3}{6} + \cdots \frac{x^n}{n!} + \cdots$$

Use this series to calculate $e^{0.3}$. Here set the value of n to be 100.
Compare your answer with that which is produced by the Matlab function `exp`.

Answer
The Matlab program can be written as follows:

```
n = 100;
x = 0.3;
ex = 1 + x;
for ix = 2:n
    ex = ex + x^ix / factorialN(ix);
end
```

In this program, `ex = 1.3499`.
Similarly, the value that is produced by `exp(0.3) = 1.3499`.

7.1.2.3   for *Loop for Vectors*

Example 16

Write a Matlab program to calculate summation of a vector. Your program should be able to calculate the summation of the vector irrespective of its length. The summation of a vector is given by the following equation:

$$summation = \sum_{i=1}^{n} v(i)$$

where $v(1)$ is the first element of the vector v and n is the number of elements in the vector.

Answer
The Matlab program can be written as follows:

```
v = [1,3,6,9];
n = length(v);
summation = 0;
for i = 1:n
    summation = summation + v(i);
end
```

Initially, we need to find the length of the vector v. The length of the vector v is 4. Then we need to define a scalar variable within which to save the summation of the vector v. We will call this scalar variable summation and set it to an initial value of 0.

To find the summation of the vector, we need to add up the elements one-by-one and then save the result of the addition in the summation variable. This is the reason we will use a for loop.

In the first iteration of the for loop, Matlab adds the first element of the vector v to the summation variable. The value of summation here is $0 + 1 = 1$.

In the second iteration, Matlab adds the second element of the vector v to the summation variable. The value of summation here is $1 + 3 = 4$.

In the third iteration, Matlab adds the third element of the vector v to the summation variable. The value of summation here is $4 + 6 = 10$.

In the fourth iteration, Matlab adds the fourth element of the vector v to the summation variable. The value of summation here is $10 + 9 = 19$.

You can use tables to follow the execution of the program as follows:

Iteration	i	v(i)	summation
First	1	1	1
Second	2	3	4
Third	3	6	10
Fourth	4	9	19

Exercise 3[1]

Follow the execution of the program given in Example 13 on a step-by-step basis by using the debug tools that are available in Matlab.

Exercise 4[1]

Write a Matlab program to calculate the mean of a vector. Your program should be able to calculate the mean of the vector irrespective of its length. The mean of a vector is given by the following equation:

$$\text{mean} = m = \frac{1}{n} \sum_{i=1}^{n} v(i)$$

where $v(1)$ is the first element of the vector v and n is the number of elements in the vector.

Example 17

Write a Matlab program to calculate the standard deviation of a vector. Your program should be able to calculate the summation of the vector irrespective of its length. The standard deviation of a vector is given by the following equation:

$$\sigma = \sqrt{\frac{1}{n-1}\sum_{j=1}^{n}(v(i)-m)^2}$$

$$m = \frac{1}{n}\sum_{j=1}^{n}v(i)$$

The Greek letter σ, pronounced sigma, is normally used to represent the standard deviation, the term $v(1)$ is the first element of the vector v, n is the number of elements in the vector, and m is the mean of the vector.

Answer

The Matlab program can be written as follows:

```
v = [1,3,6,10];
n = length(v);
summation = 0;
for i = 1:n
    summation = summation + v(i);
end
m = summation/n; %m is the average
sigma = 0;
for i = 1:n
    sigma = sigma + (v(i)-m)^2;
end
sigma = sqrt(sigma/(n-1));
```

Exercise 5[2]

Using tables, on paper, manually go through the execution of the following program and find the value of y. Then check your answer using Matlab.

```
x = [1,2];
h = [3, 4];
nx = length(x);
nh = length(h);
N = nx + nh-1;
x = [x zeros(1,N-nx)];
h = [h zeros(1,N-nh)];
y = zeros(1,n);
for n = 1:n
  for m = 1:n
    y(n) = y(n) + x(m)*h(n-m+1);
  end
end
```

Example 18

A three-point moving average is defined as

$$b(j) = \frac{1}{3}\sum_{i=1}^{3}(a(i-1) + a(i) + a(i+1)), \quad j = 1,2,3\ldots n$$

For example, let the vector $\mathbf{a} = [1, 4, 3, 2, 7, 5, 6, 9, 8, 10]$. n is the number of elements in $\mathbf{a}$.

The three-point moving average of $\mathbf{a}$ is therefore given by $b(1) = (1+4)/2 = 2.5$. At the left-hand edge of the data there is no previous element $a(i-1)$ to use in the averaging. This is why we are only using two points to calculate the average here, rather than three.

$b(2) = (1 + 4 + 3)/3 = 2.6667$
$b(3) = (4 + 3 + 2)/3 = 3$
$b(4) = (3 + 2 + 7)/3 = 4$
$b(5) = (2 + 7 + 5)/3 = 4.6667$
$b(6) = (7 + 5 + 6)/3 = 6$
$b(7) = (5 + 6 + 9)/3 = 6.6667$
$b(8) = (6 + 9 + 8)/3 = 7.6667$
$b(9) = (9 + 8 + 10)/3 = 9$

$b(10) = (8 + 10)/2 = 9$. At the right-hand edge of the data, there is no subsequent element $a(i+1)$ to use in the averaging. This is why we are only using two points to calculate the average here, rather than three.

Note that the first and last points of the vector are special cases.
Write a Matlab program to process data a using the three-point averaging method.

Answer
The Matlab program to perform this task can be written as follows:

```
a = [1, 4, 3, 2, 7, 5, 6, 9, 8, 10];
b(1) = (a(1) + a(2))/2;
for i = 2:9
    b(i) = (a(i-1) + a(i) + a(i+1))/3;
end
b(10) = (a(9) + a(10))/2;
```

Exercise 6[2]

A five-point moving average is defined as

$$b(j) = \frac{1}{5}\sum_{i=1}^{5}(a(i-2) + a(i-1) + a(i) + a(i+1) + a(i+2)), \quad j = 1,2,3\ldots n$$

For example, let **a** = [1, 4, 3, 2, 7, 5, 6, 9, 8, 10]. The five-point moving average of *a* is

$b(1) = (1 + 4 + 3)/3 = 2.6667$
$b(2) = (1 + 4 + 3 + 2)/4 = 2.5$
$b(3) = (1 + 4 + 3 + 2 + 7)/5 = 3.4$
$b(4) = (4 + 3 + 2 + 7 + 5)/5 = 4.2$
$b(5) = (3 + 2 + 7 + 5 + 6)/5 = 4.6$
$b(6) = (2 + 7 + 5 + 6 + 9)/5 = 5.8$
$b(7) = (7 + 5 + 6 + 9 + 8)/5 = 7$
$b(8) = (5 + 6 + 9 + 8 + 10)/5 = 7.6$
$b(9) = (6 + 9 + 8 + 10)/4 = 8.25$
$b(10) = (9 + 8 + 10)/3 = 9$

Note that once again there are special cases at the edges of the dataset. Here the first two and the last two data points in the vector are special cases, as there are insufficient data points at the edges of the data to calculate a full five-point local average. You will see that at the first and last data points, it is only possible to calculate a three-point local average. At the second and the second to last data points, it is possible to do slightly better, and here we can calculate a four-point local average. For all the other data points in the middle of the vector, a full five-point local average can be calculated.

Write a Matlab program to process data **a** using the five-point moving average method.

7.1.3   The Construction of a Nested for Statement

7.1.3.1 Introduction to Nested for Loops

The syntax of a for statement is

```
for iteration Variable1 = initial value1: increment1: final value1
    for iteration Variable2 = initial value2: increment2: final value2
        commands
    end
end
```

The number of iterations for the outer for loop $N1 = \left\lfloor \frac{\text{final value1} - \text{initial value1}}{\text{increment1}} \right\rfloor + 1$
The number of iterations for the inner for loop $N2 = \left\lfloor \frac{\text{final value2} - \text{initial value2}}{\text{increment2}} \right\rfloor + 1$ where $\lfloor . \rfloor$ rounds down a real number toward the nearest lower integer. The number of iterations for the nested for loops is $N = N1 \times N2$.

Let us explain the nested for loops for you by using some examples.

7.1.3.2 Nested for Loops for Arrays

Nested loops can be used to process scalars, vectors, arrays, and logic variables. Here we will explain the process of using nested loops to process arrays, since nested loops are typically used with arrays.

Example 19

Write a Matlab program to calculate the summation of an array. Your program should be able to calculate the summation of the array irrespective of its dimensions. The summation of the array is given by the following equation:

$$summation = \sum_{i=1}^{m} \sum_{j=1}^{n} V(i,j)$$

where m represents the number of rows in the array and n represents the number of columns in the array.

Answer

The following Matlab program calculates the summation of an array:

```
V = [1, 3, 6; 4, 9 10];
m = size(V,1);
n = size(V,2);
summation = 0;
for i = 1:m
  for j = 1:n
    summation = summation + V(i,j);
  end
end
```

The number of elements in the array V is six. The number of rows m is two, and the number of columns n is three.

You can use tables to follow the execution of the preceding program.

Iteration	i	j	summation
First	1	1	1
Second	1	2	4
Third	1	3	10
Fourth	2	1	14
Fifth	2	2	23
Sixth	2	3	33

Exercise 7[1]

Follow the execution of the program given in Example 15 on a step-by-step basis by using the debug tools that are available in Matlab.

Example 20

Find the value of the array A in the following Matlab program:

```
A = [1, 4, 6; 2, 3, 5; 7, 8, 9];
for i = 2:3
    A(i,:) = A(i,:) - A(i-1,:);
end
```

Answer

Initially, the value of the array A is $\begin{bmatrix} 1 & 4 & 6 \\ 2 & 3 & 5 \\ 7 & 8 & 9 \end{bmatrix}$.

In the first iteration of the `for` loop, the first row is subtracted from the second row. The result of the subtraction is saved in the second row. The value of the array A is now

$$\begin{bmatrix} 1 & 4 & 6 \\ 1 & -1 & -1 \\ 7 & 8 & 9 \end{bmatrix}.$$

In the second iteration of the `for` loop, the second row is subtracted from the third row. The result of the subtraction is saved in the third row. The value of the array A

now is $\begin{bmatrix} 1 & 4 & 6 \\ 1 & -1 & -1 \\ 6 & 9 & 10 \end{bmatrix}$.

Exercise 8[2]

Find the value of the array A in the Matlab program

```
A = [1, 4, 6; 2, 3, 5; 7, 8, 9];
for i = 2:3
    A(i-1,:) = A(i,:) - A(i-1,:);
end
```

Exercise 9[2]

Find the value of the array A in the Matlab program

```
A = [1, 4, 6; 2, 3, 5; 7, 8, 9];
for j = 2:3
    A(:,j) = A(:,j) - A(:,j-1);
end
```

Exercise 10²

Find the value of the array A in the following Matlab program:

```
m = 3;
n = 3;
A = zeros(m,n);
for i = 1:m
    for j = i:n
        A(i,j) = i + j;
    end
end
```

Exercise 11¹

Use the debug tools that are available in Matlab to follow the execution of the following program:

```
m = 3;
n = 2;
A = zeros(m,n);
for i = 1:m
    for j = i:n
        A(i,j) = 3*i + 2*j;
    end
end
```

Lesson 7.2   The Construction of Combined for and if Statements

Objectives

- To learn how to construct combined for and if statements.
- To learn how to use the continue keyword with the for loop statement.
- To learn how to use the break keyword with the for loop statement.

Topics

7.2.1 The Construction of Combined for and if Statements
7.2.2 The continue Keyword
7.2.3 The break Keyword

7.2.1 The Construction of Combined for and if Statements

Example 1

Write a Matlab program to find the maximum value of a vector variable. The program should be able to find the maximum value of the vector irrespective of its length.

Answer

The following program finds the maximum of the vector v.

```
v = [1, 5, -5, 6, 1];
maximum = v(1);
for i = 2:length(v)
  if ( v(i) > maximum )
    maximum = v(i)
  end
end
```

The operation of the program is as follows. Initially, the vector is v defined.
The first element in the vector v(1) is set to be equal to the scalar variable maximum.
The rest of the elements in the vector v are checked one-by-one. If an element is greater than the current maximum, then the value of the maximum variable is updated and set to the value of that element.
You can use the following table to follow the execution of the program.

Iteration	i	v(i)	maximum
First	2	5	5
Second	3	−5	5
Third	4	6	6
Fourth	5	1	6

Note that there is already a built-in Matlab function called max which can be used to determine the maximum value of a vector.

Exercise 1[1]

Write a Matlab program to find the minimum value of a vector variable. The program should be able to find the minimum value of the vector irrespective of its length.

Example 2

Write a Matlab program to sort a vector into ascending order (smallest numbers first) using the bubble sort method. The program should be able to sort the vector irrespective of its length.

Answer

The following program sorts the vector v into ascending order.

```
v = [1, 5, -5, 6];
n = length(v);
for i = 1:1:n-1
  for j = 1:1:n-1
    if v(j) > v(j+1);
       temp = v(j);
       v(j) = v(j+1);
       v(j+1) = temp;
    end
  end
end
```

Initially, Matlab determines the length of the vector v using the `length()`Matlab command, and here it sets the value of the scalar variable n to 4, which is used for the loop count.

The algorithm then compares a number in the vector with its next-door neighbor.

If the value of the number is less than or equal to that of its next-door neighbor, then no action is taken. This is shown in iterations 1, 6, 8, and 9.

If the value of the number is greater than that of its next-door neighbor, then both numbers are swapped. This is shown in iterations 2, 3, 4, 5, and 7.

You can use the following table to follow the execution of the program.

Iteration	i	j	v
1	1	1	[1, 5, -5, -6]
2	1	2	[1, -5, 5, -6]
3	1	3	[1, -5, -6, 5]
4	2	1	[-5, 1, -6, 5]
5	2	2	[-5, -6, 1, 5]
6	2	3	[-5, -6, 1, 5]
7	3	1	[-6, -5, 1, 5]
8	3	2	[-6, -5, 1, 5]
9	3	3	[-6, -5, 1, 5]

Note that the built-in Matlab function `sort` can be used to sort a vector into ascending order.

Exercise 2[1]

Write a Matlab program to sort a vector into descending order (largest numbers first). The program should be able to sort the vector irrespective of its length.

Example 3

Write a Matlab program to calculate y(x) according to the equation

$$y(x) = \begin{cases} 2x & x < 3 \\ 3x & x = 3 \\ 5x & x > 3 \end{cases}$$

where x is a vector and it is given as $x = 0:1:10$;

Answer
The following program calculates y according to the preceding equation.

```
x = 0:1:10;
N = length(x);
for k = 1:N
  if (x(k) < 3)
    y(k) = 2*x(k);
  elseif (x(k) == 3)
    y(k) = 3*x(k);
  else
    y(k) = 5*x(k);
  end
end
```

Note the values of x and y that are produced by Matlab.

Exercise 3[1]

Use Matlab's debugging tools to follow the execution of the program that is given in Example 3.

7.2.2   The continue **Keyword**

The continue keyword passes control to the next iteration of the for loop in which it appears, skipping any remaining statements in the body of the for loop.

Example 4

Find the value of x that is produced by this program:

```
x = 1;
for i = 1:3;
  if i == 2
    continue
  end
  x = x + 1;
end
```

Answer

Initially, the value of x is 1.

In the first iteration i = 1, so the condition i == 2 is false. The command continue is therefore not executed. Then Matlab executes the command x = x + 1. Now the value of x is 2.

In the second iteration i has been incremented and so now i = 2. The condition i == 2 is therefore true. The command continue is now executed. Matlab skips the remaining commands in the body of the for loop and therefore the command x = x + 1 is not executed. Hence the value of x remains at 2.

In the third iteration i = 3, so the condition i == 2 is false. The command continue is therefore not executed. Then Matlab executes the command x = x + 1. Now the value of x is 3.

Exercise 4[1]

Use Matlab's debugging tools to follow the execution of the program that is given in Example 4.

Example 5

Write a Matlab program to calculate y according to the equation

$$y = \sum_{k=-10}^{10} \frac{1}{k^2 + 2k} \quad \text{where } k \text{ is an integer and } k \neq 0, -2$$

Answer

The following program calculates y according to the preceding equation.

```
y = 0;
for k = -10:10;
  if k == 0 || k == -2
    continue
  end
  y = y + 1 / (k^2 + 2*k);
end
```

Note that because of the use of the if statement that is combined here with the continue keyword, in the code that is shown Matlab skips the execution of the command y = y + 1 / (k^2 + 2*k) for the values where k is 0 and −2.

7.2.3 The break Keyword

The break keyword terminates the execution of for loop. In nested loops, break exits from the innermost loop only.

Example 6

Find the value of x produced by this program:

```
x = 1;
for i = 1:3;
  if i == 2
    break
  end
  x = x + 1;
end
```

Answer

Initially, the value of x is 1.

In the first iteration i = 1, so the condition i == 2 is false. The command break is therefore not executed. Then Matlab executes the command x = x + 1. Now the value of x is 2.

In the second iteration i has been incremented, so now i = 2. Therefore the condition i == 2 is now true. The command break is therefore executed. Matlab terminates the execution of the for loop. The command x = x + 1 is not executed.

The final value of x therefore remains at 2.

Exercise 5[1]

Use Matlab's debugging tools to follow the execution of the program that is given in Example 6.

Example 7

Write a Matlab program to produce the numbers of a Fibonacci series whose values are less than 100.

Answer

The following program produces the numbers of a Fibonacci series whose values are less than 100.

```
f(1) = 0;
f(2) = 1;
for i = 3:10000
   c = f(i-1) + f(i-2);
   if c >= 100
      break
   end
   f(i) = c;
end
```

Exercise 6[3]

Write a Matlab function that determines a number if its factorial is given. The function has one input argument and returns one value. For example, if the number 120 is given to the function, it returns the value 5. Give this function a meaningful and descriptive name.

Exercise 7[3]

Write a Matlab function that determines a number if its Fibonacci is given. The function has one input argument and returns one value. For example, if the number 89 is given to the function, it returns the value 12. Give this function a meaningful and descriptive name.

Example 8

Write a Matlab program that produces the prime numbers that are less than 30.

```
2  3  5  7  11  13  17  19  23  29
```

A prime number is defined as an integer positive number that is greater than 1 and has exactly two divisors. For example, the number 3 has only two divisors (1, 3); hence it is a prime number. The number 4 has three divisors (1, 2, 4); hence it is not a prime number.

Answer

The following program produces prime numbers that are less than 30.

```
prime_numbers = 2;
n = 30
for i = 3:n
  is_a_prime = true;
  for j = 2:i/2
    if mod(i,j) == 0
      is_a_prime = false;
      break
    end
  end
  if is_a_prime == true
    prime_numbers = [prime_numbers i];
  end
end
```

Initially, we define number 2 as the first prime number. Then we check the integer numbers from 3 to 30 one by one in ascending order so as to determine whether that number is prime or not. To check if the number i is a prime, we find its divisors from 2 to i/2 using the function mod. For example, to check if the number 9 is a prime, we find its divisors from 2 to 4. For example, mod(9,2) gives a value of 1. This means that 2 is not an exact divisor of 9. However, mod(9,3) gives a value of 0. This means that 3 is an exact divisor of 9 and therefore 9 is not a prime number.

Note: The Matlab function primes generates a list of prime numbers.

Exercise 8[1]

Use Matlab's debugging tools to follow the execution of the program that was given in Example 8.

Exercise 9[3]

Write a Matlab program that produces the first 100 prime numbers.

Example 9

The Matlab program given in Example 8 considers a number i to be a prime if it does not have divisors between 2 and i/2. The program checks all the numbers 2, 3, 4, 5, 6, ...i/2. This is a time-consuming method. Measure the execution time that is required to produce the set of prime numbers that are less than 10,000.

Answer

The following code produces the set of prime numbers that are less than 10,000 and also measures the execution time that is required for this program. You can measure the execution time for a piece of code by placing it between the Matlab commands tic and toc.

```
tic
prime_numbers = 2;
n = 10000
for i = 3:n
  is_a_prime = true;
  for j = 2:i/2
    if mod(i,j) == 0
      is_a_prime = false;
      break
    end
  end
  if is_a_prime == true
    prime_numbers = [prime_numbers i];
  end
end
toc
```

The time required to execute the preceding program on a PC was 0.105537 seconds, as shown in the following output window.

Exercise 10[3]

The Matlab program that is given in Example 8 considers a number i to be a prime if it does not have any divisors with values between 2 and i/2. The program checks all the numbers 2, 3, 4, 5, 6, ...i/2. This is a time-consuming method. For example, to determine if the number 17 is a prime, you need to check the numbers 2, 3, 4, 5, 6, 7, 8 to see if they are exact divisors of the number 17.

A faster method is to check only the *prime* numbers between 2 and i/2 to see if they are exact divisors for i. For example, to determine if the number 17 is a prime, you need to check the prime numbers 2, 3, 5, 7 to see if they are exact divisors of the number 17.

Write a Matlab program to produce the prime numbers that are less than 10,000 using this faster method, and measure the execution time for the program.

Exercise 11[3]

Write a Matlab function that produces the factors of a number. This function has one scalar argument and returns a vector. The operation of this function is similar to that of the existing `factor` function in Matlab. Name this function `factorN`. In this exercise, you are not allowed to use the existing Matlab function `factor` in your code.

Exercise 12[3]

Write a Matlab function that calculates the greatest common divisor of two numbers. This function has two scalar arguments and returns one scalar variable. The operation of this function is similar to that of the existing `gcd` function in Matlab. Name this function `gcdN`. In this exercise, you are not allowed to use the existing Matlab `gcd` function in your code.

You can calculate the greatest common divisor of two numbers as follows:

1. Find the prime factors of the first number.
2. Find the prime factors of the second number.
3. Find the common factors of the two numbers.
4. Multiply the common factors. This produces the greatest common divisor.

For example, to calculate the greatest common divisor for the numbers 20 and 16 use the preceding four steps:

1. The prime factors of 20 are 2, 2, and 5.
2. The prime factors of 16 are 2, 2, 2, and 2.
3. The common factors are 2 and 2.
4. The greatest common divisor is $2 \times 2 = 4$.

Exercise 13[3]

Write a Matlab function that calculates the least common multiple of two numbers. This function has two scalar arguments and returns one scalar variable. The operation of this vector is similar to the existing `lcm` function in Matlab. Name this function `lcmN`. In this exercise, you are not allowed to use the existing Matlab `lcm` function in your code.

You can calculate the least common multiple of two numbers as follows:

1. Find the prime factors of the first number.
2. Find the prime factors of the second number.
3. Find the common factors of the two numbers.
4. Find the rest of the factors of the two numbers.
5. Multiply the common factors by the rest of the factors. This produces the least common multiple.

For example, to calculate the least common multiple for the numbers 20 and 16 use the preceding five steps:

1. The prime factors of 20 are 2, 2, and 5.
2. The prime factors of 16 are 2, 2, 2, and 2.
3. The common factors are 2 and 2.
4. The rest of the factors are 2, 2, and 5.
5. The least common multiple is $2 \times 2 \times 2 \times 2 \times 5 = 80$.

Exercise 14[3]

Write a Matlab function that has one input scalar argument and returns a square matrix. Name this function inverted_pyramid. Examples of outputs produced by this function are shown below. If the input argument is an odd integer, the function returns a square matrix as shown. If the input argument is an even integer, the function displays a warning message and returns an empty matrix. If the input argument is a real number with a fraction, the function displays a warning message and returns an empty matrix.

```
>>x   = inverted_pyramid(1)
      0

>>x   = inverted_pyramid(2)
      []
      the input argument must be an odd integer value

>>x   = inverted_pyramid(2.5)
      []
      the input argument must be an odd integer value

>> X  = inverted_pyramid(3)
      1  1  1
      1  0  1
      1  1  1

>> X  = inverted_pyramid(5)
      2  2  2  2  2
      2  1  1  1  2
      2  1  0  1  2
      2  1  1  1  2
      2  2  2  2  2

>> X  = inverted_pyramid(7)
      3  3  3  3  3  3  3
      3  2  2  2  2  2  3
      3  2  1  1  1  2  3
      3  2  1  0  1  2  3
      3  2  1  1  1  2  3
      3  2  2  2  2  2  3
      3  3  3  3  3  3  3
```

```
>> X   = inverted_pyramid(9)
       4  4  4  4  4  4  4  4  4
       4  3  3  3  3  3  3  3  4
       4  3  2  2  2  2  2  3  4
       4  3  2  1  1  1  2  3  4
       4  3  2  1  0  1  2  3  4
       4  3  2  1  1  1  2  3  4
       4  3  2  2  2  2  2  3  4
       4  3  3  3  3  3  3  3  4
       4  4  4  4  4  4  4  4  4
```

And so on.

The commands

```
>> X = inverted_pyramid(91);
>> mesh(X)
```

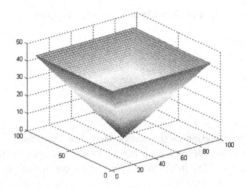

produce an inverted pyramid graph, which is shown in the figure on the right.

Lesson 7.3   The Construction of a while Loop Statement

Objectives
- To learn how to construct a while loop statement.
- To learn how to construct combined while and if statements.
- To learn how to use the continue keyword with the while loop statement.
- To learn how to use the break keyword with the while loop statement.
- To learn more about recursive functions.

Topics
7.3.1 Introduction to the while Loop Statement
7.3.2 Examples of the while Loop Statement
7.3.3 Recursive Functions

7.3.1   Introduction to the `while` Loop Statement

The syntax of a `while` loop statement is

```
while (statement)
  commands
end
```

Matlab executes the `commands` inside the `while` loop as long as `statement` remains `true`. Let us explain the `while` loop for you by using some examples.

Example 1

Find the value of r that is produced by the following program:

```
r = 2;
while (r < 10)
    r = 2*r;
end
```

Answer
Initially, the value of r is 2.

This is the first iteration of the `while` loop. The statement ($r < 10$) in the `while` loop is therefore `true`. Hence Matlab executes the commands in the body of the `while` loop. The command r = 2*r in the loop body is therefore evaluated. The new value of r is thus 2*2 = 4.

This is the second iteration of the `while` loop. With r = 4, the statement ($r < 10$) in the `while` loop is still `true`. Hence Matlab executes the commands in the body of the `while` loop. The command r = 2*r in the loop body is therefore evaluated once again. The value of r is now 2*4 = 8.

This is the third iteration of the `while` loop. With r = 8, the statement ($r < 10$) in the `while` loop is still `true`. Hence Matlab executes the commands in the body of the `while` loop. The command r = 2*r in the loop body is therefore evaluated once again. The value of r is now 2*8 = 16.

With r = 16, the statement ($r < 10$) in the `while` loop is now `false`. Matlab therefore terminates the `while` loop. The command r = 2*r in the loop body is therefore not evaluated and the final value of r remains at 16.

You can use the following table to follow the execution of the preceding program.

Iteration	r
1	4
2	8
3	16

Example 2

Find the value of r that is produced by the following program:

```
r = 2;
while (r < 10)
  if (r == 8)
    r = r - 1
    continue
  end
  r = 2*r
end
```

Answer

The continue keyword passes control to the next iteration of the while loop in which it appears, thereby skipping any remaining statements in the body of the while loop.

Initially, the value of r is 2. The statement (r < 10) in the while loop is true. Hence Matlab executes the commands in the body of the while loop. This is the first iteration of the while loop. The statement (r == 8) is false. The two commands in the body of the if statement are therefore not evaluated. The command r = 2*r in the loop body is evaluated. Hence the new value of r is 2*2 = 4.

In the second iteration, with r = 4, the statement (r < 10) in the while loop is still true. Hence Matlab executes the commands in the body of the while loop. The statement (r == 8) is false. The two commands in the body of if statement are therefore not evaluated. The command r = 2*r in the loop body is evaluated. The new value of r is 2*4 = 8.

In the third iteration, with r = 8, the statement (r < 10) in the while loop is still true. Hence Matlab executes the commands in the body of the while loop. This time, the statement (r == 8) is true. The two commands in the body of the if statement are now evaluated. The command r = r - 1 is therefore evaluated. The new value of r is 7. Matlab then executes the continue command, passes control to the next iteration of the while loop, and skips the remaining commands in the body of the while loop.

In the fourth iteration, with r = 7, the statement (r < 10) in the while loop is still true. Hence Matlab executes the commands in the body of the while loop. The statement (r == 8) is false. The two commands in the body of the if statement are not evaluated. The command r = 2*r in the loop body is evaluated. The value of r is now 2*7 = 14.

With r = 14, the statement (r < 10) in the while loop is now false. Hence Matlab terminates the while loop. The final value of r remains at 14. You can use the following table to follow the execution of the program.

Iteration	r
1	4
2	8
3	7
4	14

Example 3

Find the value of r that is produced by the following program:
```
r = 2;
while (r < 10)
  if (r == 8)
    r = r - 1
    break
  end
  r = 2*r
end
```

Answer

The break keyword terminates the execution of the while loop. In nested loops, break exits from the innermost loop only.

Initially, the value of r is 2. The statement (r < 10) in the while is therefore true. Hence Matlab executes the commands in the body of the while loop. This is the first iteration of the while loop. The statement (r == 8) is false. The two commands in the body of the if statement are not evaluated. The command r = 2*r in the loop body is evaluated. The new value of r is 2*2 = 4.

In the next iteration, with r = 4, the statement (r < 10) in the while is still true. Hence Matlab executes the commands in the body of the while loop. This is the second iteration of the while loop. The statement (r == 8) is false. The two commands in the body of the if statement are not evaluated. The command r = 2*r in the loop body is evaluated. The new value of r is 2*4 = 8.

In the next iteration, with r = 8, the statement (r < 10) in the while is still true. Hence Matlab executes the commands in the body of the while loop. This is the third iteration of the while loop. The statement (r == 8) is now true. The two commands in the body of the if statement are evaluated. The command r = r-1 is therefore evaluated. The new value of r is 7. Matlab then executes the break command, and terminates the execution of while loop. The final value of r is therefore 7.

Iteration	r
1	4
2	8
3	7

7.3.2 Examples of the while Loop Statement

Example 4

Write a Matlab program to produce the numbers of a Fibonacci series whose values are less than 100.

Answer

The following program produces the numbers of a Fibonacci series whose values are less than 100.

```
f(1) = 0;
f(2) = 1;
counter = 3;
while( ( f(counter-1) + f(counter-2) ) < 100)
  f(counter) = f(counter-1) + f(counter-2);
  counter = counter + 1;
end
```

Example 5

Write a Matlab function that determines a number if its Fibonacci is given. The function has one input argument and returns one value. For example, if the number 89 is given to the function, it returns the value 12. Give this function a meaningful and descriptive name.

Answer

The following function determines a number if its Fibonacci is given.

```
function n = inverse_fibonacci(fib)
f(1) = 0;
f(2) = 1;
counter = 3;
while( ( f(counter-1) + f(counter-2) ) <= fib)
  f(counter) = f(counter-1) + f(counter-2);
  counter = counter + 1;
end
n = counter - 1;
end
```

You can call this function from the **Command Prompt** by typing

```
>> n = inverse_fibonacci(89)
```

Example 6

Write a Matlab function that determines a number if its factorial is given. The function has one input argument and returns one value. For example, if the number 120 is given to the function, it returns the value 5. Give this function a meaningful and descriptive name.

Answer
The following function determines a number if the factorial is given.

```
function n = inverse_factorial(f)
fn = 1;
counter = 1;
while( (fn*counter) < f)
  fn = fn * counter;
  counter = counter + 1;
end
n = counter;
end
```

You can call this function from the **Command Prompt** by typing

```
> > n = inverse_factorial(120)
```

7.3.3   Recursive Functions

The while loop is used frequently in programming recursive functions. This is shown using the following exercises.

Exercise 1[2]

The following recursive function sorts a vector into ascending order. The number of elements in the vector must be $n = 2^m$, where m is an integer positive number, $m = 1, 2, 3, 4 \ldots$ and $n = 2, 4, 8, 16 \ldots$.

Using the debugging tools that are available in Matlab, follow the execution of the sort_recursive() function that is shown below using the input data $x = [1, -1]$.

```
function y = sort_recursive(x)
n = length(x);
if log2(n) ~= fix(log2(n))
  disp('the data length must be 2^n');
  y = [];
  return
end
if length(x) == 2
  if x(1) > x(2)
    temp = x(1);
    x(1) = x(2);
    x(2) = temp;
  end
  y = x;
```

```
    else
      x1 = x(1:n/2);
      x2 = x(n/2 + 1:n);
      y1 = sort_recursive(x1);
      y2 = sort_recursive(x2);
      countery1 = 1;
      countery2 = 1;
      countery = 1;
      n2 = length(x1);
      while (countery1 < (n2 + 1) && countery2 < (n2 + 1) )
        if ( y1(countery1) < = y2(countery2) )
          y(countery) = y1(countery1);
          countery1 = countery1 + 1;
          countery = countery + 1;
        else
          y(countery) = y2(countery2);
          countery2 = countery2 + 1;
          countery = countery + 1;
        end
      end
      if ( countery1 > n2 )
        y(countery:n) = y2(countery2:n2);
      else
        y(countery:n) = y1(countery1:n2);
      end
    end
end
```

Exercise 2[2]

Using the debugging tools that are available in Matlab, follow the execution of the sort_recursive() function that was shown above, this time using the input data x = [− 1, 1, − 3].

Exercise 3[2]

Using the debugging tools that are available in Matlab, follow the execution of the sort_recursive() function that was shown above, this time using the input data x = [7, 1, − 3, − 5].

Exercise 4[2]

Using the debugging tools that are available in Matlab, follow the execution of the sort_recursive() function that was shown above, this time using the input data x = [7, 1, − 3, − 5, − 6, 8, 10, − 10].

Exercise 5[3]

Explain in detail the operation of the sort_recursive( )function and describe how it sorts data into ascending order.

Answers to Selected Exercises

Lesson 7.1

Exercise 4

```
v = [1,3,6,9];
n = length(v);
summation = 0;
for i = 1:n
   summation = summation + v(i);
end
m = summation / n;
```

Exercise 6

```
a = [1, 4, 3, 2, 7, 5, 6, 9, 8, 10];
b(1) = ( a(1) + a(2) + a(3) ) / 3;
b(2) = ( a(1) + a(2) + a(3) + a(4) ) / 4;
for i = 3:8
   b(i) = ( a(i-2) + a(i-1) + a(i) + a(i+1) + a(i+2) ) / 5;
end
b(9) = ( a(7) + a(8) + a(9) + a(10) ) / 4;
b(10) = ( a(8) + a(9) + a(10) ) / 3;
```

Lesson 7.2

Exercise 1

```
v = [1, 5, -5, 6, 1];
minimum = v(1);
for i = 2:length(v)
   if ( v(i) < minimum)
      minimum = v(i)
   end
end
```

Exercise 2

```
v = [1, 5, -5, 6];
n = length(v);
```

```
for i = 1:1:n-1
  for j = 1:1:n-1
    if v(j) < v(j+1);
      temp = v(j);
      v(j) = v(j+1);
      v(j+1) = temp;
    end
  end
end
```

Exercise 6

```
function n = inverse_factorial(f)
fn = 1;
if f == 1
  n = 1;
  return
end
for i = 2:1000
  fn = fn * i;
  if fn == f
    break
  end
end
n = i;
end
```

Exercise 7

```
function n = inverse_fibonacci(f)
fib(1) = 0;
fib(2) = 1;
if f == 0
  n = 1;
  return
elseif f == 1
  n = 2;
  return
end
for i = 3:1000
  fib(i) = fib(i-1) + fib(i-2);
  if fib(i) == f
    break
  end
end
```

```
n = i;
end
```

Exercise 9

```
prime_numbers = 2;
counter = 1;
n = 3000;
for i = 3:n
  is_a_prime = true;
  for j = 2:i/2
    if mod(i,j) == 0
      is_a_prime = false;
      break
    end
  end
  if is_a_prime == true
    prime_numbers = [prime_numbers i];
    counter = counter + 1;
  end
  if counter == 100
    break
  end
end
```

Exercise 10

```
tic
prime_numbers = 2;
n = 10000;
for i = 3:n
  is_a_prime = true;
  for j = 2:length(prime_numbers)
    if mod(i,prime_numbers(j)) == 0
      is_a_prime = false;
      break
    end
  end
  if is_a_prime == true
    prime_numbers = [prime_numbers i];
  end
end
toc
```

The time required to execute the preceding program on a PC is 0.048949 seconds.
Note that the execution time here has been approximately halved.

Projects

Project 1: Conway's Game of Life

The Game of Life is an example of a zero-player game, as it has no sentient players and is determined by its initial state. It was devised by the British mathematician John Horton Conway in 1970 and is an example of a cellular automaton. Matlab has an inbuilt implementation of the Game of Life that is called `life`. To see a demo of this game, type at the Matlab **Command Prompt**

```
>> life
```

Then press the **Start** button. The game consists of a grid of square cells. Each cell has one of two possible states, either alive or dead. A dead cell has a white color and a live cell has a blue color. Each cell has eight neighbors, namely the adjacent cells that are North, South, East, West, North West, North East, South West, and South East to the cell in question, respectively. This is shown in the following figure. The Matlab code to produce this figure is also given.

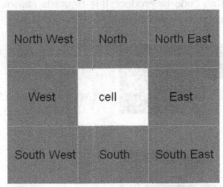

```
clear; clc; close all;
X = zeros(3,3);
X(2,2) = 1;
imagesc(X)
colormap([[0.5,0.5,0.5]; [1,1,1]])
hold on
%construct grid, horizontal lines
plot([0.5, 3.5], [1.5, 1.5],'g')
plot([0.5, 3.5], [2.5,2.5],'g')
```

```
%vertical lines
plot([1.5, 1.5], [0.5, 5.5],'g')
plot([2.5, 2.5], [0.5, 5.5],'g')
axis off
text(1.8,1,'North', 'FontSize',18)
text(1.8,2,'cell', 'FontSize',18)
text(1.8,3,'South', 'FontSize',18)
text(2.8,2,'East', 'FontSize',18)
text(0.8,2,'West', 'FontSize',18)
text(0.6,1,'North West', 'FontSize',18)
text(2.6,1,'North East', 'FontSize',18)
text(0.6,3,'South West', 'FontSize',18)
text(2.6,3,'South East', 'FontSize',18)
```

The rules for the Conway's Game of Life are the following.

Every cell interacts with its eight neighbors. At each step, the following transitions occur:

1. Any live cell with fewer than two live neighbors dies, as if caused by under-population.
2. Any live cell with two, or three, live neighbors lives on to the next generation.
3. Any live cell with more than three live neighbors dies, as if by overcrowding.
4. Any dead cell with exactly three live neighbors becomes a live cell, as if by reproduction.
5. Any live cell located at the edge of the grid dies.

For example, the following figure on the left shows a 5×5 grid, which contains six live cells denoted by the white color and nineteen dead cells denoted by the black color. The Matlab code to produce this figure is shown. The indices of the cells are shown in the figure on the right.

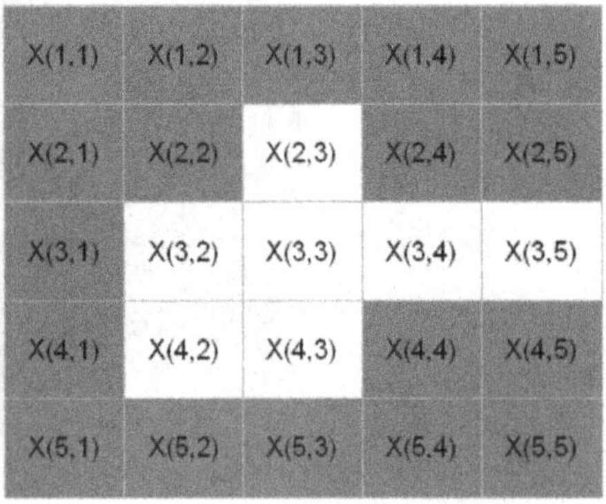

```
clear; clc; close all;
X = zeros(5,5);
X(2,3) = 1;
X(3,2) = 1;
X(3,3) = 1;
X(3,4) = 1;
```

```
X(3,5) = 1;
X(4,3) = 1;
imagesc(X), colormap(gray(256))
hold on
%horizontal lines
plot([0.5, 5.5], [1.5, 1.5],'g')
plot([0.5, 5.5], [2.5, 2.5],'g')
plot([0.5, 5.5], [3.5, 3.5],'g')
plot([0.5, 5.5], [4.5, 4.5],'g')
%vertical lines
plot([1.5, 1.5], [0.5, 5.5],'g')
plot([2.5, 2.5], [0.5, 5.5],'g')
plot([3.5, 3.5], [0.5, 5.5],'g')
plot([4.5, 4.5], [0.5, 5.5],'g')
axis off
```

Example

The initial state of the grid is shown again in the following figure on the left. This initial state is arbitrary, and you can designate any cell as being dead, or alive, just as you like. This is called the first generation.

The second generation is produced according to the rules that were given above, and this is shown in the following figure on the right.

With respect to the first-generation figure, shown below left:

The live cell (2,3) has three live neighbors and it will be alive in the second generation.
The live cell (3,2) has three live neighbors and it will be alive in the second generation.
The live cell (3,3) has four live neighbors and it will be dead in the second generation.
The live cell (3,4) has four live neighbors and it will be dead in the second generation.
The live cell (3,5) is located at the edge of the grid and it will be dead in the second generation.
The live cell (4,3) has three live neighbors and it will be alive in the second generation.
The dead cell (2,2) has three live neighbors and it will be alive in the second generation.
The dead cell (4,2) has three live neighbors and it will be alive in the second generation.

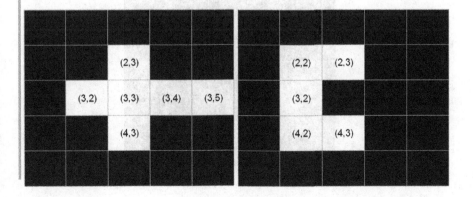

The third generation is shown in the following figure. This has been produced according to the rules for the following specific cases of the cells that were present in the second generation, with respect to the figure that is shown on the above right:

The live cell (2,2) has two live neighbors and it will be alive in the third generation.
The live cell (2,3) has two live neighbors and it will be alive in the third generation.
The live cell (3,2) has four live neighbors and it will be dead in the third generation.
The live cell (4,2) has two live neighbors and it will be alive in the third generation.
The live cell (4,3) has two live neighbors and it will be alive in the third generation.

The fourth generation is shown in the following figure:
This has been produced according to the rules for the following specific cases of the cells that were present in the third generation, with respect to the figure that is shown above.

The live cell (2,2) has one live neighbor and it will be dead in the fourth generation.
The live cell (2,3) has one live neighbor and it will be dead in the fourth generation.
The live cell (4,2) has one live neighbor and it will be dead in the fourth generation.
The live cell (4,3) has one live neighbor and it will be dead in the fourth generation.

Write a Matlab program to generate a 9 × 9 grid and initialize it with

```
rng('default')
X = randi(2,9,9) - 1;
```

A value of 0 for an element in the X array corresponds to a dead cell. A value 1 for an element in the X array corresponds to a live cell. The first generation should appear similar to this figure.

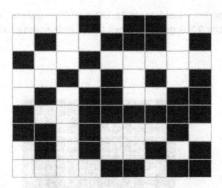

This is the Matlab code that may be used to generate the figure that is shown above.

```
close all; clc; clear
rng('default')
rng('default')
X = randi(2,9,9)-1;
imagesc(X)
colormap(gray(256))
hold on
%horizontal lines
plot([0.5, 9.5], [1.5, 1.5],'g','LineWidth',2)
plot([0.5, 9.5], [2.5, 2.5],'g','LineWidth',2)
plot([0.5, 9.5], [3.5, 3.5],'g','LineWidth',2)
plot([0.5, 9.5], [4.5, 4.5],'g','LineWidth',2)
plot([0.5, 9.5], [5.5, 5.5],'g','LineWidth',2)
plot([0.5, 9.5], [6.5, 6.5],'g','LineWidth',2)
plot([0.5, 9.5], [7.5, 7.5],'g','LineWidth',2)
plot([0.5, 9.5], [8.5, 8.5],'g','LineWidth',2)
plot([0.5, 9.5], [9.5, 9.5],'g','LineWidth',2)
plot([0.5, 9.5], [0.5, .5],'g','LineWidth',2)
%vertical lines
```

```
plot([0.5, 0.5], [0.5, 9.5],'g','LineWidth',2)
plot([1.5, 1.5], [0.5, 9.5],'g','LineWidth',2)
plot([2.5, 2.5], [0.5, 9.5],'g','LineWidth',2)
plot([3.5, 3.5], [0.5, 9.5],'g','LineWidth',2)
plot([4.5, 4.5], [0.5, 9.5],'g','LineWidth',2)
plot([5.5, 5.5], [0.5, 9.5],'g','LineWidth',2)
plot([6.5, 6.5], [0.5, 9.5],'g','LineWidth',2)
plot([7.5, 7.5], [0.5, 9.5],'g','LineWidth',2)
plot([8.5, 8.5], [0.5, 9.5],'g','LineWidth',2)
plot([9.5, 9.5], [0.5, 9.5],'g','LineWidth',2)
axis off
```

Your Matlab program should generate the next five generations and plot them on a grid. The edges of the 9×9 grid are shown below in the white color.

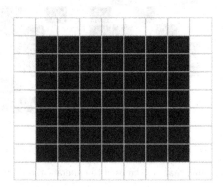

Project 2: Conway's Game of Life—Wrapped Edges

The Game of Life consists of a grid of square cells. The cells that are located at the edges of the grid were not processed in the previous project, and they were considered to be dead in the next generation. In reality, those cells are processed in a similar way to the other cells. In order to process those cells, which are located at the edges of the grid, we consider the grid to be wrapped. This means that the left-hand border of the grid is actually connected to the right-hand border. Similarly, the top border is wrapped around so that it is connected to the bottom border. The top left cell is a neighbor of the bottom right cell. The top right cell is a neighbor of the bottom left cell.

Examples of a wrapped grid are shown in the following four figures. These figures show a cell and its eight neighbors.

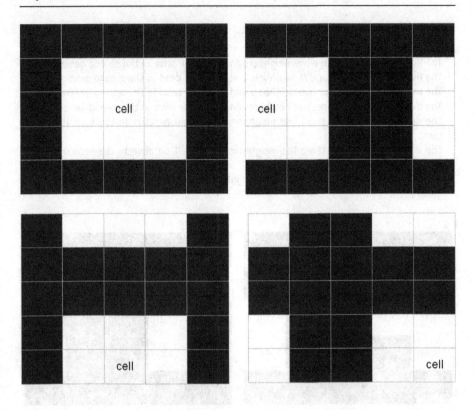

Example

The figure on the left shows the first generation for the Game of Life. The rules that determine the live and dead cells for the next generation are as follows:

1. Any live cell with fewer than two live neighbors dies, as if caused by under-population.
2. Any live cell with two or three live neighbors lives on to the next generation.
3. Any live cell with more than three live neighbors dies, as if by overcrowding.
4. Any dead cell with exactly three live neighbors becomes a live cell, as if by reproduction.

The first generation is shown in the left-hand figure.

The second generation is shown in the right-hand figure. This was produced according to the preceding rules, when applied for the following specific cases of the cells that were present in the first generation, that is, all the following descriptions are with respect to the figure that is shown below-left:

The live cell (2,1) has three[1] live neighbors and it will be alive in the second generation.

---

[1] Note the wrap here. The three live neighbors of (2,1) in the first generation figure that is presented above-left are (3,1), (3,2), and (3,5).

The live cell (3,1) has five[2] live neighbors and it will be dead in the second generation.

The live cell (3,2) has three live neighbors and it will be alive in the second generation.

The live cell (3,5) has four live neighbors and it will be dead in the second generation.

The live cell (4,1) has four live neighbors and it will be dead in the second generation.

The live cell (4,5) has three live neighbors and it will be alive in the second generation.

The dead cell (2,2) has three live neighbors and it will be alive in the second generation.

The dead cell (4,2) has three live neighbors and it will be alive in the second generation.

The dead cell (2,5) has three live neighbors and it will be alive in the second generation.

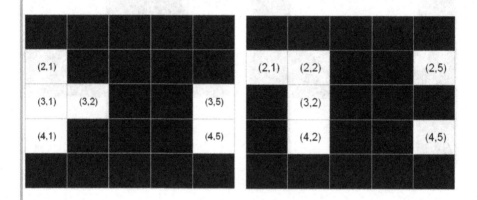

The third generation is shown in the following figure. This has been produced according to the rules for the various specific cases of the cells that were present in the second generation, that is, all of the following are with respect to the figure that is shown above-right:

The live cell (2,1) has three live neighbors and it will be alive in the third generation.

The live cell (2,2) has two live neighbors and it will be alive in the third generation.

The live cell (2,5) has one live neighbor and it will be dead in the third generation.

The live cell (3,2) has three live neighbors and it will be alive in the third generation.

The live cell (4,2) has one live neighbor and it will be dead in the third generation.

The live cell (4,5) has one live neighbor and it will be dead in the third generation.

The dead cell (1,1) has three live neighbors and it will be alive in the third generation.

The dead cell (3,3) has three live neighbors and it will be alive in the third generation.

The dead cell (4,1) has three live neighbors and it will be alive in the third generation.

---

[2] The five live neighbors of (3,1) in the first generation are (2,1), (3,2), (4,1), (3,5), and (4,5).

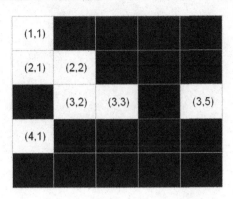

And so on.
Write a Matlab program to generate a 9 × 9 grid and initialize it with

```
rng('default')
X = randi(2,9,9) − 1;
```

A value of 0 for an element in the X array corresponds to a dead cell. A value of 1 for an element in the X array corresponds to a live cell. The first generation should look similar to this figure.

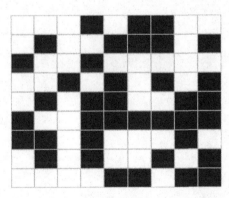

Your Matlab program should generate the next five generations and plot them on a grid. The cells located at the edges of the grid should be treated as wrapped cells and therefore should be processed as explained previously.

8 Matlab Debugging, Profiling, and Code Indentation

Lesson 8.1 Matlab Debugging

Objectives
- To learn the differences between syntax errors and runtime errors.
- To learn how to debug Matlab script files.
- To learn how to use the **Breakpoint** tool to debug Matlab code.
- To learn how to run one line of a program using the **Step** tool.

Topics
8.1.1 Syntax and Runtime Errors
    8.1.1.1 Syntax Errors
    8.1.1.2 Runtime Errors
8.1.2 Debugging Matlab Code
    8.1.2.1 Setting Up a Breakpoint
    8.1.2.2 Stepping Through the Program

8.1.1 Syntax and Runtime Errors

There are two types of errors that appear in Matlab expressions: syntax errors and runtime errors. Together, we generically refer to these errors as being bugs in the Matlab code. The debugging process is the procedure of finding these bugs and fixing them.

Matlab by Example. DOI: http://dx.doi.org/10.1016/B978-0-12-405212-3.00008-6

8.1.1.1 Syntax Errors

Let us start with the first error type, which is the syntax error. These errors mainly occur as a result of the misspelling of variable or function names or from missing quotes or parentheses (or the accidental extraneous typing of an additional one of these). Examples of such errors are given below:

```
>> x = x*(1 + 2*x));   % extra parenthesis
>> x = 1; x = x(x + 1)  % The multiplication sign is missing
>> y = `hello          % missing quote
>> z = 1; disp(Z);      % Matlab is case sensitive, so Z is not the
                        % same as z.
```

Note that you can type more than one Matlab command in a single line, but these commands should be separated by a comma (,) or a semicolon (;).

When you type a Matlab command in the **Command Window**, Matlab checks for syntax errors before running the command. If the command passes the syntax error check, then Matlab executes this command; otherwise, Matlab displays a message reporting that there is a syntax error and that it should be fixed before attempting to run this command again. Also, Matlab may give you some information that helps in identifying and fixing this error.

Suppose that you attempt to run a Matlab script file that contains syntax errors. Matlab does not run this file and responds by reporting that the file contains syntax errors. It rather helpfully provides you with the line number that contains the first syntax error that it has found in the file, and it also advises you about how to fix this error.

8.1.1.2 Runtime Errors

Runtime errors are found by Matlab during the execution of a program, and they are generally more difficult to fix than simple syntax errors. The ability to fix runtime errors is something that improves with experience and is best learned by way of an example.

Let us try to write a Matlab program that calculates the absolute values of a vector. The input vector in this example consists of the integer values from -10 to $+10$. Hence as a result of calculating the absolute values of this vector, all the positive input values from the range -10 to $+10$ should be unchanged (and zero will also be unchanged) and all negative input values will have their negative signs removed, leaving just their magnitude, for example, the value -3 will become 3. that is, the input vector is

$$
\begin{array}{ccccccccccc}
-10 & -9 & -8 & -7 & -6 & -5 & -4 & -3 & -2 & -1 & 0 \\
1 & 2 & 3 & 4 & 5 & 6 & 7 & 8 & 9 & 10 &
\end{array}
$$

which should produce an output vector as follows:

10 9 8 7 6 5 4 3 2 1 0
    1 2 3 4 5 6 7 8 9 10

Launch the Matlab **Editor**. Type the code below into the **Editor** window. Save the script file with the name *absolute.m*.

It is advisable to start any Matlab script file with the commands clear; clc;. These two respective commands delete any unwanted variables in the Matlab memory and also clear the **Command Window**. The command close all closes all figures in Matlab.

```
clear; clc; close all
x = - 10:10;
for k = 0:length(x)
  if (x(k) > 0)
    x(k) = - x(k);
  end
end
disp(x)
```

Run the program. Matlab complains that there are errors in the code. Matlab reports the error as follows:

```
??? Attempted to access x(0); index must be a positive integer or logical.
Error in ==> absolute at 4
  if (x(k) > 0)
```

Matlab starts indexing any vector with the index 1. This is unlike several other programming languages, such as C, which start the indexing process with index zero. So, we have identified this runtime mistake, which must be fixed by changing the index in the third line (beginning for k =) from the current value of 0 to a value of 1, as shown in the following code segment:

```
clear; clc;
x = -10:10;
for k = 1:length(x)
  if (x(k) > 0)
    x(k) = -x(k);
  end
end
disp(x)
```

Fix the bug and run the program over again. Matlab gives the results as shown in the following figure, which are not as expected. The numbers that are produced should all be positive, but they are not. So we need to fix this bug. and we will use Matlab's debugging capabilities to track down the location and exact nature of the bug.

8.1.2   Debugging Matlab Code

8.1.2.1   Setting Up a Breakpoint

Matlab has a feature that allows the user to control the execution of an M-file program. This feature helps in tracking down the bugs and fixing them. For example, you can introduce a **Breakpoint** in a program, and the execution of the code temporarily stops at this **Breakpoint**. Then you can check the values of the Matlab variables at this point and try to figure out the cause of the bug.

To debug your program, go to the **Editor** window. Using the mouse, left-click in the space between the column of line numbers and the code itself (where there is a column of dashes "−") and place the **Breakpoint** in the position pointed at by the arrow in the following diagram. A red circle then appears as shown. This can be toggled on and off by clicking again in the same place. If you practice toggling this here, make sure you leave the **Breakpoint** set to ON, with the red dot showing as in the following figure.

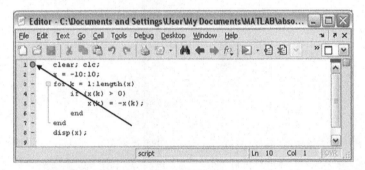

Go to the **Menu→Debug→Run absolute.m**.

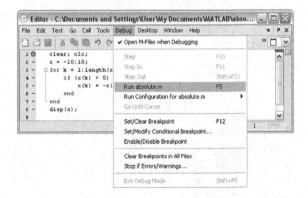

Note that as a result of doing this, the Matlab **Command Prompt** changes to

```
k >>
```

which informs you that Matlab is now running in debug mode.

Matlab starts executing the program and stops at line 1.

```
Editor - C:\Documents and Settings\User\My Documents\MATLAB\abso...
File  Edit  Text  Go  Cell  Tools  Debug  Desktop  Window  Help
1    clear; clc;
2    x = -10:10;
3    for k = 1:length(x)
4        if (x(k) > 0)
5            x(k) = -x(k);
6        end
7    end
8    disp(x);
9
                              script              Ln  1      Col  1
```

8.1.2.2 Stepping Through the Program

To direct Matlab to run the command in line 1, click on the **Step** icon (pointed at by the arrow in the following figure).

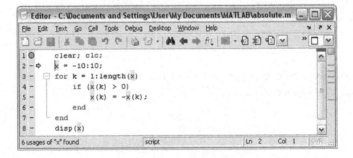

Matlab runs the first line and then proceeds to line 2.

```
Editor - C:\Documents and Settings\User\My Documents\MATLAB\absolute.m
File  Edit  Text  Go  Cell  Tools  Debug  Desktop  Window  Help
1       clear; clc;
2    ⇨  x = -10:10;
3       for k = 1:length(x)
4           if (x(k) > 0)
5               x(k) = -x(k);
6           end
7       end
8       disp(x)
6 usages of "x" found          script              Ln  2      Col  1
```

An alternative way to step through the program is by pressing the **F10** key on the keyboard. Press **F10** to make Matlab run line 2 of the code.

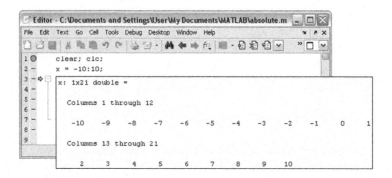

Move the mouse and place the cursor directly over the variable x. A yellow box pops up and tells you the values of x.

Alternatively, you can get the values of this vector variable by double-clicking on x in the **Workspace** window.

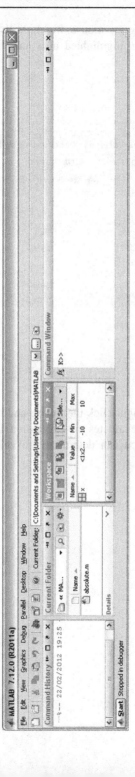

Press **F10** to run line 3. Using the mouse, highlight the expression $(x(k) > 0)$. Place the mouse cursor over the highlighted area and right-click. Choose **Copy** from the **Context Menu**.

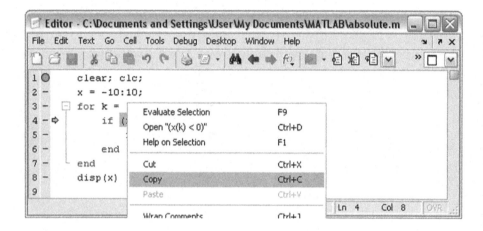

In the **Command Window**, right-click the mouse and choose **Paste**. Then press **Enter** on the keyboard. Matlab evaluates the expression and informs us that it has a value of 0. In this manner you can determine the value of any expression or variable.

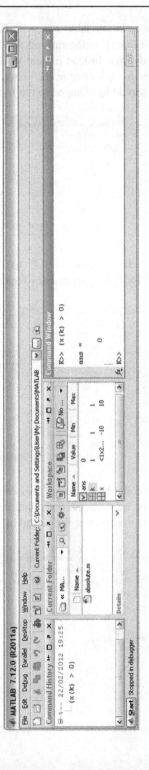

The value of the first element in the variable x is -10. Press **F10**. The code steps to line 7. It should have entered the if statement and gone to line 5 to change the sign of the first element, but it did not. Instead it went to line 7. By noting this, we can discover that there is a programming error in the condition for the if statement. The greater than character "$>$" should be changed to the less than character "$<$".

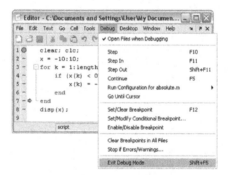

Fix this bug by changing the character "$>$" to "$<$". Then go to the **Menu→Debug→Exit Debug Mode**. This terminates the debugger in Matlab.

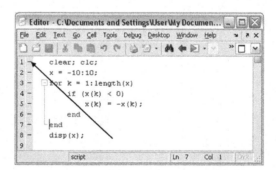

The bug is now fixed. Remove the **Breakpoint**. This can be carried out by using the mouse. Left-click in the space between the code and the line number 1 (pointed at by the arrow in the figure) to toggle the **Breakpoint** to off. The red dot disappears.

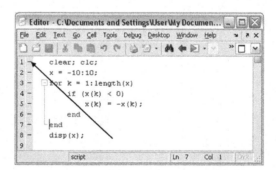

Run the code by clicking the **Run** icon. Matlab executes the program and produces the correct output.

Lesson 8.2   Debugging Matlab Functions

Objectives
- To learn how to debug both script files and functions.
- To learn how to use the **Step In** tool to debug functions.
- To learn how to use the **Step Out** tool to run functions.

Topics

8.2.1   Debugging Matlab Function

In Lesson 8.1, you learned the basics of debugging a script M-file. In this lesson, we will explain the steps involved in tracking down bugs in an M-file function.

The process of debugging a function is probably best explained by way of an example. Here we will try to write a function to calculate the factorial of a number, and we will name this function `factorialN`. The factorial of a number n is defined as

$$n! = n \times (n-1) \times (n-2) \times (n-3)\ldots\ldots\ldots\ldots(3) \times (2) \times (1)$$

The factorial of the number 1 is 1 by definition.
The factorial of 2 is $2 \times 1 = 2$.
The factorial of 3 is $3 \times 2 \times 1 = 6$, and so on.

8.2.1.1   Creating a Script File to Call a Function

In order to debug a function, it must first be called from a script M-file. So, in this example task we should write two M-files: the first is a script M-file whose purpose is to call the function, and the second is an M-file containing the factorial function itself.

Launch Matlab. Create a new M-file for the script file that will actually call the function. To create an M-file go to **Menu→File→New→Script**. Type the following code in the file editor. Choose a suitable name for the file, as you learned how to do in Lesson 1.2, and then save it. For example, we shall choose the name *callfun.m*.

```
%This script file calls the factorialN function
clear; clc;
n = 3;
factorial_of_n = factorialN(n)
```

8.2.1.2   Creating a Function

Now create a new M-file for the `factorialN` function. Type the following code in the M-file. Save the file with the name *factorialN.m*.

```
%This function calculates the factorial of the number n
function fact_of_n = factorialN(n)
fact_of_n = 0;
for i = 2:n
    fact_of_n = fact_of_n * i;
end
end
```

Save both the script file *callfun.m* and the function file *factorialN.m* in the same folder.

8.2.1.3   Debugging the Function

Run the script M-file *callfun.m*. The results of running this script M-file should be an output value of 6, the factorial of 3, where $3! = 3 \times 2 \times 1$. The actual result is as shown, and you will note that it is not as expected.

```
factorial_of_n =
     0
```

So what is the mistake that we have made here? Let us proceed to debug our program in a step-by-step manner.

Go to the file *callfun.m*. Set a **Breakpoint** at line 3 of the code as shown, in the same manner that was explained in the previous lesson.

To start the debugging process, on the keyboard, press **F5**, which is the shortcut key for **Run**.

To step to line 4, press **F10**, which is the short-cut key for **Step**.

8.2.1.3.1   Step In Tool

The Matlab debugger has the ability to track bugs inside functions. To step into the `factorialN` function, go to **Menu→Debug→Step In**.

An alternative way to step inside the function is to press the short-cut key **F11** on the keyboard.

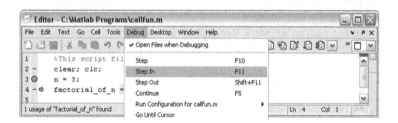

Matlab goes to the *factorialN.m* file and stops before executing the first command in the `factorialN` function, which is line 4 here as shown in the following figure.

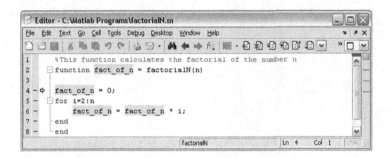

Press **F10** to execute the command in line 4. To check the value of the variable `fact_of_n`, first highlight the variable using the mouse, right-click, and then choose **Evaluate Selection**.

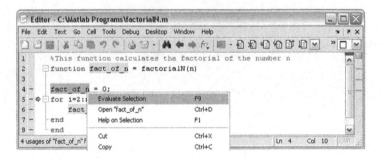

Matlab displays the value of the `fact_of_n` variable in its **Command Window** as shown.

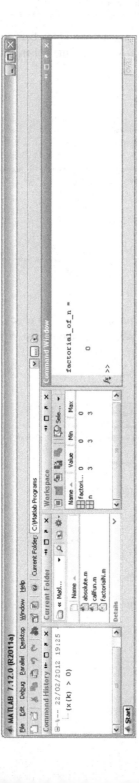

Press **F10** to **Step** and enter the `for` loop. To execute the first command inside the loop, press **F10** again. Check the content of the `fact_of_n` variable. You should find that, unexpectedly, it is still 0. However, the content of the variable should be 2. This is because the value of the `fact_of_n` variable at line 4 is initially set to 0. The value of the `fact_of_n` variable should have been set to 1 if the program is going to work properly. This is because if we multiply any number by 0 it will always produce a result of 0.

Now exit Matlab's debug mode. To do this, go to **Menu→Debug→Exit Debug Mode**.

Go to line 4 of the `factorialN` function and change the value of the `fact_of_n` variable from 0 to 1. Save the M-file function.

Go to the *callfun.m* file again and press **F5** to run the file. Press **F10** to execute the command in line 3. Press **F11** to step inside the `factorialN` function.

Press **F10** until Matlab executes the command in line 6 inside the `factorialN` function. Check the content of the `fact_of_n` variable. It now has a value of 2 as expected and the code in this line then corresponds to values of 2 × 1.

8.2.1.3.2 Step Out Tool

It seems that the program now works correctly and as expected. To run the function all together in a single step, go to **Menu→Debug→Step Out**.

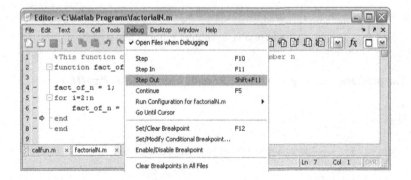

This executes the rest of the commands in the `factorialN` function and returns the control to the *callfun.m* file. This script file now produces the output which would be expected.

```
factorial_of_n = 0
```

Lesson 8.3   Advanced Matlab Debugging Tools

Objectives
- To learn how to use the **Conditional Breakpoint** debugging tool.
- To learn how to use the **Go Until Cursor** debugging tool.
- To learn how to use the **Continue** debugging tool.

Topics
8.3.1 Introduction
8.3.2 The Conditional Breakpoint Debugging Tool
8.3.3 The Go Until Cursor Debugging Tool
8.3.4 The Continue Debugging Tool

8.3.1   Introduction

In the Matlab debugging, Lessons 8.1 and 8.2, you have learned the basics of debugging script and function M-files. In both lessons, you were introduced to the **Step**, **Step In**, and **Step Out** debugging techniques in order to find runtime errors in Matlab code. In this lesson, we will explain to you some other advanced techniques for debugging your program, and once again it is probably best to start by giving an example.

Suppose that we would like to write a program that calculates the following summation:

$$S(n) = \sum_{n=-100}^{100} \frac{n+1}{n} \quad \text{where } n \text{ is an integer number and } n \neq 0$$

The program code is given below. Save this script file as **PartIII.m**.

```
%{
This program calculates the summation
```

$$S(n) = \sum_{n=-100}^{100} \frac{n+1}{n} \text{ where n is an integer number and n} \sim = 0$$

```
%}
clear; clc
summation = 0;
N = 100;
for n = - N:N
   if (n ~ = 0)
     summation = summation + (n + 1)/n;
   end
end
```

```
disp('The Summation is')
disp(summation)
```

We would like to check here that the case n = 0 is not included in the summation and also whether the if statement works properly.

8.3.2 The Conditional Breakpoint Debugging Tool

We can use the Matlab debugging tool **Set/Modify Conditional Breakpoint** to check the execution of the program when n = 0. Using the mouse, go to line 15 and highlight n. Go to the **Menu→Debug→Set/Modify Conditional Breakpoint...** as shown in the following figure.

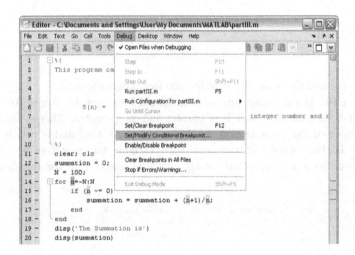

The window shown pops up. To set the condition n = 0, type n == 0 in the text box.

Using the keyboard, press **F5** to run the code. Matlab starts executing the script M-file and stops at line 15 when n is equal to 0.

Check the value of n. Is the value of n = 0 as expected?

Note here that the color of a **Conditional Breakpoint** is yellow.

Press **F10**. Matlab then jumps from line 15 to line 18. Lines 16 and 17 have not been executed, which is correct and as expected. This is because of the presence of the if statement, so the code is only executed if n is not equal (~ =) to 0. The content of the summation variable has therefore not changed when n = 0. So it can be seen that the program works fine for the case when n = 0.

8.3.3 The Go Until Cursor Debugging Tool

Suppose that we would like to run the entire `for` loop. To do this, left-click on the code in line 19. Go to the **Menu→Debug→Go Until Cursor**. Check the value of the variable `n`. It should have a value of 100.

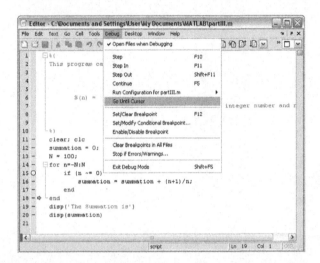

8.3.4 The Continue Debugging Tool

We would now like to run the program all the way to the end until it terminates. To do this, go to the **Menu→Debug→Continue**, or press the shortcut key **F5**.

The program executes completely and displays the results, which should be as follows.

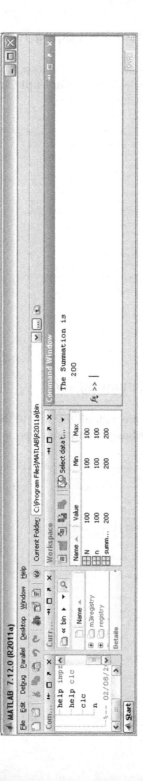

Exercise 1[2]

We would like to find the greatest value of n that can be used in the sum

$$s = 1^2 + 2^2 + 3^2 + \ldots + n^2$$

and still get a value of s that is less than 100.

A Matlab program has been written in an attempt to calculate s and n, and this is given below.

```
clear; clc
s = 1;
n = 0;
while (s < 100)
    n = n + 1;
    s = s + n^2;
end
s
n
```

Note the lack of semicolons ";" in the last two lines, so that these values of s and n are actually displayed. When the code is executed by Matlab, it gives the following output

```
s = 141
n = 7
```

But the correct values for s and n should be

```
s = 91
n = 6
```

The Matlab code that has been given above obviously does not work properly. Use Matlab's debugging tools to fix this program.

Lesson 8.4   The Matlab Profiler Tool

Objectives

- To learn the use of the Matlab **Profiler** tool to measure the execution time of code in script files and functions.
- To learn how to benchmark your computer.

Topics

8.4.1 The Matlab Profiler
    8.4.1.1 Launching the Matlab Profiler
8.4.2 Timing Matlab Code
8.4.3 Benchmarking Your Computer

8.4.1   The Matlab Profiler

As Matlab programmers, our aim is not always just to write a Matlab program that correctly solves the problem in hand, but sometimes it is also very important to make sure that this code uses the lowest possible resources of a computer in terms of memory usage and computational power. In this lesson, we are interested in investigating the possibility of reducing the number of computations that are required to execute a Matlab program. In other words, we wish to optimize a Matlab program in order to reduce its execution time. Here we shall not discuss the various techniques which may be used to optimize Matlab code, but we will discuss the use of Matlab tools for determining which particular sections in the code consume excessive amounts of the total execution time, thus enabling the possibility of optimizing these specific code sections.

A Matlab program consists of a script M-file that may call a number of different Matlab functions. We want to find out the time that is required to execute the script file and all the functions that it calls. We can use this information to optimize our code and make it run faster. Matlab contains a tool that provides us with this information, called the **Profiler**.

In this lesson, we will use an example program to explain the use of the Matlab **Profiler** tool.

Launch Matlab. Create a new Script file. Type the following code into this file. Save this script file as *main.m*.

```
%Code for Lesson 4:Profiling
clear; clc;
t = 0:0.01:100000;
x = log10(t);
y2 = power2(x);
y3 = power3(x);
```

Create a new M-file. Type the following code into this file. Save this file as
power2.m.

```
%This function calculates the square of its input.
function result = power2(y)
result = (y.^2);
end
```

Create a new M-file. Type the following code into this file. Save this file as
power3.m.

```
%This function calculates the cube of its input.
function result = power3(y)
result = (y.^3);
end
```

8.4.1.1   Launching the Matlab Profiler

To launch the Matlab **Profiler** go to **Menu→ Tools→ Open Profiler**.

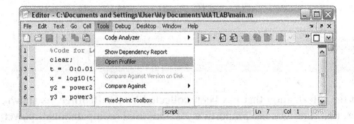

A new window pops up. Click **Start Profiling** as shown in the following figure.

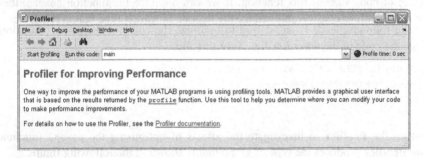

Matlab starts executing the main program and collects information about the
time required to execute this program and any functions it calls.

Matlab displays the information that is collected by the **Profiler** tool as a graph.
We can obtain the following information from this Profile Summary graph for this
particular example:

The time required to execute the entire main program is 0.835 seconds.

The time required to execute the main program, but excluding the functions, is 0.294 seconds and this is indicated by the color ▮▮.
The time required to call the functions themselves is 0.5410 seconds (0.835 − 0.294 = 0.5410) and this is indicated by the color ▮▮.
The time required to call the function power3 is 0.480 seconds.
The time required to call the function power2 is 0.061 seconds.

Note that these numbers are specific to the computer hardware upon which the code is running and will of course vary when the program is executed on different computers.

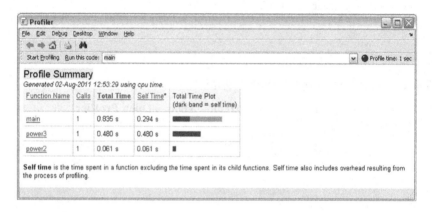

From the information that has been collected by the **Profiler**, as shown, we can conclude that the largest proportion of the total computational power that is required by the main program is actually consumed by the specific function power3. In this manner, we can identify particularly computationally intensive pieces of code such as this function. If we can optimize the function power3, then we can therefore considerably reduce the overall execution time that is required.
The following code is an attempt to optimize the code for the power3 function. Type the code in the*power3.m* file. Save this file.

```
%This function calculates the cube of its input.
function result = power3(y)
result = y .*y .*y;
end
```

Run the **Profiler** to investigate the effects of optimizing the power3 function. The **Profiler** produces the type of graph that is shown in the following figure.
From this graph we can see that the time that is required to execute the power3 function has been reduced from 0.480 seconds to 0.077 seconds. The execution time for this function has been reduced by a factor of approximately six times.
The overall execution time for the main program has now been reduced from 0.835 seconds to 0.415 seconds. Thus we can see that, by this optimization of the slowest function within the program, the overall execution time for the main program has been reduced to less than half.

Profiler

File Edit Debug Desktop Window Help

Start Profiling Run this code: main   Profile time: 0 sec

Profile Summary
Generated 02-Aug-2011 12:54:05 using cpu time.

Function Name	Calls	Total Time	Self Time*	Total Time Plot (dark band = self time)
main	1	0.415 s	0.276 s	
power3	1	0.077 s	0.077 s	
power2	1	0.062 s	0.062 s	

Self time is the time spent in a function excluding the time spent in its child functions. Self time also includes overhead resulting from the process of profiling.

8.4.2 Timing Matlab Code

The Matlab commands tic and toc can be used to measure the execution time for an M-file. This can be done by inserting the command tic at the beginning of the code and the command toc at the end of the code. To measure the execution time for the above *main.m* program, modify it as follows:

```
%Code for Lesson 4:Profiling
clear; clc;
tic
x = 0:0.01:100000;
y2 = power2(x);
y3 = power3(x);
toc
```

Run the file. Matlab reports the time required to execute the *main.m* file and produces the result:

```
Elapsed time is 0.207983 seconds
```

8.4.3 Benchmarking Your Computer

Benchmarking software involves the use of a computer program that runs a set of standard tests to measure the computing performance of a computer. The performance of a computer depends on a number of different factors, such as processor type, memory speed and size, bus speed, graphics card, and so on.

Matlab has the built-in bench tool that is used to measure the performance of a computer and compare the results with that of other standard machines. To benchmark your computer using Matlab, type at the **Command Prompt**

```
>> bench
```

Matlab runs a number of tests to evaluate the performance of your computer. Matlab shows the results of the benchmarking both graphically and numerically in two separate windows as shown. The benchmarking of your machine is of course specific to your particular computer hardware and will probably differ from the results shown here.

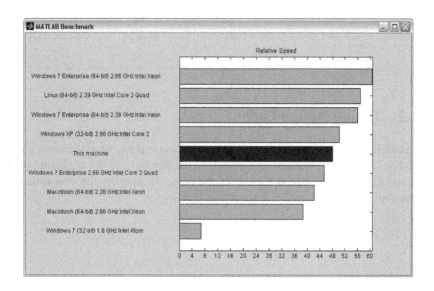

Lesson 8.5   Matlab Code Indentation

Objectives
- To learn how to improve code readability using indentation.
- To learn how to use the **Smart Indent** tool in Matlab.

Topics
8.5.1 Matlab Code Indentation
8.5.2 Smart Code Indentation

8.5.1   Matlab Code Indentation

You can use the **Tab** key on the keyboard to make Matlab code tidier. The following are illustrative examples on how to write tidy Matlab code that is easier to read than nonindented code.

Example 1

Good programming practice is best learned by presenting some examples. Let us write a Matlab program that calculates a mathematical function y which is given by the following expression:

$$y = \begin{cases} 2x & x < 3 \\ 3x & x = 3 \\ 5x & x > 3 \end{cases}$$

Answer
For the input vector x = 0:1:10. (This produces a vector that is indexed from 0 to 10, in increments of 1)

```
x = [0  1  2  3  4  5  6  7  8  9  10].
```

The corresponding values of the vector variable y are

```
y = [0  2  4  9  20  25  30  35  40  45  50].
```

The following Matlab program calculates the mathematical function y. Note here the proper commenting of the code, proper use of indentation for the code, and the general ease with which you can read it.

```
%{
This program calculates y according to the equation
```

$$y = \begin{cases} 2x & x < 3 \\ 3x & x = 3 \\ 5x & x > 3 \end{cases}$$

```
where x = 0:1:10;
%}
x = 0:1:10;
%n is the number of elements in the vector x
n = length(x);
for k = 1:n
  if (x(k) < 3)
    y(k) = 2*x(k);
  elseif (x(k) == 3)
    y(k) = 3*x(k);
  else
    y(k) = 5*x(k);
  end
end
disp(y)
```

Compare the readability of the following two sets of code. The program that is shown on the left is a well-indented program. The program that is shown on the right uses no indentation at all. Both cases shown have exactly the same textual content; the only difference lies in the way that the commands have been laid out. Which piece of code do you think is easier to follow?

```
clear; clc;                          clear; clc;
x = 0:1:10;                          x = 0:1:10;
n = length(x);                       n = length(x);
for k = 1:n                          for k = 1:n
  if (x(k) < 3)                      if (x(k) < 3)
    y(k) = 2*x(k);                   y(k) = 2*x(k);
  elseif (x(k) == 3)                 elseif (x(k) == 3)
    y(k) = 3*x(k);                   y(k) = 3*x(k);
  else                              else
    y(k) = 5*x(k);                   y(k) = 5*x(k);
  end                               end
end                                 end
disp(y);                            disp(y);
```

Here are 12 examples that show you how to indent Matlab code properly. This improves the readability of your programs.

Example 2

In the case of an if statement

```
z = 2;
r = 0;
```

```
if z > 1
   r = 2 * z;
end
```

Example 3

In the case of an `if else` statement

```
z = 2;
r = 0;
if z > 1
   r = 2*z;
else
   r = 3*z;
end
```

Example 4

In the case of an `if elseif else` statement

```
z = 2;
r = 0;
if z > 1
   r = 2*z;
elseif z < 1
   r = 3*z;
else
   r = 4*z;
end
```

Example 5

In the case of a `switch` statement

```
n = 4;
x = 1;
r = 0;
j = 0;
switch j
   case 1
      x = x + 1;
   case 2
      r = x + 2;
      n = 5;
   otherwise
      n = 6;
end
```

Example 6

In the case of a for loop statement
```
n = 3;
r = 0;
for k = 1:n
  x(k) = 3.^k;
  r = r + 1;
end
```

Example 7

In the case of a while loop statement
```
n = 4;
r = 0;
while (r < n)
  r = r + 1;
end
```

Example 8

In the case of nested for loops
```
n = 2;
r = 0;
for k = 1:n
  for j = k:n
    x(k,j) = 3.^(k+j);
    r = x(k,j);
  end
end
```
The indentations resulting from the use of the **Tab** key make the contents of the for loops much more easily visible.

Example 9

In the case of nested if statements
```
z = 2;
r = 0;
if z > 3
  r = 2*r;
  if r > 4
    s = z.^3;
  end
end
```

Example 10

In the case of a `for` loop inside an `if` statement
```
z = 2;
r = 0;
if z < 3
  r = 2*r;
  for j = 1:2
    r = r + 2.^r;
  end
end
```

Example 11

In the case of an `if` statement inside a `for` loop
```
n = 4;
x = 1:1:n;
r = 0;
for k = 1:n
  if (x(k) < 3)
    y(k) = 2*x(k);
    r = y(k) + 1;
  end
end
```

Example 12

In the case of an `if else` statement inside a `for` loop
```
n = 4;
x = 1:1:n;
r = 0;
for k = 1:n
  if (x(k) < 3)
    y(k) = 2*x(k);
  else
    y(k) = 5*x(k);
    r = 1;
  end
end
```

Example 13

In the case of an `if elseif else` statement inside a `for` loop
```
n = 4;
```

```
x = 1:1:n;
r = 0;
for k = 1:n
   if (x(k) < 3)
      y(k) = 2*x(k);
   elseif (x(k) == 3)
      y(k) = 3*x(k);
   else
      y(k) = 5*x(k);
      r = 2;
   end
end
```

Exercise 1[2]

Find the value of r in the previous set of Examples 2 to 13 without using Matlab. Then check your answers using Matlab.

8.5.2 Smart Code Indentation

If you find these rules lengthy and hard to follow, you can use the Matlab **Smart Indent** tool to tidy your code as follows. Type the code below into the **Editor**.

```
%{
This program calculates y according to the equation
```
$$y = \begin{cases} 2x & x < 3 \\ 3x & x = 3 \\ 5x & x > 3 \end{cases}$$
```
where x = 0:1:10;
%}
%clear Matlab memory and Command Window screen
clear; clc;
x = 0:1:10;
%The number of elements in the vector x
N = length(x);
for k = 1:N
if (x(k) < 3)
y(k) = 2*x(k);
elseif (x(k) == 3)
y(k) = 3*x(k);
else y(k) = 5*x(k);
end
end
disp(y);
```

Highlight all of the code that you have just typed using the mouse. Then go to **Menu→Text→Smart Indent**.

The result of using the **Smart Indent** tool is as shown in the following figure.

You now have tidy and more readable Matlab code.

Exercise 2[1]

Determine which of the following pieces of code is not well indented, and then indent it correctly. Explain your answer.

a.

```
x = 1;
y = 2;
r = 0;
if x == 1
    if y == 2
        r = 3;
    end
end
```

b.

```
x = 1;
y = 2;
r = 0;
if x == 1
    if y ==2
    r = 3;
    end
end
```

c.

```
x = 1;
y = 2;
r = 0;
if x == 1
    if y ==2
    end
        r = 3;
end
```

d.

```
n1 = 10;
n2 = 20;
r  = 0;
for i=1:n1
    x = i;
    for j=1:n2
        y = j;
        if x == y
            break
        else
            r = 1;
        end
    end
end
```

e.

```
n1 = 10;
n2 = 20;
r  = 0;
for i=1:n1
    x = i;
    for j=1:n2
        y = j;
            if x == y
                break
            else
                r = 1;
            end
    end
end
```

f.

```
n1 = 10;
n2 = 20;
r  = 0;
for i=1:n1
    x = i;
    for j=1:n2
        y = j;
        if x == y
            switch i
                case 1
                    r = 2;
            end
        else
            r = 1;
        end
    end
end
```

g.

```
n1 = 10;
n2 = 20;
r  = 0;
while(n1 < n2)
    r = r + 1
        n1 = n1 + 1;
        switch r
        case r
            r = r + 1;
        end
end
```

Exercise 3[2]

Find the value of r for the programs in Exercise 2 firstly without using Matlab. Then check your answers using Matlab.

Answers to Selected Exercises

Lesson 8.3

Exercise 1

```
clear; clc
s = 0;
n = 0;
while (s < 100)
    n = n + 1;
    s = s + n^2;
end
s = s - n^2;
n = n - 1;
s
n
```

9 Structures in Matlab

Chapter Outline

Lesson 9.1   Structures in Matlab

Objectives
- To learn how to construct a structure in Matlab.
- To learn how to write a structure function in Matlab.

Topics
9.1.1 The Need for the Structure Class
9.1.2 Functions for Structures

9.1.1 The Need for the Structure Class

You have studied vectors and arrays in this book. You can use the vectors and arrays to save a collection of identical classes. For example, the vector x saves a collection of numbers with the `double` class, as shown below:

```
>> x = 1:9;
```

In this second example, the array Y saves a collection of numbers with the `logical` class.

```
>> Y = reshape(x,3,3) > 5;
```

Matlab by Example. DOI: http://dx.doi.org/10.1016/B978-0-12-405212-3.00009-8

In this third example, the variable z saves a collection of characters each with the char class.

```
>> z = 'hello world';
```

Exercise 1[1]

Use the Matlab command whos to find the classes of x, y, and z variables above.

You may need to use a single variable to save a collection of nonidentical data types. For example, you may need to use a single variable to save the parameters of a circle such as its radius, center point, and color. Matlab provides you with the structure class to do this.

For example, the circle's parameters can be represented in Matlab by using two different methods. The first method is to use three different variables with different class types to save the circle's various parameters. The second method is to use a single variable, which has the class structure in order to save the circle's different parameters.

Method 1

In this method you need to create three different variables to save the circle's parameters. For example, the following code represents a circle with a radius of 5, a center of (1, 2), and a color of red. These three parameters are defined as a scalar variable, a vector variable, and a string variable.

```
circle_radius =   5;
circle_centre =   [1,2];
circle_colour =   'red';
```

To display the circle_radius variable, type at the Matlab **Command Prompt**

```
>> circle_radius
```

Matlab responds with

```
circle_radius =
                5
```

To display the circle_center variable, type at the Matlab **Command Prompt**

```
>> circle_center
```

Matlab responds with

```
circle_center =
1                    2
```

To display the `circle_color` variable, type at the Matlab **Command Prompt**

```
>>circle_color
```

Matlab responds with

```
circle_color =
            red
```

Method 2

In this method, you will use the `structure` class to save the three parameters of the circle within a single variable. Type at the Matlab **Command Prompt**

```
circle.radius =   5;
circle.center =  [1,2];
circle.color =   'red';
```

To display the contents of the `circle` variable, type at the Matlab **Command Prompt**

```
>>circle
```

Matlab responds with

```
circle =
        radius:5
        center:[1 2]
        color:'red'
```

Question In your opinion, which method is more convenient for saving the circle's parameters?

The class of the `circle` variable is `struct`. To find the class of the `circle` variable, type at Matlab **Command Prompt**

```
>>whos circle
```

Matlab responds with

```
Name    Size  Bytes  Class    Attributes
circle  1×1   402    struct
```

The `circle` structure has three fields: `radius`, `center`, and `color`.

Matlab requires more memory to save a structure variable than would be the case for saving multiple individual variables. For example, representing the circle's parameters in the previous example by using three scalar variables requires 24 bytes of memory. Whereas representing the circle's parameters using a three-field structure variable as shown actually requires 402 bytes of memory.

9.1.2   Functions for Structures

You can write a function to call a structure class variable and process it. This is illustrated using the following two examples.

Example 1

A rectangle has four parameters: width, height, center, and color. Suppose that the values of the four parameters are width = 200, height = 100, center = (250, 150), and the color is red. You can represent this rectangle in Matlab as follows:

```
rect.width =   200;
rect.height =  100;
rect.centre =  [250,150];
rect.colour =  'red';
```

The following figure shows the rectangle and its four corners: North West (NW), North East (NE), South West (SW), and South East (SE).
Write a Matlab function to draw this rectangle.

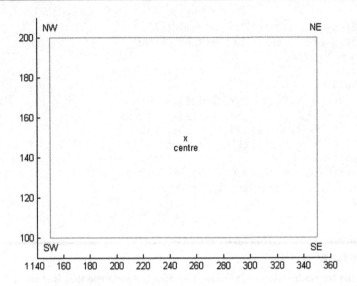

Answer

The function to draw the rectangle and the code to call this function are shown below. The horizontal direction here is considered to be the x axis, whereas the vertical direction is considered to be the y axis.

```
clc; close all
rectangle.width = 200;
rectangle.height = 100;
rectangle.center = [250,150];
rectangle.color = 'red';
x = draw_rectangle(rectangle);
function state1 = draw_rectangle(rect)
if (isstruct(rect) ~ = 1)
    state1 = 'The argument is not a structure';
    return;
end
switch rect.color
    case 'red'
       clr = 'r';
    case 'green'
       clr = 'g'
    otherwise
       clr = 'b'
end
NW_x = rect.center(1) - rect.width/2;
NW_y = rect.center(2) + rect.height/2;
SW_x = rect.center(1) - rect.width/2;
SW_y = rect.center(2) - rect.height/2;
NE_x = rect.center(1) + rect.width/2;
NE_y = rect.center(2) + rect.height/2;
```

```
SE_x = rect.center(1) + rect.width/2;
SE_y = rect.center(2) - rect.height/2;
n = 10; %margin
figure
hold on
plot([NW_x, NE_x], [NW_y, NE_y], clr)
plot([SW_x, SE_x], [SW_y, SE_y], clr)
plot([NW_x, SW_x], [NW_y, SW_y], clr)
plot([NE_x, SE_x], [NE_y, SE_y], clr)
hold off
axis([NW_x-n, NE_x+n, SE_y-n, NE_y+n])
state1 = 'The argument is a structure';
end
```

Exercise 2[2]

Use the Matlab function rectangle() to draw the rectangle that is shown in Example 1. The color of the rectangle that is drawn should be black.

Example 2

A school student is 17 years old. The student has studied mathematics, physics, and English courses. The student's marks in these three courses are 70, 80, and 90, respectively. Write Matlab code to represent the student's age and marks using a structure.

Answer

```
student.age =      17;
student.math =     70;
student.physics =  80;
student.English =  90;
```

Example 3

Write a Matlab function to calculate the average mark for the student.

Answer

```
function mark_average = student_average(student)
if (isstruct(student) ~= 1)
    disp('The argument is not a structure');
    return;
end
mark_average = (student.math + student.physics + student.English) / 3;
end
```

To call the `student_average( )` function, type at Matlab **Command Prompt**

>> student_average(student)

Matlab responds with

ans =
        80

Exercise 3[1]

Write a Matlab function to calculate the standard deviation for the student's marks in Example 3.

Lesson 9.2   A Vector of Structures

Objective
* To learn how to construct a vector of structures in Matlab.
Topic
9.2.1 A Vector of Structures

9.2.1   A Vector of Structures

You can use Matlab to create a vector of structures. Let us explain this concept to you by way of an example.

Example 1

Three students study in a college. The following table shows their ages and marks in three subjects. Use a vector of structures to represent the students' information as given.

Student Name	Age	Math Mark	Physics Mark	English Mark
Alex	25	70	55	58
John	23	77	90	75
Mike	24	80	64	87

Answer

```
student(1).name = 'Alex';
student(1).age = 25;
student(1).math = 70;
student(1).physics = 55;
student(1).English = 58;
student(2).name = 'John';
student(2).age = 23;
student(2).math = 77;
student(2).physics = 90;
student(2).English = 75;
student(3).name = 'Mike';
student(3).age = 24;
student(3).math = 80;
student(3).physics = 64;
student(3).English = 87;
```

To display the fields of the vector, type at the Matlab **Command Prompt**

```
>> student
```

Matlab responds with

```
student =
1 X 3 struct array with fields:
name
age
math
physics
English
```

To display the contents of the first structure in the vector, type at the Matlab **Command Prompt**

```
>> student(1)
```

Matlab responds with

```
ans =
name: 'Alex'
age: 25
math: 70
physics: 55
English: 58
```

To display Alex's mark in mathematics, type at the Matlab **Command Prompt**

```
>> student(1).math
```

Matlab responds with

```
ans =
    70
```

To display the mathematics marks for all the students in the vector, type at the Matlab **Command Prompt**

```
>> a = [student.math]
```

Matlab responds with

```
a =
    70  77  80
```

Example 2

Write a Matlab program to calculate the mean of the mathematics marks for the students given in Example 1.

Answer
Type at the Matlab **Command Prompt**

```
mathMarks =       [student.math];
meanMathMarks =   mean(mathMarks)
```

Example 3

Write a Matlab program to calculate the mean of all the subject marks for the students given in Example 1.

Answer
Type at the Matlab **Command Prompt**

```
mathMarks =       [student.math];
physicsMarks =    [student.physics];
EnglishMarks =    [student.English];
AllMarks =        [mathMarks,physicsMarks,EnglishMarks];
meanAllMarks =    mean(AllMarks)
```

Example 4

Write a Matlab command to remove the mathematics marks from the vector structure that is shown in Example 1.

Answer
Type at Matlab **Command Prompt**

```
>> rmfield(student,'math')
```

Matlab responds with

```
ans =
1 X 3 struct array with fields:
 name
 age
 physics
 English
```

Example 5

Write a Matlab command to remove the student Alex from the vector structure that is shown in Example 1.

Answer
Alex is the first structure in the vector. To remove the student Alex, type at the Matlab **Command Prompt**

```
>> student = student(1:2);
```

Answers to Selected Exercises

Lesson 9.1

Exercise 2

```
clc; close all
rect.width = 200;
rect.height = 100;
rect.center = [250,150];
SW_x = rect.center(1) - rect.width/2;
SW_y = rect.center(2) - rect.height/2;
rectangle('Position',[SW_x, SW_y, rect.width, ...
rect.height],'Curvature',[0,0])
n = 10; %margin
axis([SW_x - n, SW_x + rect.width + ...
n, SW_y - n, SW_y + rect.height + n])
```

Exercise 3

```
function stddev_marks = student_stddev(student)
if (isstruct(student) ~= 1)
    disp('The argument is not a structure');
    return;
end
marks = [student.math, student.physics, student.English];
stddev_marks = std(marks);
end
```

To call the `student_stddev()` function, type at Matlab **Command Prompt**

```
student.age =        21;
student.math =       70;
student.physics =    80;
student.English =    90;
student_stddev(student)
```

Matlab responds with

```
ans =
    10
```

Project: The Fox and Rabbit Game

The fox and rabbit game is a zero-player game. It is played on a 5×5 grid of square cells. This grid represents a jungle and is shown in the following figure. The game contains one rabbit, which is represented by a green cell, and one fox, which is represented by a red cell. The Matlab code that may be used to produce this figure is shown.

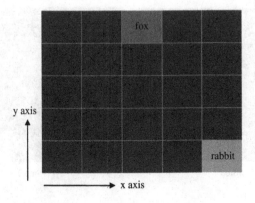

```
clear; clc; close all;
X = zeros(5,5);
X(1,3) = 1;
X(5,5) = 2;
imagesc(X), colormap([0,0,1; 1,0,0; 0,1,0])
hold on
%horizontal lines
plot([0.5, 5.5], [1.5, 1.5],'g')
plot([0.5, 5.5], [2.5, 2.5],'g')
plot([0.5, 5.5], [3.5, 3.5],'g')
plot([0.5, 5.5], [4.5, 4.5],'g')
%vertical lines
plot([1.5, 1.5], [0.5, 5.5],'g')
plot([2.5, 2.5], [0.5, 5.5],'g')
plot([3.5, 3.5], [0.5, 5.5],'g')
plot([4.5, 4.5], [0.5, 5.5],'g')
axis off
```

The game is played as follows:

1. Place the rabbit in a random location on the grid.
2. Place the fox in a random location on the grid.
3. The game involves only five steps.
4. In each step
   a. Move the rabbit one step randomly in one of the eight different directions.
   b. Move the fox one step randomly in one of the eight different directions.
   c. If the fox and rabbit cells become neighbors, the fox eats the rabbit. The fox wins and the game terminates.
5. If the number of steps reaches five and the rabbit survives during these five steps, the rabbit wins and the game terminates.
6. The borders of the grid are wrapped. This is explained in Chapter 7, Project 2.

The following figures show one scenario of the game in which the fox wins within three steps.

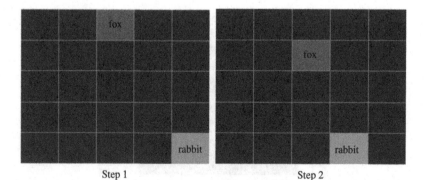

Step 1   Step 2

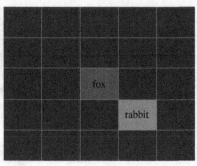

Step 3

The following figures show a second scenario of the game in which the fox again wins, this time within four steps. Note the movement in wrapped directions and the fact that here the winning "kill" itself is achieved across a border wrap.

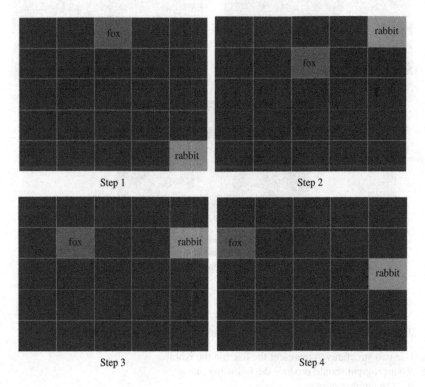

The following figures show a third scenario of the game in which this time the rabbit survives for all five steps and hence wins.

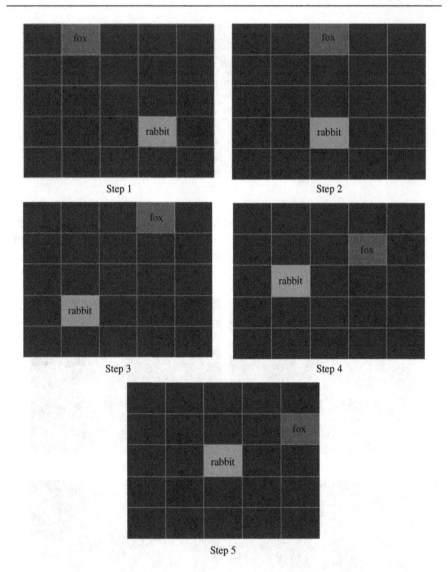

Step 1   Step 2

Step 3   Step 4

Step 5

The following requirements for programming your game must be met:

1. Use two structures to represent the fox and the rabbit.
2. Your program should produce the following outputs:
   a. The number of steps.
   b. Who won the game?
   c. A figure to show each step of the game.

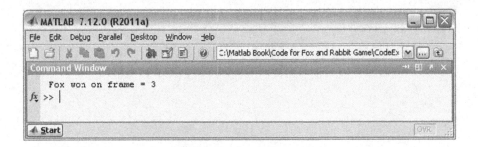

An example of figures produced by the game is shown.

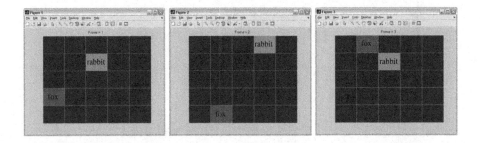

10 Calculus in Matlab

Chapter Outline

Lesson 10.1   Introduction to Symbolic Math Toolbox

Objectives
- To familiarize Matlab users with the Symbolic Math toolbox.
- To learn the `sym` class in Matlab.
- To learn how to construct symbolic equations in Matlab.
- To learn how to display symbolic equations using the `pretty` command.
- To learn how to plot symbolic equations in Matlab using the `ezplot` function.

Topics
10.1.1 Symbolic Math Toolbox
10.1.2 Constructing a `sym` Variable
10.1.3 Constructing a Symbolic Expression
10.1.4 Finding the Value of a Symbolic Expression
10.1.5 Plotting of a Symbolic Expression in Matlab Using the `ezplot` Function

---

10.1.1   Symbolic Math Toolbox

Matlab has a number of toolboxes that contain specialized functions. To check the toolboxes installed in your machine, type at the **Command Prompt**

```
>>ver
```

Matlab by Example. DOI: http://dx.doi.org/10.1016/B978-0-12-405212-3.00010-4

Matlab lists the installed toolboxes and their versions. For our computer, Matlab responds with

```
MATLAB                    Version7.12  (R2011a)
Symbolic Math Toolbox  Version5.6   (R2011a)
```

This indicates that the Symbolic Math toolbox is installed in our computer. You will need this toolbox to be installed in your Matlab software system in order to follow Chapter 10 of this book.

10.1.2   Constructing a sym **Variable**

So far you have learned a number of different data classes in Matlab such as double, logical, string, and struct. Here you will learn the sym class. You will need this class to use the Symbolic Math toolbox. For example, type at the **Command Prompt**

```
>> x = sym(1/2)
```

Matlab responds with

```
  x =
     1/2
```

Matlab creates a sym variable and set its value to ½. Note here that the value of the x variable is ½ not 0.5.

Let us create a second sym variable and set its value to ¼. Type at the **Command Prompt**

```
>> y = sym(1/4)
```

Matlab responds with

```
y =
   1/4
```

Let us add the values of the x and y variables together and assign the result to a third variable that once again has the same sym data class.

```
>> z = x + y
```

Matlab responds with

```
z =
   3/4
```

Note that the class of the z variable here is sym.

To convert the value of the z variable to double and assign it to another variable, type at the **Command Prompt**

```
>> r = double(z)
```

Matlab responds with

```
r =
    0.7500
```

To display the available variables in Matlab and their classes, type at the **Command Prompt**

```
>> whos
```

Matlab responds with

```
Name  Size  Bytes  Class   Attributes
r     1×1   8      double
x     1×1   60     sym
y     1×1   60     sym
z     1×1   60     sym
```

Matlab also enables you to create a sym free variable without assigning a value to it. For example,

```
>> syms s
```

Matlab responds with

```
s =
    s
```

10.1.3   Constructing a Symbolic Expression

Matlab enables you to construct a symbolic expression and assign it to a sym variable. For example, to construct the symbolic expression $y = x^2 + 3x + 2$, type at the **Command Prompt**

```
>> syms x
>> y = x^2 + 3*x + 2
```

Matlab responds with

```
y =
x^2 + 3*x + 2
```

To display the symbolic expression in mathematical format, type at the **Command Prompt**

```
>>pretty(y)
```

Matlab responds with

```
    2
x + 3x + 2
```

10.1.4   Finding the Value of a Symbolic Expression

Suppose that you have the symbolic expression $y = x^2 + 3x + 2$, and the value of $x = 1$. You can determine the value of y by substituting the value of x in the symbolic expression as given by $y(1) = 1^2 + 3 \times 1 + 2 = 6$.

The value of $y(1)$ can be determined using Matlab. Type at the **Command Prompt**

```
>>d = subs(y,1)
```

Matlab responds with

```
d =
    6
```

10.1.5   Plotting a Symbolic Expression Using the ezplot Function

To plot the symbolic expression $y = x^2 + 3x + 2$ that was constructed above, type at the **Command Prompt**

```
>>ezplot(y)
```

The Matlab command ezplot is pronounced as "easy plot." Matlab responds by creating the following figure.

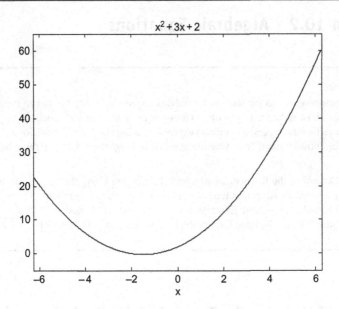

You can specify the domain for the function $y = x^2 + 3x + 2$. For example, to set the domain to $-5 < x < 2$, type at the **Command Prompt**

```
>>ezplot(y,[-5,2])
```

Matlab responds with

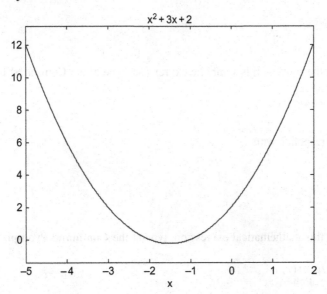

Lesson 10.2   Algebraic Equations

Objectives
- To learn how to find the roots of a symbolic expression using the `solve` function.
- To learn how to factor a symbolic expression using the `factor` function.
- To learn how to expand a symbolic expression using the `expand` function.
- To learn how to simplify a symbolic expression using the `simplify` function.

Topics
10.2.1 Determine the Roots of an Algebraic Expression Using the `solve` Function
10.2.2 Factorize an Algebraic Expression Using the `factor` Function
10.2.3 Expand an Algebraic Expression Using the `expand` Function
10.2.4 Simplify an Algebraic Expression Using the `simplify` Function

---

10.2.1   Determine the Roots of an Algebraic Expression Using the `solve` Function

Suppose that you have the algebraic expression $y = x^2 + 3x + 2$. You can construct a symbolic expression to represent this mathematical expression in Matlab as follows:

```
>> syms x
>> y = x.^2 + 3*x + 2;
```

To find the roots of this symbolic expression, type at the **Command Prompt**

```
>> r = solve(y)
```

Matlab responds with

```
r =
    - 2
    - 1
```

To plot this mathematical expression, type at the **Command Prompt**

```
>> ezplot(y, [ - 3,0])
>> grid on
```

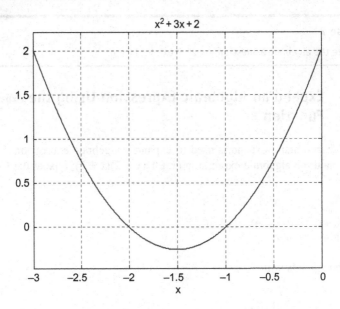

$x^2 + 3x + 2$

Note that the symbolic expression $y = x^2 + 3x + 2$ has the value 0 when the values of x are -2 and -1 as shown in the figure above.

Exercise 1[2]

Use the `roots` Matlab function to determine the roots of the expression $y = x^2 + 3x + 2$.

10.2.2 Factorize an Algebraic Expression Using the `factor` Function

The Matlab command `factor` is used to factorize an algebraic expression. For example, to factorize the algebraic expression $x^2 + 3x + 2$, type at the **Command Prompt**

```
>> syms x
>> y = x^2 + 3*x + 2;
>> f = factor(y)
```

Matlab responds with

```
f =
    (x + 2)*(x + 1)
```

Exercise 2[1]

Factorize the algebraic expression $y = x^3 + 6x^2 + 11x + 6$.

10.2.3   Expand an Algebraic Expression Using the expand Function

The Matlab command expand is used to expand a algebraic expression. For example, to expand the algebraic expression $(x + 1)(x + 2)(x + 3)$, type at the **Command Prompt**

```
>> syms x
>> g = (x + 1)*(x + 2)* + (x + 3);
>> h = expand(g)
```

Matlab responds with

```
h =
      x^3 + 6*x^2 + 11*x + 6
```

To display the symbolic expression h in a standard mathematical format, type at the **Command Prompt**

```
>> pretty(h)
```

Matlab responds with

```
3      2
x + 6x + 11x + 6
```

10.2.4   Simplify an Algebraic Expression Using the simplify Function

The Matlab command simplify is used to simplify an algebraic expression. For example, to simplify the algebraic expression

$$\frac{x^3 + 6x^2 + 11x + 6}{x^2 + 3x + 2}$$

type at the **Command Prompt**

```
>> syms x;
>> m = (x^3 + 6*x^2 + 11*x + 6)/(x^2 + 3*x + 2);
>> n = simplify(m)
```

Matlab responds with

```
n =
    x + 3
```

Remember:

$$\frac{x^3 + 6x^2 + 11x + 6}{x^2 + 3x + 2} = \frac{(x+1)(x+2)(x+3)}{(x+1)(x+2)} = (x+3)$$

Lesson 10.3   Differentiation and Integration

Objectives
- To learn how to find the derivative of a mathematical expression using the `diff` function.
- To learn how to find the integration of a mathematical expression using the `int` function.

Topics

10.3.1 Differentiation of a Mathematical Expression Using the `diff` Function

10.3.2 Integration of a Mathematical Expression Using the `int` Function

   10.3.2.1 Unlimited Integration of a Mathematical Expression Using the `int` Function

   10.3.2.2 Delimited Integration of a Mathematical Expression Using the `int` Function

10.3.1   Differentiation of a Mathematical Expression Using the `diff` Function

You can find the first, second, third, and so on derivatives of a mathematical expression using Matlab. For example, to find the first derivative of the function $y = x^2 + 3x + 2$, type at the **Command Prompt**

```
>> syms x
>> y = x^2 + 3*x + 2;
>> df1 = diff(y)
```

Matlab responds with

```
df1 =
    2*x + 3
```

To find the second derivative of the function $y = x^2 + 3x + 2$, type at the **Command Prompt**

```
>>df2 = diff(y,2)
```

Matlab responds with

```
df2 =
      2
```

To find the third derivative of the function $y = e^{x^2} + \cos(x)$, type at the **Command Prompt**

```
>>syms x
>>z = exp(x^2) + cos(x);
>>df3 = diff(z,3)
```

Matlab responds with

```
df3 =
      sin(x) + 12*x*exp(x^2) + 8*x^3*exp(x^2)
```

Exercise 1[1]

Find the first derivative of the mathematical expression $y = \ln(x)$.

10.3.2 Integration of a Mathematical Expression Using the int **Function**

There are two types of integration: delimited and unlimited. We will discuss both types here.

10.3.2.1 *Unlimited Integration of a Mathematical Expression Using the* int *Function*

You can find the unlimited integration of a mathematical expression using the Symbolic Math toolbox. Note that the unlimited integration produces a mathematical expression.

Example 1

Find the integration of the function $y = x^2 + 3x + 2$.

Answer
Type at the **Command Prompt**

```
>> syms x
>> y = x^2 + 3*x + 2;
>> int1 = int(y)
```

Matlab responds with

```
int1 =
        (x*(2*x^2 + 9*x + 12))/6
```

To expand the symbolic expression saved in the variable int1, type at the **Command Prompt**

```
>> int1 = expand(int1)
```

Matlab responds with

```
int1 =
        x^3/3 + (3*x^2)/2 + 2*x
```

To display the symbolic expression int1 as a mathematical format, type at the **Command Prompt**

```
>> pretty(int1)
```

Matlab responds with

```
 3        2
x        3x
—  +    ——  + 2x
 3        2
```

Exercise 2[1]

Find the integration of the mathematical expression $y = \frac{1}{x}$.

10.3.2.2 Delimited Integration of a Mathematical Expression Using the `int` Function

You can find the delimited integration of a mathematical expression using the Symbolic Math toolbox. Note that the delimited integration produces a number.

Example 2

Find the delimited integration of the function

$$a = \int_{-3}^{4} x^2 + 3x + 2\, dx$$

Answer
Type at the **Command Prompt**

```
>> syms x
>> y = x^2 + 3*x + 2;
>> a = int(y, -3, 4)
```

Matlab responds with

```
a =
    329/6
```

The class of the `a` variable is `sym`. To convert this variable to double, type at the **Command Prompt**

```
>> a = double(a)
```

Matlab responds with

```
a =
    54.8333
```

Example 3

Find the delimited integration of the function

$$z = \int_{0}^{\infty} e^{-x}\, dx$$

Type at the **Command Prompt**

```
>> syms x
>> z = exp(-x);
>> b = int(z, 0, Inf)
```

Matlab responds with

    b =
        1

Exercise 3[1]

Find the integration of the mathematical expression $r = \int_{-\infty}^{\infty} e^{-x^2} dx$

Exercise 4[1]

Find the integration of the mathematical expression $d = \int_{-10}^{10} e^{-x^2} dx$ using the quad Matlab function.

Lesson 10.4   Differential Equations

Objectives
- To learn how to solve a differential equation using the dsolve function.
- To learn how to use initial conditions to solve a differential equation.

Topics
10.4.1 Solving a First Order Differential Equations Using the dsolve Function
10.4.2 Solving a Second Order Differential Equations Using the dsolve Function

---

10.4.1   Solving a First Order Differential Equation Using the dsolve **Function**

You can find the solution of a first order differential equation using the Math Symbolic toolbox.

Example 1

Find the solution of the differential equation

$$\frac{dy}{dt} + 2y = 3$$

Answer
To solve this differential equation, type at the **Command Prompt**

```
>> s = dsolve('Dy + 2*y = 3')
```

Matlab responds with

```
s =
    C2/(2*exp(2*t)) + 3/2
```

To check the value of the C2 variable, type at the **Command Prompt**

```
>> C2
```

Matlab responds with

```
???Undefined function or variable'C2'.
```

To calculate the value of C2, you need to have the initial conditions of the differential equation.

To display the symbolic expression s in a standard mathematical format, type at the **Command Prompt**

```
>> pretty(s)
```

Matlab responds with

```
C2
-- -- -- -- -- --   + 3/2
2exp(2 t)
```

Example 2

Find the solution of the differential equation

$$\frac{dy}{dt} + 2y = 3, \quad y(0) = 10$$

Answer
To solve this differential equation, type at the **Command Prompt**

```
>> s = dsolve('Dy + 2*y = 3', 'y(0) = 10')
```

Matlab responds with

s =
    17/(2*exp(2*t)) + 3/2

To plot the solution of the differential equation, type at the **Command Prompt**

```
>> ezplot(s)
```

Matlab responds and produces the figure.

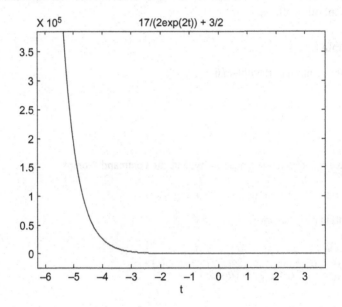

X 10⁵   17/(2exp(2t)) + 3/2

Example 3

Find the solution of the differential equation

$$\frac{dy}{dt} + 2y = 3x, \quad y(0) = 10$$

Answer
To solve this differential equation, type at the **Command Prompt**

```
>> s = dsolve('Dy + 2*y = 3*x', 'y(0) = 10')
```

Matlab responds with

```
s =
    (3*x)/2 – (3*x – 20)/(2*exp(2*t))
```

10.4.2   Solving a Second Order Differential Equation Using the `dsolve` Function

You can find the solution of a second order differential equation using the Math Symbolic toolbox. Also, you can solve higher order differential equations using the Math Symbolic toolbox.

Example 4

Find the solution of the differential equation

$$\frac{d^2y}{dt^2} + 2\frac{dy}{dt} + 3y = 4x$$

Answer
To solve this differential equation, type at the **Command Prompt**

```
>> s = dsolve('D2y + 2*Dy + 3*y = 4*x')
```

Matlab responds with

```
s =
(4*x)/3 + (C14*cos(2^(1/2)*t))/exp(t) +
(C15*sin(2^(1/2)*t))/exp(t)
```

Example 5

Find the solution of the differential equation

$$\frac{d^2y}{dt^2} + 2\frac{dy}{dt} + 3y = 4x, \quad y(0) = 1, \quad y'(0) = 2$$

Answer
To solve this differential equation, type at the **Command Prompt**

```
>> s = dsolve('D2y + 2*Dy + 3*y = 4*x', 'y(0) = 1', 'Dy(0) = 2')
```

Matlab responds with

```
s =
(4*x)/3 + (C14*cos(2^(1/2)*t))/exp(t) + (C15*sin(2^(1/2)*t))/exp(t)
```

Exercise 1[1]

Find the solution of the differential equation

$$\frac{d^3 y}{dt^3} + 4\frac{d^2 y}{dt^2} + 5\frac{dy}{dt} + 10y = 4x$$

Lesson 10.5   Laplace and Fourier Transforms

Objectives
- To learn how to find the Laplace transform of a function using the `laplace` function.
- To learn how to find the inverse Laplace transform of a function using the `ilaplace` function.
- To learn how to find the Fourier transform of a function using the `fourier` function.
- To learn how to find the inverse Fourier transform of a function using the `ifourier` function.

Topics
10.5.1 Laplace Transform
10.5.2 Inverse Laplace Transform
10.5.3 Fourier Transform
10.5.4 Inverse Fourier Transform

10.5.1   Laplace Transform

You can find the Laplace transform of a mathematical function using the Symbolic Math toolbox.

Example 1

Find the Laplace transform for the function

$$y = e^{-3t}$$

Answer
Type at the **Command Prompt**
```
>> syms t
>> y = exp(- 3*t);
>> Lap_y = laplace(y)
```

Matlab responds with

```
Lap_y =
        1/(s + 3)
```

10.5.2   Inverse Laplace Transform

You can find the inverse Laplace transform of a mathematical function using the Symbolic Math toolbox.

Example 2

Find the inverse Laplace transform for the function

$$\frac{1}{s+3}$$

Answer
Type at the **Command Prompt**

```
>> syms s
>> d = 1./(s + 3);
>> inv_d = ilaplace(d)
```

Matlab responds with

```
inv_d =
        1/exp(3*t)
```

Note that $e^{-3t} = \frac{1}{e^{3t}}$

10.5.3   Fourier Transform

You can find the Fourier transform of a mathematical function using the Symbolic Math toolbox.

Example 1

Find the Fourier transform for the function

$$y = e^{-3t^2}$$

Answer
Type at the **Command Prompt**

```
>> syms t
>> y = t.*exp(- 3*t^2);
>> Fourier_y = fourier(y)
```

Matlab responds with

```
Fourier_y =
            - (3^(1/2)*pi^(1/2))/(3*exp(w^2/12))
```

10.5.4   Inverse Laplace Transform

You can find the inverse Laplace transform of a mathematical function using the Symbolic Math toolbox.

Example 2

Find the inverse Fourier transform for the function

$$e^{-\omega^2}$$

Answer
Type at the **Command Prompt**

```
>> syms w
>> dw = exp(- w^2);
>> inv_dw = ifourier(dw)
```

Matlab responds with

```
inv_dw =
            1/(2*pi^(1/2)*exp(x^2/4))
```

Answers to Selected Exercises

Lesson 10.2

Exercise 1

```
>> r = roots([1,3,2])
```

Lesson 10.3

Exercise 1

```
>> syms x
>> y = log(x);
>> df1 = diff(y)
```

Exercise 2

```
>> syms x
>> y = 1./x;
>> int1 = int(y)
```

Exercise 3

```
>> syms x
>> y = exp(- x.^2);
>> r = int(y, - Inf,Inf)
```

Exercise 4

```
>> d = quad('exp(- x.^2)', - 10,10)
```

Lesson 10.4

Exercise 1

```
>> s = dsolve('D3y + 4*D2y + 5*Dy + 10*y = 4*x')
```

Printed in the United States
By Bookmasters